Log on now to enjoy MFP Online for a full semester

Purchase of this textbook entitles you to a limited, one-semester license to web-based *MFP* software. To use this license, your *MFP* textbook must be purchased as a brand new book from an authorized bookseller, and must be packaged in the publisher's original shrink wrap. ***Important: See label affixed to inside front cover - new books will always have a silver coating on the label; be sure to verify that the label has not been tampered with. If the label on your book has been scratched off, the Access Code has been used and it will expire without notice.*** Previously used Access Codes will not work. You may access *MFP* from any computer, but you cannot login to more than one session simultaneously, or share your access code with another person.

Why you should keep your book when you're done this semester.
Many schools use MFP for more than one course. For later courses, you can renew your license with your professor's permission at no charge. Directions are on the website on the *Contact Us* page. The information needed to renew is on your access code sticker inside the front cover of this book. No one else can use your code, please don't cause problems for other students by selling them a book they can't use.

Get help--bother us, not your professor.
If you have a problem logging in, send us an email: **support@mediaflightplan.com**. We can't help with your homework, but we can fix just about anything else.

Step 1: ***MFP*** **Access Code** Find the label on the inside front cover of your book - do not remove it. Carefully scratch-off the silver coating to reveal your 25 character MFP Access Code. If you inadvertently scratch off some characters, send the ones you can read to **support@mediaflightplan.com** and we'll help you.

Step 2: Logging onto ***MFP***
Go to Exercise 13 (Tutorial) and read the instructions carefully.

Media Flight Plan 6

A Strategic Approach to Media Planning Theory and Practice
Sixth Edition

Printing 2.0

Dennis G. Martin, Emeritus, Brigham Young University
Robert D. Coons, Campbell-Ewald

SOFTWARE NOTICE
For access to the MFP Online simulation, your Media Flight Plan text must be a new book purchased from an authorized bookseller, and packaged in the publisher's original shrink wrap.

ISBN: 978-0-9632515-9-6

Provo, Utah (12.10)
www.mediaflightplan.com

Important Software Notice

For access to the new *MFP* databases, your *Media Flight Plan* text must be a new book purchased from an authorized bookseller, and packaged in the publisher's original shrink wrap. First inspect the label affixed to the inside front cover. ***If this text has been unwrapped and if the coating on the access code has been scratched off, you must assume the code has been used, and the MFP web server will flag it as invalid.*** Please make sure that you have a new shrink-wrapped book, and that the Access Code/Login has not been used or tampered with. Previously used Access Codes will not work. You cannot use *MFP* on more than one computer at a time, or share your access code with another person. Loss or sharing of your Access Code/Login with another person requires repurchase of *Media Flight Plan*.

Acknowledgments

The authors express appreciation to the following for their professionalism and excellence:

Media Flight Plan Text & Workbook:

Jon Trelfa, Web Programming and Design
Virginia Martin-Rutledge, Chief Editor
Professer Jay Newell, Editorial Consultant, Iowa State University
Professor Ode Amaize, Consultant, Zayed University, Abu Dhabi
Professor Daniel Stout, Surf Shoppe Case Study Author & Editorial Consultant,
University of Nevada, Las Vegas

MFP Online Simulation Beta Testing Consultants:

Sarah, Emilie, and Ashley Coons
Robert M. Sainsbury
Maiah G. Rutledge

Table of Contents

Section I *Media Flight Plan* Text Chapters

Section II *Media Flight Plan* Exercises

Section III *Media Flight Plan* Case Studies

Preface

Deer Creek Publishing has invested unprecedented resources into developing the first web-based *Media Flight Plan* software and textbook. Our sixth edition provides access to data from real-world syndicated sources including MRI, CMR, SRDS, and Nielsen data – all integrated online with exercises and case studies - and, as far as possible, presented in the same format found in the professional marketing/media world. Although change is inevitable with new editions, adopting professors have asked us to maintain the original *MFP* philosophy. That philosophy is first, to provide a text that encourages students to learn theoretical and applied principles of media planning. Second, to help students learn how to apply media theory intelligently and thoughtfully. And finally, to create software simulations that help simplify the complex world of reach curves, frequency distributions and media efficiency models.

Rapid change in the media world has increased the demand for more powerful yet user-friendly software. We are confident that we have made improvements consistent with the changing world of marketing and media planning without sacrificing simplicity or accuracy. At the same time, we have continued to provide emphasis on the fundamentals needed by practitioners in their daily work lives.

The new *Media Flight Plan* web-based software includes a new main-screen interface, new reach/frequency estimates, and offers new media choices and a new cost database. This workbook contains some new cases, and new case materials are also found online.

Despite technological advances, the authors believe the most valuable knowledge a student can take from studying this discipline goes beyond rote memorization of media terms, formulae, and rate book skills. The Media Flight Plan philosophy is to move students beyond mechanical application of media skills. A text such as this is designed to push intellectual boundaries, to encourage analytical thinking and rigorous problem solving. Students must learn to apply both theory and applied media principles intelligently. Following a series of text chapters and exercises, we conclude this text with a set of marketing intensive case studies. Together, all of these elements combine to deliver an integrated marketing/media planning experience.

When employers interview a candidate for an advertising or marketing position, more than any other quality they want a person who knows how to analyze and solve marketing/media problems. They want to hire individuals educated to think strategically. Moreover, they will insist on someone who knows how to articulate this strategy in writing. *Media Flight Plan* will continue to focus on strategic planning as the most important knowledge goal. When used as intended, *Media Flight Plan* helps eliminate busy work and focus student time and energy on marketing problem solving and strategic planning. While we may not succeed in simplifying all of the complexities of media planning, our goal is to deliver as much reality as possible while providing a real-world experience that blends the practical with both applied and theoretical knowledge.

Section I

Media Flight Plan
Text Chapters

Basic Marketing and Media Language

A prerequisite for working with media research data is to have a command of the language and to learn the basic theory behind the language. First, however, you have to commit to learning the language. Sharing a common, precise language helps media planners, buyers, sellers, and researchers communicate clearly and effectively. As you work with the terms and concepts in this chapter, try to grasp *what they mean* instead of trying to memorize every detail. This will help with the formulas later in the chapter. First, learn the meaning – knowing what to do will follow naturally because you've got a basic knowledge of the concepts.

Universe (Population): A universe is the total group of persons in a specific geographic area that share a common characteristic. An example would be "Women age 18-49" or "Adults living in D counties." Universes have a geographic limit—*Total US* or *Detroit Metro*. Universes can be made of *Households*, and although *Households* aren't persons, they can be treated as if they are--any formula that works for a demographic group also applies to households. The terms *Universe* and *Population* are interchangeable—different research services use one or both. Universes are important—they are the basis for many calculations in the media world. Here is an example of the universes used by the Nielsen Company for their national television measurement service:

Estimates of U.S. TV Households and Persons in TV Households (Millions)#

	HOUSE-HOLDS	WRK WOM 18+	WOMEN 18+	18-34	18-49	25-54	35-64	55+	MEN 18+	18-34	18-49	25-54	35-64	55+	TEENS TOTAL 12-17	FEMALE 12-17
COMPOSITE	99.40	47.80	101.70	30.72	62.66	59.33	52.31	30.64	93.36	30.63	61.24	57.49	49.45	24.17	22.14	10.87
TERRITORY																
NORTHEAST	20.67	10.60	21.96	6.53	13.41	12.72	11.32	6.74	19.72	6.42	12.88	12.12	10.52	5.15	4.22	2.07
EAST CENTRAL	13.35	6.11	13.41	3.94	8.08	7.67	6.93	4.19	12.12	3.83	7.78	7.33	6.51	3.27	3.00	1.47
WEST CENTRAL	15.69	7.57	15.49	4.63	9.47	9.02	7.93	4.74	14.35	4.62	9.35	8.85	7.65	3.77	3.48	1.70
SOUTHEAST	19.61	9.36	19.90	5.82	11.88	11.28	10.15	6.36	17.86	5.67	11.38	10.73	9.39	4.95	4.18	2.06
SOUTHWEST	11.39	5.24	11.47	3.67	7.31	6.83	5.90	3.21	10.57	3.64	7.12	6.61	5.57	2.56	2.87	1.41
PACIFIC	18.69	8.92	19.47	6.15	12.51	11.81	10.08	5.40	18.73	6.45	12.73	11.85	9.81	4.47	4.40	2.15
COUNTY SIZE																
A	39.24	20.08	41.52	13.00	26.35	24.92	21.42	11.77	38.22	13.15	25.85	24.19	20.18	9.15	8.45	4.15
B	30.48	14.61	30.68	9.42	19.12	18.02	15.77	9.06	27.97	9.26	18.53	17.36	14.84	7.10	6.63	3.27
C& D	29.68	13.11	29.50	8.30	17.19	16.39	15.11	9.81	27.17	8.22	16.86	15.95	14.44	7.92	7.06	3.46
CABLE/VCR STATUS																
CABLE PLUS ADS	75.16	37.91	77.82	23.21	47.62	45.65	40.57	23.40	71.66	23.20	46.82	44.52	38.42	18.44	16.19	7.95
CABLE PLUS WITH PAY	47.53	25.98	50.66	16.11	33.07	31.79	27.54	12.79	47.75	16.07	32.67	30.79	26.50	10.73	11.58	5.69
BROADCAST ONLY	24.24	9.89	23.88	7.51	15.04	13.68	11.74	7.24	21.70	7.43	14.42	12.97	11.03	5.73	5.95	2.92
VCR OWNERSHIP	84.20	43.64	88.13	27.52	56.74	54.20	47.60	23.51	82.43	27.30	55.35	52.16	45.08	19.87	20.35	9.99
HHLD SIZE																
1	24.43	5.08	14.35	1.61	3.90	4.49	5.36	9.43	10.08	2.55	5.71	6.06	5.18	3.50	0.00	0.00
2	31.81	15.33	32.69	7.04	14.23	15.30	17.37	14.81	28.50	6.61	11.81	12.52	13.49	14.08	0.99	0.49
3+	43.16	27.40	54.66	22.07	44.53	39.53	29.58	6.40	54.79	21.47	43.72	38.91	30.78	6.59	21.15	10.38
4+	26.06	16.46	34.57	14.68	29.80	25.65	18.48	2.96	35.53	14.00	30.11	26.32	20.48	2.95	17.30	8.49
PRESENCE OF NON-ADULTS																
ANY UNDER 18	37.12	21.81	42.32	18.43	38.28	33.99	22.93	2.29	36.50	13.74	32.04	29.59	22.07	2.15	22.14	10.87
ANY UNDER 12	28.19	15.72	31.77	16.23	29.43	25.83	14.90	1.52	26.67	11.28	24.32	22.67	14.94	1.27	10.47	5.14
ANY UNDER 6	16.98	8.98	19.46	12.50	18.24	15.07	6.68	0.78	16.20	8.69	15.12	13.73	7.30	0.63	3.65	1.79
ANY 6-11	18.16	10.04	20.16	8.32	18.59	17.60	11.36	1.07	17.01	5.51	15.39	14.88	11.19	0.85	8.77	4.31
ANY 12-17	17.16	10.87	20.19	5.19	17.84	16.33	14.48	1.18	17.82	4.40	14.94	13.69	13.06	1.21	22.14	10.87
HOUSEHOLD INCOME																
$30-39,999	12.18	5.90	11.97	4.12	7.67	7.05	5.85	3.43	11.43	4.29	7.72	7.03	5.32	3.01	2.76	1.35
$40-59,999	19.60	11.62	20.35	6.90	14.11	13.43	11.30	4.53	20.85	7.31	14.74	13.96	11.48	4.47	4.98	2.44
$60-74,999	10.00	6.75	11.04	3.50	8.02	7.94	6.71	1.93	11.79	4.02	8.52	8.17	6.94	2.14	3.05	1.49
$75.000+	18.78	13.36	22.00	5.98	14.98	15.32	14.37	4.26	23.44	6.51	15.63	15.59	15.25	4.85	5.12	2.51

Universes can be added as long as they are *mutually* exclusive. Mutually exclusive means no part of the cells being added overlap. For example, add the 18-34 cell for Men and Women to get Adults 18-34.

You can also subtract cells as long as the cell being subtracted is completely contained in the cell it is subtracted from. Therefore, if you needed Women 50+, you could obtain that figure by subtracting Women 18-49 from Women 18+.

Impression: An impression is one *opportunity* for one individual to see an advertisement. If you are watching a television program, you have the opportunity to see any spots placed within it, or if you are reading a magazine, you have the opportunity to see the ads contained therein. *There is no guarantee a viewer, reader, or listener will actually be exposed to the ad*. This is an important concept to remember. Some audience members will miss all or part of the ad as they leave the room to get a snack, or flip over a large portion of a magazine to get to a particular item of interest.

Audiences to advertisements are rarely measured. Typically, it is audiences to media vehicles (i.e. individual programs or magazine titles) that are measured. Movement toward measurement of commercial audiences is being made in national television, but the industry is not there yet. Program commercial minute ratings are produced for minutes of a program that contain at least one second of a commercial, weighted by the number of commercial seconds--not exactly the same as 'commercial ratings', but much closer using program ratings as a surrogate)

Fortunately, since research studies are almost always done using "opportunities to see" as the measurement standard, research results can be transferred to the "real world" and understood in terms of the everyday media environment.

Exposure: An exposure occurs when a person "consumes" an ad. As noted previously, this is rarely measured. Doing so is problematic or prohibitively expensive in most cases, and since both media planners and researchers commonly use the impression standard, it's not an issue that affects trade. Exposure is sometimes used as a synonym for impression. Technically speaking, it is not. When "exposure" is used as a synonym for impression, think "exposure to the medium" and not "exposure to the ad."

Net Reach or **Reach**: A count of persons with at least one impression. The number of impressions received is irrelevant to reach; each person is only counted one time. Because that number doesn't tell the planner much by itself, it is most often expressed as a percentage of the *universe*. Here is the first media formula you'll need to know:

$$reach = \frac{\#\ persons\ reached}{\#\ persons\ in\ universe} x\ 100$$

There is only one "requirement" for this formula, which is that all the numbers must be on the same "scale." You'll often see counts presented in research as thousands (000) or millions (MM or 0'000), but for some media, like radio and cable, the numbers are often in units or hundreds (00). You may have to convert either reached persons or the universe into the measurement of the other in order to get the correct answer.

Reach is a flexible concept—it works for any demographic, including households. It also works for media schedules, campaigns, or individual programs or magazines. In any case, each person is only counted once—either they received an impression or not; and the persons counted as exposed must share the same unit base as the universe in order to get the correct reach. (Remember, exposed to the campaign or program, *not* to the ads) .

Reach for an individual program, magazine, radio program, or other media vehicle has a special name. It is called a *rating*.

Rating: The portion of a demographic universe that is exposed to a specific media vehicle expressed as a percentage of that universe:

$$rating = \frac{\#\ persons\ exposed\ to\ vehicle}{\#\ persons\ in\ universe} x\ 100$$

Ratings are usually rounded to one decimal place.

Ratings from different universes cannot be averaged, because the demographic universes used as denominators are different. To arrive at the correct Adult 25-54 rating from Women 25-54 and Men 25-54, you must convert the ratings back to persons for both demographics, and add them together. The total is divided by the sum of the universes. If the rating for Women 25-54 was a 5.0, and for Men 25-54 a 3.0, simple averaging would give a 4.0 rating. That is incorrect. Assuming universes of 10 million and 8 million for women and men 25-54 respectively:

10,000,000 x 0.05 (rating converted to decimal)	=	500,000
8,000,000 x 0.03	=	240,000
Total Impressions	=	740,000
740,000 / (10,000,000+8,000,000) x 100	=	4.1, the correct answer

The tenth of a rating point difference in this example may seem insignificant. However, you need to consider that hundreds of millions of dollars in media inventory are traded daily. Tenths of a point literally add up to millions of dollars.

You may discover other ways to correctly calculate combined ratings. For now, however, to avoid confusion we'll stay with a single method that we know will always work.

HUT, PUT, PUR, PUMM: These acronyms stand for "Households Using Television," "Persons Using Television," "Persons Using Radio" and "Persons Using Measured Media." All express a similar concept: the total number of persons (or households) using television (or radio) during a particular time period expressed as a percentage of the universe. PUMM is a special case of PUR, used in radio markets that are measured with meters. In those markets, only stations transmitting a special signal can be measured. When all outlest stranslate the signal, PUMM is equal to PUR. These measures are used to get a sense of overall medium usage, and are often used by media buyers to forecast ratings for future time periods. Here are the formulas:

HUT= # households using TV during time period / total households in universe x 100
PUT = # persons usin g TV during time period / total persons in universe x 100
PUR = # persons using radio during time period / total persons in universe x 100
PUMM= # persons using measured radio during time period / total persons in universe x 100

These formulas work for any demographic universe.

Does the formula for HUT/PUT or PUR/PUMM look strangely familiar? It should—like "rating," these are also cases of "reach" that have special names. In essence, HUT is the reach of all television programs being aired during the same time period. PUR/PUMM is the equivalent for persons listening to radio.

Program ratings and HUT/PUT are related through a third measure, called *share*.

Share: Share indicates the portion of the available television (or radio) audience that is viewing a particular television program (or radio station). It is calculated this way:

$$share = rating \div PUT\ x\ 100$$

As with other formulas, the calculation is the same for all demographics. In the case of households, HUT is substituted for PUT, and if you're calculating a radio share, PUR (or PUMM) is substituted for PUT.

Shares are important because they help put ratings in perspective. Without share, planners and buyers might be misled to believe that "bigger is better." Programmers of television and radio networks would be tempted to cancel some strong programs based solely on ratings. In actuality some lower rated programs are outperforming programs with higher ratings. A "real life" example will clarify this idea.

During primetime, a popular program, *NCIS,* has a rating of 6.8. Later in the evening, *The Tonight Show*, with Jay Leno has a rating of 4.2. Which is stronger? The answer is we don't know unless we see how well each draws from the available audience. The statistic that shows available audience is HUT/PUT (PUR for radio). And strength of audience draw is represented by share. It so happens that the primetime HUT for *NCIS*on the night in question was 69.7. HUT for *The Tonight Show* was 34.8. Calculating share for each, the winner is:

Tonight Show share = 4.2 ÷ 34.8 x 100 = 12

NCIS share = 6.8 ÷ 69.7 x 100 = 10

From these calculations, we see that *The Tonight Show* is doing quite well despite its lower rating. In fact, it's actually a bit stronger in its fringe-prime time slot than *NCIS* in prime. Figuratively speaking, *HUT/PUT represents the size of the available pie*, while *share represents the size of the slice. The Tonight Show* enjoyed the bigger slice.

Net vs. Gross

All of the terms defined thus far can be termed "net"—in each case a person is only counted one time, regardless of the number of times they are reached or exposed. It's sort of like counting the people who come to the dessert table or the bar at a banquet. Knowing the number of unique people at the bar or dessert table lets us know how many people were served in each location, but we still want to know how much beer or how many pies will be needed. That's because we all know people who make trips for seconds and thirds. Media planning is similar in that duplication occurs—some persons will have multiple opportunities to see our ad. Planners need to know how the "advertising pie" is being distributed—how many people are getting more than one slice, and ultimately how many media pies ("weight") should be put on the table.

Media concepts that include duplication usually include the term *gross* in the label. That's a tip-off that every impression is counted instead of every person. Let's extend the concepts we've learned so far and see what their duplicated partners are, and how all of them assist planners and buyers to analyze and see the whole planning picture.

Gross Impressions: The total number of opportunities to see provided by a campaign or plan. Remember that an impression is an opportunity to see an ad, and almost always represents the audience to a particular program or magazine, not to the ad itself. In an ad campaign, multiple programs, magazines and other media opportunities are used—and many persons in the target audience have more than one opportunity to see an ad. The sum of all those opportunities is the total number of gross impressions. Gross impressions for a campaign or media plan often run into very large numbers. You'll often see Gross Impressions (abbreviated GI or GIMP) reported in thousands or even millions.

The term Gross Impressions by itself isn't terribly useful—and it's difficult to comprehend, since the numbers are so large. It's like asking you to imagine what a stack of billion dollar bills looks like—you know it's a lot of money, but most of us don't have experience that would allow us to visualize the concept of "billions."

Where are you most likely to run into Gross Impressions? Gross Impressions are commonly used is to calculate CPM, a relative measure of cost we'll see a little later in this chapter. Another (somewhat cynical) usage for Gross Impressions is in sales materials companies use to "wow" their suppliers and franchisees. The objective is generally to impress clients with the amount of activity that is occurring (sometimes even to make a smallish schedule look bigger than it is).

Given the unwieldy nature of Gross Impressions, what do planners, buyers and clients use as a currency and descriptor of media weight? The answer is Gross Rating Points, which, as you might guess, is the "gross" counterpart of the "net" rating.

Gross Rating Points (GRPs): Gross Rating Points are commonly abbreviated in writing and in speech as "GRPs"—but can also be pronounced in humorous ways, the most common of which is "gurps." You might also hear "grips" depending on what area of the country you're in.

GRPs can be calculated several ways. We'll talk about a couple so you can see how various media terms are related. The first way is to divide total gross impressions by the universe and multiply by 100:

GRPs = gross impressions ÷ universe x 100

While this might look like the calculation for reach, it is different than reach because there is duplication involved. A person can be counted more than once, and many are. That is the reason that 100 GRPs is not the same as reaching 100 percent of the universe. Some will have been exposed to the campaign multiple times, some will only have received one impression, and some no opportunity for exposure at all.

A little algebra applied to the above equation demonstrates another basic GRP concept:

100 GRPs = a number of gross impressions equal to the size of the universe

1 GRP = a number of impressions equal to one percent of the universe

So, for a demographic group of 20 million persons, 20 million impressions equal 100 gross rating points, and 200,000 gross impressions equal 1 GRP.

A common way to calculate GRPs is to simply add up the ratings of the media vehicles. Assume your target is Women 18-24. You buy 3 spots in a TV show with a 5.0 rating, and 2 spots in a magazine with a 4.5 rating:

3 spots	@ 5.0	= 15.0
2 insertions	@ 4.5	= 9.0
TOTAL		= 24.0 GRPs

Some important issues are implied here. First, *all the ratings summed together must have the same demographic base*. You cannot add Men 25-54 GRPs and Women 18-24 GRPs, just as you cannot add their ratings. And secondly, even though ratings are a "net" measure, when they are summed, they become "gross" (hence gross rating points). They are not equal to reach any longer because of duplication. This schedule produces 24 gross rating points, but may only reach 12 or 15 percent of the target audience.

TRPs (Target Rating Points): Are the same thing as Gross Rating Points. Some agencies use the term TRPs to refer to GRPs for a specific demographic, and reserve GRPs for households.

Average Frequency: Used to describe the average number of times a reached individual was exposed to a campaign (remember—exposure to medium, **NOT** an ad). It is calculated simply by dividing the gross impressions by the persons reached, or by dividing the gross rating points (GRPs) by reach:

average frequency = gross impressions ÷ persons reached
average frequency = GRPs ÷ reach

Here are two examples:

7,800,000 gross impressions ÷ 6,000,000 reached = 1.3 average frequency

300 GRPs ÷ 75 reach = 4.0 average frequency

One more reminder: All the values used *must* have the same demographic base. Rearranging the GRP/reach equation for average frequency, we see the most ubiquitous formula in the media world:

REACH x FREQUENCY = GRPs

Frequency Distributions, Effective Reach and Effective Frequency

Reach/Frequency models used at agencies to estimate the reach of media schedules also model *frequency distributions*. A frequency distribution simply lists the number of persons reached at each level of frequency. The techniques used to model this information are outside the scope of this discussion, but there are very good discussions of reach/frequency modeling that have been published[1].

Frequency distributions are generally used to understand *effective reach* and *effective frequency*, two concepts based on communication/learning theory. The idea is that repetition is required to "learn" or "remember" an advertising message. The level of repetition or frequency required is dependent on many factors, such as complexity of the message, clutter (level of advertising in general, and specifically competing messages), relevance, ad environment and others. When target audience members have received the appropriate level of advertising (i.e. the required number of impressions) the ad becomes "effective." This frequency level is called *effective frequency*, and the proportion of the universe exposed at that level is called *effective reach*. The model below shows a frequency distribution for a schedule of 100 GRPs in primetime TV for Adults 25-54. **The "F" column means exactly this frequency level, and F+ means exposed this many times or more.**

	F	F+
0	54.7	100.0
1	20.8	45.3
2	10.8	24.5
3	6.0	13.7
4	3.4	7.6
5+	4.2	4.2

Some programs use "N" or "X" instead of "F". This example shows figures in percentages. You can see that the total reach of the schedule (persons reached one or more times) is 45.3%. If we had determined that the effective frequency level was "two or more times," then the effective reach for this schedule would be 24.5%. Setting an effective frequency level is as much art as science. There are numerous methods for estimating this level in use at different agencies. Most are based on the judgment of the research group.

You should be aware that many ad agencies lean toward a different view of advertising, often referred to as "recency theory[2]." This model places far less emphasis on frequency, and emphasizes exposure close to the sale. In fact there is convincing evidence for this model, especially with consumer products. Because the effort is directed toward placing impressions close to the sale, continuous advertising to as many people as possible becomes more important. Continuity is important because different people are continuously coming to market. And reach is important because pinpointing different individuals coming to market is difficult.

Media Costs and Comparisons

As planners and media buyers start looking at various media options, the issue of performance comes up—how to get the most "bang for the buck." Many things must be considered when planning or buying media. For example, will the vehicle environment (sitcom vs. drama; beauty column vs. food column, etc.) affect the communication objectives? Are the sight, sound and motion of television, the thought-evoking capabilities of radio, or the luxurious appearance of an upscale magazine the best environment for telling the story?

Such questions will be set aside for now — these are strategic considerations discussed in other parts of this textbook. Although these and other considerations are taken into account in real-life analysis, cost comparisons must be made.

It's difficult to tell if a program with a 5.0 rating costing $130,000 per spot is a better or worse buy than two 2.0 rated programs costing a total of $118,000. To make such comparisons easily, planners and buyers commonly use two measures, *cost per thousand* and *cost per point*. Both are essentially the same statistic. What makes them useful is that they put disparate sums of money onto a common cost basis.

Cost Per Thousand (CPM): The cost of delivering 1000 gross impressions. Cost per thousand is calculated by taking the total cost of a schedule, dividing that amount by the total impressions and multiplying by 1000:

CPM = total cost (in dollars) ÷ total gross impressions x 1000

Example: Two magazine insertions cost $45,000, and produce an estimated 4,000,000 impressions. They are combined with a radio schedule costing $10,000, and producing 2,500,000 impressions. What is the CPM of the schedule?

Total cost = $45,000 + $10,000 = $55,000
Total gross impressions = 4,000,000 + 2,500,000 = 6,500,000

Substituting: CPM = 55,000 ÷ 6,500,000 X 1000 = $8.46

Cost Per Point (CPP): Cost per point is the cost of one gross rating point. Its calculation is similar to CPM. Take the total cost of the schedule and divide by the total gross rating points:

CPM = total cost (in dollars) ÷ total GRPs

Using this formula, we can answer the earlier question of which program option was a better buy, 5.0 GRPs for $130,000 or 4.0 GRPs for $118,000:

$130,000 ÷ 5.0 GRPs = $26,000 CPP

$118,000 ÷ 4.0 GRPs = $29,500 CPP

Mathematically, the 5.0 rated show is a better buy. However, it's quite possible the other shows would be bought based on other criteria, such as the quality of the audience or appropriateness of environment.

CPP and CPM are related in the same way that GRPs (gross rating points) and gross impressions are related—through the universe that is common to both. They are basically the same measure. If you know the universe, you can easily convert from one to the other:

CPP = (CPM X Universe) ÷ 1,000 and...

CPM = (CPP ÷ Universe) X 1,000

For both of these formulas, the universe must be in units (not thousands or millions).

So which is best? The answer is neither. The one you will use depends on what information you have, or client/buyer preference. In practice, CPPs are most often used for broadcast media, while CPMs are used more frequently for print.

Additional Print Terms

There are a few additional terms you should be familiar with when dealing with print media. While these concepts could be applied to other media, they are most commonly used with print.

Composition: Composition refers to the "make-up" of a magazine audience. It is calculated by dividing the desired demographic audience by the total audience of the publication, then multiplying by 100:

Composition = target audience ÷ total audience x 100

A magazine with 250,000 "Women with children" readers and a total audience of 2,000,000 has a "Women with children" composition of 12.5%:

$$250{,}000 \div 2{,}000{,}000 \times 100 = 12.5\%$$

Composition is used to find publications that are "popular" with a particular group—in other words, which magazines have the highest *concentration* of the target. While most commonly used with magazines, the concept of composition can obviously be applied to other media.

Circulation: Is simply the number of copies distributed by a publication. It is a measure of absolute size. Planners use circulation analysis to understand the overall health of a publication, and to find publications with certain characteristics, such as those with circulation emphasizing a particular area of the country. The Audit Bureau of Circulation (ABC) audits circulation statistics for consumer magazines. Individual publications pay to have their circulation audited.

Coverage: This media term is usually used in connection with newspapers. It refers to the portion of households in a market that are in the publication's delivery area. Because newspaper readership varies widely from market to market, buyers frequently buy newspapers to reach a particular coverage level in a market.

Coverage can be confusing because it also has other meanings. When used with magazines, for example, it really means 'rating'. And with television programs, it means the percentage of households that are in markets where the program is broadcast.

Internet Terms

Relatively speaking, the Internet is a "young" advertising medium. It has many attractive characteristics, such as high targetability, and interactivity. Because of its unique character, unique measures have been developed to adapt advertising to the Internet. As measures become more formalized and better defined, industry groups are moving the Internet measures toward measures used in other media. Impressions are the primary measure used to plan web internet although it is possible to estimate ratings and GRPs with some services.

In order to understand current Internet measurements, it is necessary to consider the basics of how users navigate the Internet. Navigating the Internet is accomplished via a *browser*. Browsers are programs that display web pages. The popular web browsers include *Internet Explorer, Firefox,and Safari.*

It's all about the files. Whenever a web page is visited, a file is loaded. Each icon on the page, each ad, and each other element is displayed via a file request embedded in the page. Each link to another page is nothing more than a request to load another file. This brings us to the first Internet measurement, *hits*.

Hit: A request for a file. It is probably obvious now why this measurement is no longer used to measure web audiences. Each file request on a page results in a 'hit' on the host computer; some pages contain numerous hits, others just one or two.

Page Views: The number of times a page is completely delivered to a browser. This is quite an improvement over hits—each page is counted once as a unit. Although an improvement, page views still do not tell us anything about the individuals who viewed them.

Impressions: The delivery of an ad to a browser. There are various means employed by ad delivery services to determine if an ad was delivered. However, delivery of an ad does not mean a consumer viewed it. In this respect, it is similar to the previous definition of an impression—an opportunity to see.

Other Internet Measurements

All of these measures are derived by looking at computer logs. Their strength is that they are all objective physical measures. Their weakness is that they don't tell us anything about the person seeing the page or ad.

That kind of information is available from syndicated research services that use survey panels to follow web surfing habits of participants.

Participants in these panels load tracking software on their computer. They also give the research company information about themselves, such as age, gender, household income, and other characteristics. The software asks users of the computer to log in when connecting to each session of web surfing. The respondent's surfing activity is monitored by the software, which reports the activity back to the research company where it is aggregated with information from other panel members and reported to subscribers of the service.

These panels measure the activity of individuals, other statistics are available for web sites, and in some cases, individual web pages. Some of the statistics may include:

Unique visitors: Analogous to reach. This is the estimated number of unique persons that visited a particular site. Various demographic breaks are available depending on the service.

Usage statistics: Syndicated web research services also provide various measures of usage, such as time spent per day or month and average number of page visits. These are fairly self-explanatory and vary by service.

Social Media and Word of Mouth Measurement

Measurement of social media and word-of-mouth are still in their infancy--much like the Internet was 10 years ago. It's the 'wild west'. While there is plenty of evidence advertisers can have effective communication with consumers using these media, measurement is less well defined than other media.

Summary

In this chapter you've learned a number of important terms and concepts that will help you in your everyday work, whether for an agency or corporation, advertiser, or medium. These terms, formulas, and theoretical models form the basic currency on which all media are analyzed, bought and sold.

These are not all the terms you will use in your marketing or media planning career. However, if you understand these well, you will have a solid foundation to build on. You'll also find that as you encounter these new terms, they will logically follow from these building blocks.

Endnotes

[1]See, for example, Sumner, Paul, *Readership Research and Computers* 1985 Newsweek International; Greene, Jerome, *Consumer Behavior Models for Non-Statisticians: The River of Time* 1982 Praeger.

[2]For information on recency theory, see Jones, John Phillip, *When Ads Work* 1995 Simon & Schuster.

Media Math Conventions

Clients, planners, buyers and others are used to seeing media figures reported in specific ways. You should learn and use the "common language" of these reporting conventions:

Ratings: 4.5, not 4.5%. Ratings are not written with a % sign, even though they are percentages with one decimal place. The one possible exception to this rule are cable ratings, which are frequently carried to two decimal places because they are so small.

Reach: 78.3, not 78.25673 or 78.25673%. Reach is also written without a % sign, even though it is also a percentage, and rounded to a single decimal place--more than that is just silly given the margin of error inherent in the data.

Average Frequency: 2.8, not 2.83744. Again, just one place will do nicely.

(00): this is the way to indicate the numbers are in hundreds. Usually used with radio audiences and universes.

(000): indicates the numbers are in thousands. M after a number also means that the number is in thousands. M is the Roman numeral for 1000

MM: MM after a number means millions (M x M, or 1000 x 1000). To convert a number in millions (MM) to thousands (000), shift the decimal place three places to the right. Ex: 11.23 MM = 11,230 (000)

GRPs (Gross Rating Points): are written as whole numbers (e.g. 324 not 323.8), especially in a document that goes to a client.

CPM (Cost Per Thousand): is a cost. Don't forget the $ sign (e.g. $12.35 CPM)

CPP (Cost Per Point): is a cost. Remember the $ sign, and round to the nearest dollar (e.g. $12,000)

Social Media and Social Marketing

Social Media Defined

Twitter, facebook, digg, YouTube, delicious - all social media, and no doubt you can think of another dozen off the top of your head. When new media emerge, advertisers move quickly to capitalize on them. Although there are many ways to interpret social media, this definition goes to the heart of what it means to live in a socially constructed media environment:

Social media is a wireless conversation that fosters communion and sharing between human beings compared with traditional media that delivers content at the expense of conversation.

The goal for marketers is to get people talking online about products and services. Ron Jones (searchenginewatch.com) defined social media in the language of the Internet: "Social media essentially is a category of online media where people are talking, participating, sharing, networking, and bookmarking online. It's more of a two-way conversation, rather than a one-way broadcast like traditional media."

Social media has catapulted into our consciousness because it connects groups of people not only socially, but across geographic boundaries. Thanks to social media, it's easy to share your ideas, photos, videos, likes and dislikes with the world at large, or with an intimate group. You can find friends or business contacts and become part of a community. Social media gives human beings what TV never could - a chance to commune with and engage others.

For advertisers, the potential of social media derives from the loyalty and trust inherent in these conversations.

Integrating Social Media into Media Planning

Although all media plans will not call for social media, it has become an important means of communicating with consumers. Social media cannot be ignored because it empowers individuals with something to say, allowing planners to see who it is they're hoping to reach as well as understand what motivates them. The ability to understand someone, their challenges, filters, objectives, options, and experiences makes us "mentally one" with whom we hope to connect.

Because we are a consumer culture, and consumption has become an integral part of American lifestyle, it's a natural evolution to find social media integrated into the marketing of products and services. Both big and small businesses are experimenting with social media marketing, grappling with the question of how to capitalize on an especially viral way to connect people with products in more intimate, human ways. Since conversations in social media are rooted in social, not commercial life, participants share consumption experiences in an open and honest way.

For example, Chevrolet might invite Taylor Swift to drive the Chevy Volt for six months, and ask her to tweet her honest reviews and experiences, no holds barred.
Assume she tweets something like: *"Love my furious Volt. Feels like it's on rails and jolts you to 60 in a NY second. Never need 2 stop for gas."*

While fans may realize that Taylor has a financial relationship with Chevrolet, many in her network will accept her comments as truthful because of the trust she has built up over time. The advertising aspect is enhanced because she has earned personal equity with her fans as they've followed her. A potential brand builder for Chevrolet? Very likely. However, there are two sides to the social media coin. If (hypothetically) a month later Taylor had a bad experience with Mr. Goodwrench, who was rude during a scheduled maintenance visit, and she tweeted about that, everything could backfire on Chevrolet because of the loyalty and trust factor in social media. The danger to advertisers inherent in social media is that they have no control over the message. The best social media advertisers are actively involved in monitoring social conversations about their brand, responding to them in a way that turns negative experiences into positive communications by meeting the needs of disgruntled consumers. *Travel and Leisure* relates a story from Virgin Airlines, who carefully manages social conversations. "One customer had a hard time flagging down a flight attendant to order a meal," says Abby Lunardini, a spokesperson for the airline. "After she tweeted about it, our team sent a message to the crew and she was served immediately." With consumers ensconced in social media, marketers face a whole new world of transparency. Warning to advertisers: The consumer has a new tool, and it gives her the power to make or break your brand in a tweet.

As this example illustrates, social media can play a big part in brand-building. If a brand is the sum total of our product related feelings and experiences, social media has already proven itself as a vital marketing tool for the future. Online conversations can be brutally honest; they tell us a great deal about the relationship between consumers and the brands they like and dislike.

Phenomenal Growth of Social Media

Wherever we turn in today's linked world, big brands like Nike, Pepsi, Sony, HP, Home Depot, Lands' End and others are embedding social media into their marketing plans. These companies embed links to branded facebook and twitter accounts in their email marketing. Pepsi recently opted out of the Super Bowl to pursue cause-based social media. Instead of spending millions on traditional advertising during the game, Pepsi posted online conversations detailing how the company is engaging in community service.

According to *Time* magazine, "To Pepsi, and to companies around the world, the days when mass-market media is the sole vehicle to reach an audience are officially over. Instead of pouring millions into a Super Bowl commercial, Pepsi has started a social-media campaign to promote its 'Pepsi Refresh' initiative. Pepsi plans to give away $20 million in grant money to fund projects in six categories: health, arts and culture, food and shelter, the planet, neighborhoods and education."

Social marketing expert, Brian Solis, is confident that social marketing will continue to fuse with our email inboxes until one day, they become one. Solis refers to a survey indicating that many marketers are planning to double their budgets in email marketing, SEO (Search Engine Optimization) and social media compared to their spending in traditional advertising and PR well into the future, as illustrated in the following graph.

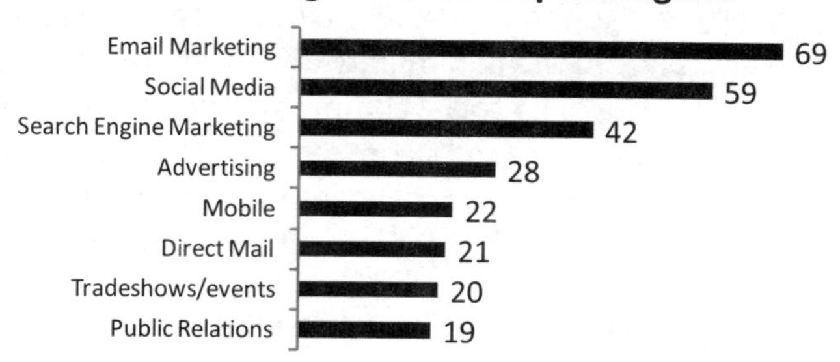

Drawbacks in Social Media

Lest the reader get the impression that social media will soon flatten the world of traditional advertising, don't hold your breath. In Darwinian fashion, advertising as an institution continues to evolve according to its own brand of natural selection. Even if social media threatens to become the predominant medium in the coming decade, mutations are inevitable, and traditional media is far from an endangered species. TV and print advertising content are always evolving and adapting to other forms of distribution. Keep in mind that they are not beholden to a TV screen or two dimensional paper. Their content can morph into new shapes and sounds distributed via laptops, Kindles, iPads, iPhones, and other tools not yet imagined, be they home based, highly portable or perhaps one day transported through nanotubes into 3-D holograms.

Audience metrics are still problematic in social media. Compared with traditional advertising - which has had many decades to evolve its measurement techniques - social media measurement is in its infancy. Despite the advantages of trust and intimacy inherent in social media, the advertiser faces a major limitation in understanding social media in a quantitative way, and will need new methods of measuring effectiveness. A TV sitcom has the potential to deliver a message to 30 million target women in 2-4 weeks, and a generally accepted measurement system, Nielsen, exists to reliably quantify it. Advertisers are well aware of the power of twitter or facebook through anecdotal evidence, however, there is no standard of measurement that can reliably quantify the size of that audience. While social media brings to advertising strengths of intimacy and communication power, traditional advertising maintains advantages that it has always enjoyed: the ability to 'get the word out' with broad reach and efficiency. Over time, advertisers will learn to make the best use of social media as it settles into its proper place in the media landscape.

Effective Social Media Demands Ethical Marketing

As marketers open the door to social media, they must be aware that they are exposed in a way like no other medium. Ethics, or lack thereof, cannot be hidden and are readily apparent in a social media world. Consumers will 'call out' both successes and failures, and they express both with passion. As social media becomes more embedded in the culture, marketing behavior must evolve to reflect the sensitivity and trust necessary in human conversation.

When brands and companies communicate socially, they must act as members of the community, responding to consumers' needs in a 'golden rule' manner--putting the needs of consumers first. Failure to be honest or to ignore the consumer will result in a backlash far beyond one customer. For example, Toyota's failures will be the subject of social media case studies for a decade. Instead of acting ethically when safety concerns were rife on facebook and YouTube, officials hedged. How could they ignore tweets like this from CaptStephen? "Toyota president said: We grew too big too fast. Big and fast is not the issue--honesty and integrity is. Obviously [Toyota] is still hedging." Consumers have a megaphone in social media. Brands must act so this megaphone is used in their favor, not against them. Toyota lost both faith and face by thinking they could hide.

As brands communicate honest experiences, consumers receive commnication they can believe in, and something they value. But consumers won't continue to share in the conversation unless the social marketer resonates honestly with their needs and expectations. Here's a good example:

> Dr. Jason Lipscomb, a nationally recognized expert in the use of social media in his dental practice, wrote, "How can I give back to the community and in return gain their trust? First of all, you behave unselfishly. When you join a social community, don't start immediately talking about your practice. You wouldn't go to a friend's cookout and try to score new patients. Social media works the same way. When you start, make sure you give back to the community by offering helpful comments and linking to articles they are interested in."

The doctor gets it. He knows that social communities are also consumer communities, and that consumers value honest conversations with a dentist who understands them. Since about 25% of all tweets discuss a product or service, his posts are perceived as part of a conversation. His interest in the community, expressed with one or two tweets a day, generates an average of seven new patients a month, at zero cost. He has also been on his local NBC and ABC stations. How? Local journalists saw his posts on twitter and thought they were interesting. An excellent example of how media can help grow a small business and give it a human voice in the community. It also illustrates how social media function as marketing research tools. The advertiser plugs into an ongoing conversation, and asks, "How's my product doing?" Responses to this question could reveal important consumer insights for building future campaigns.

Red Bull

Red Bull Fan Page Case Study

The Red Bull Fan Page is easily one of the best on facebook simply because it has been able to break out of the typical fan page mold by providing fun content that encourages fans to interact with and ultimately connect with the brand. Their uniqueness is captured in their innovative incorporation of Twitter into their Facebook fan page. Integrating a Twitter stream is not special on its own, but Red Bull doesn't just pull in tweets from their official corporate voice, as you might expect most brands do. Instead, Red Bull has aggregated tweets from sponsored athletes like skateboarder Ryan Sheckler and snowboarder Shaun White and included them directly in their facebook presence. Associating themselves with popular athletes and letting fans connect to those athletes on a separate social network gives Red Bull some instant cool points.

Red Bull has built all kinds of content and applications that help them break out of the vanilla Facebook mold that forces all brands to look and feel more or less the same. A favorite app is one that lets fans rate phone calls of people who "drunk dialed" the Red Bull 1-800 number. It's not only hilarious, but it also smartly encourages additional fan engagement.

Red Bull, popular with the teen and college-age demographic, definitely knows its audience, and they've played to that face by categorizing their page under the business type "pharmaceuticals." Clearly, this is a company that understands their audience and knows that the best way to connect with them on facebook is with humor, creativity, and fun apps that engage them.

McDonald's Among Early Adopters of Social Media

It was March 2006 when Fernando Sosa and Thomas Middleditch rapped a video in the streets of Chicago about their love of McDonald's Chicken McNuggets. Maybe you know this story.

i'm lovin' it®

The video was filmed by Matt Malinsky with a McDonald's franchise in the background. The company had nothing to do with the customer-generated video; their only involvement was the McNugget product that inspired the two 20-something fans to create a rap.

The video scored tens of thousands of views on YouTube in the first year. Arnold Worldwide, an advertising agency based in Boston, was tipped about the video. After consulting with the burger-and-fries empire, they adapted Sosa's and Middleditch's rap to a TV commercial. The media gulped it down; TV viewers raced to the stores to buy McNuggets, and one of social media's earliest case studies was born.

Home Town, Small Business Social Media Case Study: Dr. Jason Lipscomb, DDS

Following is a conversation with a dentist, Jason Lipscomb, who has learned to use social media in a beneficial way. The principles he outlines are equally applicable to any brand or marketer, large or small. Note how he focuses on fulfilling the needs of consumers, using current clients and staff to 'spread the word' and manage the social campaign, and especially how he provides value to consumers. It covers the basics.

Note: This conversation on social media was published by Kevin Henry, managing editor of Dental Economics. *He recently visited with Dr. Jason Lipscomb, a Fredricksburg, Virginia, dentist who is the co-author of the book, "Social Media for Dentists." Log on to www.socialmediadentist.com. to learn more.*

Henry: What's the most surprising statistic to you when it comes to dentistry and social media?
Dr. Lipscomb: About 34 million women go online each month to discuss everything from their purchases to — you guessed it — their dentists. About 70% of women made the decision to use a product or service online and then, according to Forrester research, 50% of them told their friends about it.

Henry: You say it's important to have an action plan before starting down the social media path. Why?
Dr. Lipscomb: Social media is made up of many parts, however it has one consistent theme — conversing and listening. Social media is word of mouth on steroids, but if you dive into it haphazardly without a plan, then your chances of succeeding are very low. An action plan should have clearly defined goals that enable you to run a highly effective and efficient campaign.

Henry: What's your best advice to dentists just starting down the social media path?
Dr. Lipscomb: Take your time and don't try to incorporate every social media platform at once. One of the biggest mistakes dentists make is trying to be everywhere at once, and they immediately become overwhelmed. The best advice I can give is to pick one or two social networking platforms and start there.

As I said before, have a game plan with a clear and concise strategy. Also make sure that you are consistent with your branding. Your Web site, blog, Twitter and Facebook accounts should all help extend your message to the community. Also when you join a social community, don't start immediately talking about your practice and the services you offer. You wouldn't go to a friend's cookout and try to get new patients. Social media works the same way. The CEO of Zappos Inc., Tony Hsieh, has nearly 1.7 million followers and he is on Twitter every day. Tony always has something interesting to say and I always read his posts. Nearly 95% of his tweets are not about Zappos at all, they are just interesting tweets or articles, but followers have grown to really like him. When you start, make sure you give back to the community by offering helpful comments and linking to articles.

Don't underestimate the power of social communities. About 25% of tweets discuss a product or service. My Twitter campaign alone brings me an average of seven new patients a month and there is zero cost. I have also been on NBC and am being interviewed by ABC this month. How? Local journalists saw my posts on Twitter and thought they were interesting. Social media can definitely help grow your practice and give you a voice in your community.

Henry: I know some dentists are using their team members as their social media coordinators. Is this a good idea? Why or why not?
Dr. Lipscomb: Your team can be a powerful asset. As long as you lay down definite ground rules, such as patient privacy, and acceptable language and behavior, using your team can be a great opportunity to communicate with the community at many different levels. Many of the young dental assistants and office

staff have grown up using social media and understand completely what is acceptable and not acceptable. I would discuss using social media with your staff, and encourage those interested to play a part in helping you grow your practice. Not only is social media an effective tool to communicate with others and become the voice of your local community, it is also a great tool that can save you hours of work if used correctly!

Henry: What's the most common misconception you find among dentists when it comes to social media?
Dr. Lipscomb: There are actually two main misconceptions that I hear over and over. The first is, "I don't have enough time," and the second is, "My Web site is first on Google . . . so I don't need to do anything else."

A well-managed campaign takes about five to 10 minutes a day and is virtually free. The most time consuming part of a social media campaign is the original set-up. After that there are plenty of ways to send messages to multiple social media networks simultaneously with the push of a button.

Most dentists think, "I have a Web site and great SEO (Search Engine Optimization) so that's all I need." This might have been true as recently as a year ago, but simply is not true anymore. Many dentists hire companies to get their Web sites to top ranking positions and believe this will bring in the traffic.

Unfortunately, many SEO specialists over-stuff Web sites with keywords and over-optimized text. Many Web sites I've seen are almost illegible because everything is written for search engine traffic. If your Web site is not attractive, not engaging, and does not collect any information from the prospective patient, it doesn't matter if your site is number 1 or number 50. You get 7 seconds to hold someone's attention.

Social media is much more powerful because you are interacting with prospective clients. You have a voice in the community, and a personality. People are more likely to go to dentist who they feel relaxed and at ease with. Earlier I mentioned that 1.4 million women cancel their appointments out of fear. Social media is a way to interact, allay fears, and build relationships with prospective clients.

SEO is important, but it cannot compete with review sites, local search, and the fact that more tweets and Facebook posts are indexed instantly by the major search engines. I have spoken with several dentists who are spending between $30,000 and $40,000 a year just to maintain a top position in the search engines. Meanwhile they don't realize that Facebook actually beat out Google for visits this year, social media surpassed e-mail this year, and YouTube had more viewership than ABC, CBS, NBC, and Fox combined.
Henry: How many times do you use social media in a day? Do you set limits or goals for yourself on a daily or weekly basis?
Dr. Lipscomb: Dentists will have the best results if they use social media a couple times a day. Many times I'll get to the office a few minutes early and send out a few quick posts, and then after lunch I'll spend a few minutes again. I don't really set limits for myself, but I do set goals. I generally like to bring in seven to 10 new patients a month. To do this I engage my Twitter community with interesting articles, surveys, videos, and usually a weekly give-away. In our book I really go into detail on how to implement the above techniques in a matter of minutes a day.

Henry: You've said that time management can make or break a social media campaign. Why?
Dr. Lipscomb: It's human nature to want to see immediate results for something that you invested time creating. Many dentists will join a social community and give up after a week. Most dentists have no idea how to even implement a social media strategy and they feel they're investing time without reaping any rewards. That's one of the main reasons we see dentists give up on social media.

To be effective you must have a plan, and you must also understand that you will have to initially invest some time. That being said, dentists still struggle with implementation. Most dentists are not marketers nor do they want to be. They want to be successful, but they want to continue using traditional techniques that are becoming less effective every day.

For a social media strategy to be effective, dentists need to implement just a couple of strategies. Realize that it will take some time to set up the campaign. For instance, if they are setting up a Twitter campaign they will need to have a professional background designed, a nice picture taken as their avatar, and a small bio written. Unless you are a graphic artist, I recommend you have a professional create your Twitter background and help you write your bio. Once this is set up and you have a professional presence, then you can create your community. Once this is finished you need to spend only about five to 10 minutes a day.

If done correctly, instead of investing thousands of dollars, a powerful Twitter campaign can get you in front of your local community EVERY day, many times a day. Once you have established a great Twitter campaign then you can establish other campaigns on other social networks. My advice is to take your time — it's amazing when you think about the ability to converse with your local community every day. And remember, when you tweet or post on Facebook, every one of your messages is being indexed by Google. Be smart, use keyword rich posts, and whenever possible add links back to your Web site or blog.

Henry: How should dentists balance social media with blogging?
Dr. Lipscomb: Blogs are very important as people expect to see valuable information in them. Their mindset is one of interest and curiosity. This is a great place for dentists to have how-to articles and videos, picture galleries, and procedure articles and videos.

Blogs are great because they lead to interaction with others. Dentists should be sure to ask for comments at the end of every blog. Search engines love comments, especially keyword rich comments. This is also true with videos. Make sure that you ask for comments about your videos. Blogs also enable you to expand on topics from your Web site. You can post case studies and help patients understand such topics as billing or insurance.

Another concern that dentists have about blogging is, "Where do I get content for my blog?" Some dentists love to write, and some would rather bang their head against a wall. I enjoy writing articles and creating video testimonials, so using social media is a natural extension for who I am. However, in our book we discuss great ways for dentists to use industry experts to write their blogs and articles for them. We have created a group of expert research companies, dental students, and retired dentists to help dentists create content for their Web sites and blogs. Articles and blogs usually run about $50 to $100 for 15 expertly-written articles. That's a good 12 months worth of articles, which can then be advertised on press release sites, etc.
Once again, as with any social media campaign, make sure that your blog's message and appearance is consistent with the rest of your social networks and Web site. Uniformity and consistency are extremely important in building a reputation.

Henry: What's the main thought you want to leave with our readers?
Dr. Lipscomb: I encourage dentists to get started now and explore the options that are available. If all you send out are direct mail campaigns and use the phone book then you are really missing out. All your competition has to do is be a little bit more interesting than a phone book ad. Traditional advertising is moving online, and today only 14% of people use phone books to find a professional. And 24 of the 25 largest newspapers are experiencing record declines in circulation and advertising revenue. Almost 90% of people Tivo television shows to avoid watching commercials. Out of all TV commercials watched (a multi-billion dollar industry) less than half generates positive ROI.

With the right tools, social media can grow your practice for pennies on the dollar compared to traditional advertising costs. It can establish you as a hero or local expert in your community. Social media also enables you to have a presence throughout the Web and not just rely on your Web site as the key selling point for your practice.

Social media is here, it's not a fad, and 96% of generation Y is already heavily involved in it . . . It's a fundamental shift in the way we communicate. Your patients and prospects are already there. Are you?

CHAPTER 3

Marketing Driven Media Plans

Situation Analysis Yields Marketing Intelligence

A marketing driven media plan recognizes that most media decisions are subordinate to marketing objectives and strategies. All advertising decisions, whether creative, positioning, or media strategies, will be much more effective when firmly rooted in marketing intelligence. The media planner must become thoroughly familiar with all available marketing facts that drive the media plan.

What is marketing intelligence? It is the discovery and evaluation of all promotional and marketing facts relating to the product – and fitting them to the media plan. *Media Flight Plan* software assumes all of your decisions will be justified with thorough marketing intelligence. This chapter provides a checklist of seven questions to help you prepare marketing-driven case studies for *Media Flight Plan* software.

SWOT (Situation Analysis): A Marketing Checklist For Media Planners

A SWOT analysis is essentially a situation analysis; it's an acronym that represents four elements of the process: **S**trengths, **W**eaknesses, **O**pportunities and **T**hreats. Whether you call it SWOT, Statement of Facts, or Situation Analysis, the seven points in this chapter will help you gather intelligent marketing information.

This list covers more questions than you will be able to research for most products. It would be wasteful of your time, and whoever reads your SWOT if you try to answer every question below. Focus only on *relevant questions that relate to your product*. Also, *avoid writing strategic recommendations or setting objectives when writing your SWOT*. The SWOT is a statement of facts – it *does not set any goals* or recommend actions.

Most of these questions deal directly with marketing, not media issues. However, a few questions will hit directly on media issues – these are to help you make the connection with marketing. Many researchers get inspiration for marketing ideas (strategies/objectives) while conducting this research. It's smart to jot down ideas for goals as you write the SWOT, but *save them for the media objectives/strategies section of your plan*.

1. Analysis Of Marketing Objectives & Strategies

A media plan must be consistent with the goals set for marketing. For example, assume a brand manager sets a goal to double current sales using a direct marketing television promotion. A media planner would need to know such goals so she could respond with an appropriate media plan. Consider these basic questions:

- The 4 P's: Product, Price, Place, Promotion. What effect do they have on the media plan? Uncover as much relevant information about these four pillars of marketing as you can.
- What is the total size of this market?
- What methods have been used to sell this product?
- Has advertising been used in the past? How? Which media?
- Where is this brand in the product life cycle? If this is a new product, developing awareness may be your highest priority. If product is mature, and competition is strong, reminder ads with higher

levels of frequency may be called for.

- What are the sales goals for the product?
- Current share of market? Share goals?
- Current awareness for brand? Awareness goals?
- Is marketing budget available?
- Geographic breakdown for sales?
- Creative concept: Does it require a specific media mix? Social Media? SEO (Search Engine Optimization)? Are print media needed? Broadcast? Internet? Event marketing? Sales promotions? Demonstration? Is your concept highly memorable? If not, is media budget adequate to support high frequency to get awareness needed?

2. Competitive Considerations

A media planner needs to know as much as possible about the marketing and media activities of competitive brands. Suppose a competitor is spending double the amount in mass media compared to your brand. Moreover, all of it is being spent in broadcast media. This may leave open an opportunity to out-spend the competition in internet. Or, it may suggest the need to concentrate marketing dollars in just a few major markets where you can match competitive spending. Ask these questions:

- Who are all the major competitive players?
- What share of market do they have?
- Compared with competition, is your brand unique or is it very similar to competitors?
- How much is the competition spending?
- Which media does the competition use? Which vehicles?
- When do major competitors spend most of their money?
- What kind of sales promotion does the competition employ?
- Non-traditional media and guerilla marketing – do your competitors paint outside the lines?

3. Creative History Of Brand

Consider a situation where you are assigned to develop a media plan for Demae, a new chain of sushi bars located in California, Nevada and Arizona. Research reveals that 60% of prospective customers, adults 25-34, perceive Demae's fare as a healthy alternative to high calorie lunches, especially during the hot summer months. The campaign follows from these facts—the summer campaign positions Demae as a healthy, yet pleasurable lunch alternative. The campaign theme: "Tuesday's Lunch Special: 300 Low Tempura Calories!" How might this affect media decisions? First, it may help decide the media mix. For example, it may be effective to reach prospects right before or during the noon hour. Awareness of the creative concept should help you later when you need to write the media mix strategy. Consider the following questions:

- How is the product currently positioned?
- What is the current copy theme? Slogan? Headlines?
- Which media are currently being used by this brand?
- Is this product high or low involvement? If involvement is medium to high – the prospect is willing to invest time to gain knowledge about the product, and has considerable interest in the consequence of the purchase. Media should be considered that allow enough copy to provide details, e.g., magazines, Internet or newspapers. If involvement is low – product is purchased on impulse or with very little time investment – radio, TV or outdoor may be effective media choices.
- Make a list of benefits and specific qualities of your product, including psychological benefits. For example, in the case of the Demae Sushi bar, benefits might include: Fresh seafood, low fat, low calorie, fresh vegetables, and no artificial flavors. Guilt-free indulgence is a clear psychological benefit.

- How do users feel about the brand? Attitudes? Lifestyles?
- How is the product/service used? Consumed? When?
- What percent of budget should be considered for national media? Spot media?

4. Target Audience

It is vital to develop both demographic and psychographic target profiles. Many products appeal to multiple groups. If your product has wide appeal, assign a value to each group. It is always useful to conduct primary research (focus groups and/or surveys) to develop an accurate target profile. *When writing case studies, be sure to check mediaflightplan.com for syndicated data and other materials provided for the case. These may include data from MRI (Mediamark Research Inc.), TNS-MI (Competitive Media Reports), SRDS, and other companies.*

5. Geography Questions

It is important to know whether a brand is distributed nationally or regionally. If distribution is national, it's important to know if sales potential varies by metro markets or by region, and which regions hold greatest promise. It would be rare for a brand or category to be equally strong in all geographic parts of the country. Also, simply because a brand is distributed nationally, distribution alone is hardly adequate justification for spending media dollars in national media. Analyze all available marketing data, and then make a judgment call. Whether you advertise in national media only, spot media only or both, geographic strategy is critical to the success of your brand. Don't be afraid to take a risk as long as you can present a strong case based on hard marketing data.

- Is brand distributed nationally, regionally, or both?
- Advertise in national media only? Can this strategy be justified with quantitative marketing data? Remember that national buys cover all markets, including any spot markets under consideration.
- Advertise in national media with heavy-up buys in key spot markets. Does data support this decision?
- What percent of budget should be considered for national media? Spot media?
- Advertise only in key spot markets? Does available quantitative data support a spot market only campaign?
- Which spot markets have the best potential? Rank markets by EV% (see chapters on factor spreadsheets), and then divide them into subgroups of 5 or 10. Justify each group of 5 or 10 based on available advertising budget and other data.
- If you conduct a spot only campaign, how many markets will your budget handle? This may require trial and error buys on *MFP* (adding a few markets at a time). Can you penetrate enough markets (% of population or % of target population) to keep brand sales strong?
- The above assumes doing a spreadsheet analysis of all spot markets, ranking them top to bottom.
- What is BDI (Brand Development Index) and CDI (Category Development Index) for each major market?
- What types of non-traditional media can be justified in national or spot markets?
- Does guerrilla marketing hold potential for this brand? Nationally? In spot markets?
- What percent of budget should be considered for non-traditional media? Which media?

Approach all of these questions based on marketing facts. For example, on the question of national budget, you could write: Possible allocation: Split budget 70% national and 30% spot. Spreadsheet analysis indicates that 18 spot markets scored above a 110 index. These 18 markets yield 30% of total brand sales.

Avoid writing any recommendations in the situation analysis. *Phrase your SWOT so that it reports facts only - no goals, objectives or strategies.*

6. Timing & Purchase Cycle

Timing is everything in media. When should you advertise this brand? Some products are highly seasonal. If there is relatively consistent demand for your product throughout the year (or for a solid block of time such as 3 months or 6 months) a CONTINUOUS media schedule may be needed. If consumers do not purchase your product every month (e.g. appliances, cars, tires, etc.) a FLIGHTING schedule may be justifiable. PULSING may be a good strategy if demand is fairly continuous, but with heavier demand in key months. Study consumption of the brand and category. Know when sales are highest and lowest. Once the SWOT discovers key timing facts, extra weight (GRPs) can be used in the heaviest consumption periods. For example, if 60% of sales occur in July, this may call for 60% of the GRP weight in July, for one month *before* July.

- Is life cycle relevant? If this is a new product introduction, when should advertising launch?
- Seasonality - which months are most important?
- Should campaign launch before or during peak sales period?
- When does competition advertise most heavily? Should you have a strategy to deal with it? Match it? Exceed it?
- What is the purchase cycle for this product? If purchased often (more than once a month), frequent reminder advertising may be appropriate.
- Will purchase cycle influence the frequency strategy in a media plan?
- Are any specific days of the week important?
- Is there a time of day when most purchases are made? Which media could reach target closest to this time?
- What time of day is product consumed or used?
- Should media weight (GRP's) follow monthly sales?
- Any sales promotion events? Is media support needed? When? Why?
- Is a specific time of month important for this product?
- Any holidays that might influence consumption?
- Can weather or climate in geographic regions be used strategically?

7. Questions About The Media Mix

Although last on the list, this is one of the most critical issues in your plan. Media mix is the combination of media and vehicles that suit this brand best. The media mix should also address which environment is best for the brand. Kid's cereal, for example, would not be appropriate for late night TV. Technical products (computers, cars, etc.) may require long copy, and the higher credibility of the magazine environment. Guerilla marketing may work marketing XBox or Playstation to teenagers, but may not work as well for many adult products. High tech products may also require interactive Internet buys. Remember to state your observations about the brand and media options under consideration – and to write them as facts, not as goals. Do not make any media recommendations yet. Ask these questions:

- How much Internet or social media is appropriate for your brand?
- Which media/vehicles match the lifestyle of your target audience?
- Will budget allow you to match or outspend the competition using the same media mix as competitors?
- Are there any weaknesses in competitor's media mix?
- Do you have enough competitive media data to create a Share of Voice (SOV) analysis?
- Does your brand enjoy clear advantages over the competition? If so, consider meeting them head-on in their own media.
- Which media would work best for this brand? Why? Any marketing incentives for using social media? Radio? TV? Outdoor? Internet? Magazines? Direct mail? Guerilla media? Media mix is the very heart of your media strategy. Sound research here is vital supported by solid rationales.

- Is purchase decision high or low involvement? If high involvement, can print media be effective?
- Is the message simple or complex?
- How, if at all, should the Internet be used for this brand?
- Is message heavy with information?
- How much time or space is needed to say it?
- Is creative concept flexible enough to work effectively across all media?
- Should product/service be demonstrated?
- Does product need to be shown visually? Why?
- Is color important in your media mix for this brand?
- Would print be effective? Would coupons induce trial? What possible cross promotions might work with other brands or categories?
- Are commuters likely to purchase? Where? When? Which media are best to reach them?
- Have you calculated effective frequency for your media mix? (If available, use Ostrow model). How many exposures are estimated to get response?

"Gotchas" that destroy SWOT credibility

Biggest offense: Inadequate research. Clients do not value opinions; they want valid information, and nothing improves validity more than evidence backed up by primary and secondary sources. Primary research generally refers to research contracted directly by the agency or client; secondary research comes from syndicated sources or published materials in the library or on the internet. Secondary sources are a good start, but don't stop there.

Using only secondary research suggests laziness. Clients expect you to tell them something they don't know. This could be accomplished with primary research. If time and money preclude a scientific study, conduct something as simple as a non-probability intercept survey in a mall, or sample a few people on the phone. A phone call to a store manager takes minimal effort, or even better, visit him/her in the store, and take photos on site, etc. For example, if you're assigned to work on the Harley Davidson business, visit the store and talk with the sales people. Hang out with customers and get inside the Harley culture. Provide evidence of all merchandising and promo strategies. If you're marketing a packaged goods product, visit the store section and map the number of shelf facings occupied by your brand and all competitors. (Facings = number of packages that "face" the customer horizontally on the shelf). How many shelves (vertically) does each brand occupy? Does your brand (or a competitive brand) capitalize on end cap displays? Talk to customers. Study them as they shop for brands in your category.

Failure to cite sources kills your credibility. If you don't cite sources, or bury your sources, credibility is weakened.

Poor organization discourages reading your plan. Avoid fluff and filling pages with opinions. Unsubstantiated thinking jumps off the page and suggests last minute effort.

Use subheads and avoid "fluff-heads" that say nothing. Write complete "headlines" and don't worry about length. Hook the reader by selling a concept with compelling suheads. Example: "Social Media Dominates Red Bull's Media Mix."

Lazy writing is a major "gotcha." Clients (and professors) can always tell when you're submitting a first draft.

Late work brands you, whatever the reason. Your reason for lateness automatically reveals a lot about you to the client. What's the best excuse for lateness? Not, "I was sick or my car broke down." Man up and tell the client, "No excuse - it won't happen again."

CHAPTER 4

Organizing a Media Plan

Anatomy of a Media Plan

This chapter illustrates all the parts of the plan in linear order with examples for each.

The chapter "Award Winning Media Plan" provides excellent examples of well-crafted media objectives, rationales, and strategies. Important Note: There are as many models for writing media plans as there are ad agencies. The winning example follows many (but not all) of the conventions shown here. Unless your professor instructs you otherwise, follow the outline shown below – it covers the basics.

The media plan is comprised of five sections: Each section should start on a new page.

Model Media Plan:

I. Executive Summary
II. SWOT-Situation Analysis
III. Creative Brief-Creative Strategy
IV. Media Objectives & Strategies
V. Appendix

I. Executive Summary

Typically one to two pages in length, this is a tight, definitive synopsis that reveals the highlights of your plan. It should highlight the strategic genius that drives your media plan, and after reading your summary, the marketing VP should know if the rest of the plan is worth reading.

II. SWOT - Situation Analysis Section (Start on a new page)

Recommended length: There is no absolute length for a situation analysis, but it typically runs 4-6 pages. Avoid prose style. Write in business/technical style using outline format. Use "call out" boxes and compelling subheads to draw the reader's attention to vital points.

A good way to approach the SWOT is to ask intelligent questions about your brand's marketing situation, and craft your answers into statements of relevant marketing/media facts that will drive your media objectives and strategies. (See SWOT – Situation Analysis in previous chapter.)

Remember, this is *not* a place for media objectives or strategies. *Avoid recommendations and rationales.* Instead, be descriptive and factual. A situation analysis reports the important facts and history relevant to the brand - *it never includes objectives or strategies about what you plan to do.*

Based on the **Marketing Checklist For Media Planners** that you studied in the previous chapter, your situation analysis or SWOT should include detailed information on the following:

- Analysis of Marketing Objectives & Strategies
- Competitive Considerations
- Creative History of the Brand
- Target Audience
- Geography Questions
- Timing & Purchase Cycle
- Questions about The Media Mix

III. Creative Brief – Creative Strategy (Start on a new page)

Along with marketing considerations, creative is equally important in driving the media plan. Media decisions must be integrated with the brand's creative strategy. Media objectives and strategies must be consistent with the creative strategy. For example, if your brand's success depends on a creative concept on facebook, this position must be clearly articulated in the brief. Some professors may require a few creative executions to accompany your brief. This can be useful in helping to integrate the media plan with the message.

Creative Brief

The Creative Brief is a one-page document defining the creative strategy. This brief includes five main points:

1. Communication Objective

State exactly what you expect the advertising to accomplish. Awareness? Trial purchase? Brand loyalty? Increase customer traffic in the retail store?

2. Creative Strategy – Brand Position

At the heart of any creative strategy, positioning describes *how you want your brand to be perceived by the consumer*. It describes your niche in the mind of the consumer. Begin by identifying your brand's existing position. For example, assume the brand is Harley Davidson's Sportster targeted primarily at thirty-something women. Harley-Davidson is an expert at inclusion marketing, and it's impossible to do inclusion marketing for the Sportster unless you understand the thirty-something female. Harley knows she wants to identify with the Harley brand – hence the Sportster is positioned as an entry-level bike with all the classic sound and power women expect from a Harley. HD understands that women want to be *included* in the Harley culture; they want to be *perceived* as legitimate Harley owners. The last thing they want is to be singled out as sissy bike owners.

3. Promise

What is the major *benefit* your product promises to the user? **Caution**: A product feature is not a benefit. For example, the Harley Sportster's 850 cc engine is a product feature. *The benefit* is power and a throaty Harley report.

4. Tone

What is the tone of voice of your advertising? Friendly? Serious? Light- hearted? Humorous? Thoughtful? Use one or two words to describe the tone.

5. Tag line

A tag line or slogan gives continuity to a campaign. Use economy of language, make it memorable, rhythmic, and make sure it reflects the advertising position.
For example:

Harley-Davidson
Live to Ride.
Ride To Live.®

IV. Media Objectives & Strategies (Start on a new page)

Media objectives and strategies are dual engines that drive the whole media plan. Considered the heart of any plan, you'll find *six basic media strategies and objectives* illustrated in depth in the next chapter. The six include:

- Target Audience & Media Mix
- Reach, Frequency & GRPs
- Scheduling & Timing
- Media Budget
- Geography
- Sales Promotion

V. Appendix

The appendix is a place for exhibits in the very back of the plan – and includes data that supports your plan but is too lengthy or complicated to include in the main section. One important rule of thumb: If it's really important, don't hide it in the appendix, because it is often quickly scanned or even ignored by the client.

CHAPTER 5

The Art of Writing Media Objectives & Strategies

Kirkham Motor Sports Cobra

Tom Kirkham and his son, Dave, owners of Kirkham Motor Sports, use a bottom-up business model. They trekked the globe seeking out parts suppliers and tooling up a factory to authentically replicate the classic Ford Shelby Cobra. They succeeded in creating the most authentic hand crafted Cobra replica in the world, now so popular they always have a waiting list. Each Cobra is a one-off classic, true to the original in every detail from aircraft braided hoses to the buffed aluminum body. It's the world's last and only aluminum skinned Cobra still hand crafted in the tradition of the famous original.

The Cobra bodies are formed, hand-finished and buffed to a near polish by highly skilled craftsmen in Warsaw, Poland, and then shipped to the US. These craftsmen learned their trade building Soviet MIG fighters in a factory now converted for Cobra production. Tongue in cheek, Dave Kirkham told one of his former MIG fighter craftsmen, "I want all the body parts to fit together with near zero tolerance - I want this car to hold water when it's finished." During his next visit to the factory, Dave found the trunk of a finished Cobra filled with water, and it didn't leak a drop. Each Cobra that roars out of the Kirkham shop has a tamper-proof nameplate and serial number. The Kirkhams were forced to brand their Cobras after critics complained they couldn't distinguish their $100,000 replicas from the original Shelby Cobras at car shows and auctions.

Think of Media Objectives/Strategies as Art

Just as Cobra Craftsmen are perfectionists, marketers and media planners must be devoted to communicating both the tangible and the psychological benefits of a brand. Similar to handcrafting a classic race car, crafting media objectives and strategies demands rigorous attention to detail, and a passion for strategic planning that builds brands into familiar icons. Not only must the media plan achieve a tight fit with marketing, indeed the entire media plan is a marketing document because media objectives and strategies are driven by exhaustive marketing research. *Media planners are charged with crafting objectives into measurable goals and fitting them seamlessly with strategies that build brand equity.*

Using product examples, the next few pages explain the process of how to write your own media objectives and strategies. Each case, while based on brand research, does take some liberties for the sake of illustration.

A full set of media objectives and strategies for Coca-Cola is provided at the end of this chapter. After studying the Coke Mini-Case, you may want to bookmark it for future reference. It offers a full set of media objectives and strategies - use them as models to help you learn the art of writing your own media plans.

Measurable Media Objectives

Measurability requires marketers to be accountable for both marketing and media goals. If the marketing objectives for the brand are clearly articulated, media objectives emerge naturally out of these goals. Driven by intelligent marketing objectives, measurable media objectives establish the direction for the brand's entire communications plan. A planner's success or failure rests on the research, imagination and passion invested into writing measurable media objectives.

Writing the Media Objective –Identifying the Goal

The secret to writing media objectives is to focus on the goal – define exactly what you want to do. Whether targeting buyers for Subway sandwiches or Biolage shampoo, first discover which media most effectively communicate with the target. Since you are almost always aiming at a moving target exposed to dozens of media, *triangulate your objective from multiple perspectives.* Connect with the target on many levels – from traditional media to product sampling to social media web sites. Conduct exhaustive consumer analysis – how can you persuade someone to act on your message unless you know her both demographically and psychographically? Target analysis ranges from digging through oceans of quantitative data to in-depth qualitative research on attitudes and lifestyles. Syndicated data and other secondary sources often do not go deep enough – that's when you begin doing your own primary research.

Writing the Media Strategy – How to Achieve the Goal

When Marshall McLuhan theorized, "the medium is the message," advertisers listened because they realized that *the medium is loaded with qualitative meaning independent of the ad copy*. For example, a commercial on *Rachel Ray* on TV engages the heart and mind very differently than does the same ad in *Everyday with Rachael Ray* magazine, or a tweet about Rachel's roasted peppers and balsamic chicken. Always craft your message to fit the medium – not the other way around. If you're an educated media planner, you no longer consider TV a no-brainer buy. You should buy media wherever the target audience is *involved*, not just where the GRPs are highest. How can I move her? Which magazines does she wait for each week? Is she on Facebook? Twitter? Which web sites does she bookmark? Which sports does she spend money on? How much time does she spend working out?

There is no "recipe" for writing objectives or strategies. Each must be custom designed based on the different marketing ingredients that make up the brand. Nevertheless, there is no better way to learn how to write objectives/strategies than to study examples of successful brands. Here are some examples using the marriage of two famous brands, Apple and Nike.

Example of Marketing Objective: *Apple and Nike will team up in a cross promotion to boost demand by 10% for two existing products. Capitalize on the synergy inherent in the personality of both brands by integrating Nike + shoes and Apple iPod nano, iPod touch, and iPhone 3G into a single product.*

The product resulting from this objective was the Nike + iPod shoe that "helps the miles unfold and lets you hear real-time voice feedback on your run – all to your favorite music including the one song that always gets you through the home stretch."

Example of a Target Audience Objective: *The primary target audience for both brands is composed of 18-24 college age females. Combining their love of popular culture along with an obsession for running and fitness, the marriage of Apple and Nike is a match made in cross-promotion heaven.*

Example of Media Objective: *Because of our target's frequent consumption of popular culture such as iTunes, heavy usage of social media like Facebook and twitter, 40% of the budget will be focused on SEO (Search Engine Optimization) and social media with 60% dedicated to sales promotion and traditional media.*

Example of a Media Strategy: *Traditional and social media will be integrated to work seamlessly to complement each other throughout the campaign. Begin campaign with an April kickoff on MTV. Nike + ads and graphics will be painted visually and musically on Facebook, Google, hulu, digg, and You Tube. Nike + shoe signs will be posted in 500 gyms in the top 50 metro markets. Radio will be used in the top 50 markets following the TV kickoff.*

Notice how objectives tell you very specifically *what* is to be accomplished, while strategies tell you *how*.

How to Write Media Objectives & Strategies

Although only a partial media plan, this Coca-Cola mini case study that follows provides a complete model of the art of writing media objectives and strategies. Keep in mind that the objectives/strategy section is the most vital part of any media plan. This is where the client will spend the most time, and it's where you either win or lose the business.

No Objective is an Island. One of the most important concepts in this case is that all six objectives/strategies are interdependent. As you study the case, take note how all six of the objectives and strategies are interwoven. Interplay between them is not only expected, it's essential since each objective affects a neighboring objective, or a related objective up or down the line. Repetition of key points is normal in this section of the plan - most objectives/strategies are linked in some way with at least two or three others. The most thoughtful media plan recognizes this interdependence and justifies it by strategically linking all the parts together.

Brevity and Wit. Note the attention to detail in the Coke Case. Media plans demand measurable, actionable objectives that drive imaginative strategies. Also note the economy of words; media objectives are short and to the point. Although typically a bit longer, media strategies are never verbose; strategies should employ the same economy of words used in objectives.

Six Recommended Media Objectives/Strategies. There is no absolute number of media objectives/strategies for any media plan, but based on experience, we recommend the following set of six. Note that each of the six requires its own objective and strategy—twelve "points" altogether.

Media Objectives & Strategies

I. Target Audience & Media Mix
II. Reach, Frequency & GRPs
III. Scheduling & Timing
IV. Media Budget
V. Geography
VI. Sales Promotion

Six Media Objectives/Strategies for Coca-Cola

I. Target Audience and Media Mix Objective: Over thirty percent of Coke's North American soft drink volume is consumed by teens 13-18. The target audience goal for this campaign is to increase the Coke brand experience (consumption) by 20% among teens 13-18 by reaching a new teen market that doesn't think or drink like any other. This campaign will create a tangible brand experience reaching over 1 million teens in 10 DMA markets using radio/TV to announce a guerilla-marketing event, the "Free Coke & Burger Bash."

Remember: **A media strategy tells how to achieve the media objective**: Study how the following media strategy delivers the Coca-Cola objective stated above:

Target Audience and Media Mix Strategy: We will break away from prior media strategies; breaking away includes announcing the "Free Coke & Burger Bash" with YouTube video and Facebook product page. In addition, youth-focused cable TV and local FM radio will also be used. March 1st launches a teaser campaign on ESPN Sports Center, MTV Real World, MTV2, VH1, SITV, FUSE and the top 5 FM rock stations in each market. Teaser ads will build excitement leading up to the "Bash" on April 1. April begins a month-long guerilla campaign with thirty Coca-Cola "Can-Vans" rotating among the biggest middle schools and high schools in Coke's top ten DMA markets. Free Coca-Cola and burgers will be offered during lunch and after-school for 1-2 weeks on locations adjacent to local schools. Winning numbers for 100 prizes daily will be printed on Coke cans and announced on www.Coca-Cola.com. Visits to Coke's web site will offer free sports gear, free McDonald's and Wendy's grub, free Cinemark movie passes, and free iTunes music downloads.

II. Reach, Frequency and GRP Objective: Achieve 80% reach during the kick-off month (350 GRPs) with average 4.5 frequency. Reach will range from 70–85% over the life of the campaign. Frequency will bottom at 3.0. The non-traditional reach goal (event marketing) is to get 40% of teens in each school to visit the Coca-Cola "Can Vans" for a burger and a Coke. Hard counts will be taken each day in each location.

Reach, Frequency and GRP Strategy: Traditional media will peak during the kick-off with 350 GRPs in TV and FM radio. Media weight will go toward a teaser campaign on ESPN *Sports Center*, MTV *Real World*, MTV2. VH1 buys include *Rock Docs* and *Tough Love*. Syfy will run *Ghost Hunters*, *Eureka* and *Stargate Universe*. FUSE includes *On the Record* and *Hip Hop Shop*. The top 5 FM rock stations will run Burger Bash ads mornings and afternoons in each market.

*** *Did you notice the integration between objective/strategy 1 and 2? Integrated marketing demands all components of your plan be stitched together. If you want to make a living as a marketer, be willing to invest the time to write intelligently. It's virtually impossible to write a top notch plan on the first draft.*

III. Scheduling and Timing Objective: Campaign kick-off begins with a teaser campaign running throughout March to preempt the competition. Traditional media run continuously in March, April, and May. "Free Coke & Burger Bash" service begins April 1. The Coke Can-Van will open 1-2 hours during lunch periods and reopen two hours after school. The "Bash" runs 1-2 weeks in April and May.

Scheduling and Timing Strategy: Teaser campaign (350 GRPs) runs during the March launch to generate interest and awareness. The broadcast schedule in April/May drops to 300 and 250 GRPs respectively. Although reach/frequency will bottom at 70/3, this is adequate to sustain awareness. Broadcast buys in TV will not run until after school is out, between 4 pm and midnight. FM radio ads will run from noon through 12 pm daily to remind teens about the Coke & Burger event.

IV. Media Budget Objective: Coke's $4.5 million budget is limited to spending in 10 DMAs. Markets will receive a percentage of total budget based on their Estimated Value (EV%) rankings from a spreadsheet analysis of all 10 markets.

Media Budget Strategy: An analysis was conducted on the 10 DMAs based on these criteria:

- Total teens (boys and girls) ages 13-18 in each market
- Soft drink category sales by market
- Coca-Cola sales by market

The $4.5 million budget is allocated as follows:

- $3,000,000 in mass media (Cable TV, FM radio, Internet buys) in 10 DMAs.
- $1,000,000 for Coke & burger products plus leasing/outfitting thirty Coke Can-Vans.
- $500,000 covers 100 prizes daily: Free sports gear, free McDonald's and Wendy's grub, free Cinemark movie passes, and free iTunes music downloads.

V. Geography Objective: Ten middle and high school markets are targeted for the "Free Coke & Burger Bash" guerilla-marketing event. All cable TV and FM radio buys are restricted to spot buys in these 10 markets. This will be a spot-only media buy.

Geography Strategy: MRI and CMR data combined with Coca-Cola's proprietary marketing database provided information for a spreadsheet evaluation of the top 40 DMAs. Market selections are predicated on EV% growth potential for Coke products. In ranking order, the 10 metros selected from the top 40 include:

Los Angeles
Chicago
Atlanta
Philadelphia
San Francisco
Houston
Seattle-Tacoma
Miami
Phoenix
Sacramento

Note: Be sure to generate a weighted spreadsheet (see exercise section of book) and include it with your SWOT. If multiple markets are being considered, **always include the spreadsheet analysis and results with your geography objective**.

The Coca-Cola spreadsheet analysis for this plan is based on four criteria:

- Total target males/females age 13-18 by market (DMA)
- Fast food sales volume by market (DMA)
- Canned soft drink sales volume by market (DMA)
- Annual discretionary spending by market (DMA)

VI. Sales Promotion Objective: Sales promotion carries the biggest responsibility in this campaign. Our goal is to increase the Coke brand experience by 20% among teens, and this increase will be accomplished through a guerilla-marketing event – the "Free Coke & Burger Bash." Internet goal: Generate 1 million visits (click-throughs) to Coca-Cola.com with 40% target penetration in all ten markets.

Sales Promotion Strategy: The "Free Coke & Burger Bash" is the primary vehicle for achieving the goal of increasing brand experience by 20% among teens. (20% increase = average 20% increased Coca-Cola consumption among teens compared to current Coke brand consumption in the 10 DMAs.) To achieve this goal, at least 40% of teens in the 10 DMAs must participate in a tangible brand experience during the "Bash" event. A tangible brand experience = one or more visits to the "Coke & Burger Bash." Thirty Coke "Can-Vans" will rotate (bi-weekly) among the highest enrollment middle schools and high schools in the top ten DMAs. Teaser ads (350 GRPs) announcing the "Bash" will run in March in teen dominated media. Ads will continue through April and May to stimulate traffic and induce trial. Fifteen second ads announcing "Free Coke & Burger Bash" will run on spot cable channels in all 10 markets.

The "Coke & Burger Bash" will open during lunch periods and after-school and last for 1-2 weeks on locations adjacent to each metro school. Number codes for 100 daily prizes will be printed on Coke cans and winners will be announced on www.Coca-Cola.com. Visits to Coke's web site will achieve 20% penetration among the target audience by offering additional chances at prizes—free sports gear, free McDonald's and Wendy's grub, free Cinemark movie passes, and free iTunes music downloads.

Companion Internet Strategy: Teen visits to the Coca-Cola web site will generate a permission-marketing database. Teens who give permission to receive email (Coke SURPRIZES) and tweets will increase brand loyalty by responding to additional Coca-Cola purchase incentives over a one-year internet marketing campaign.

Summary: Note the attention to detail, and the clear articulation of specific, measurable goals - the integration of relationship marketing, social media, sales promotion and mass media. Also note the imaginative use of targeted promotions and careful attention to media mix strategy and targeted vehicles. Everything is stitched together to ensure that every objective and strategy pushes and pulls together.

CHAPTER 6

ABC's of Witty, Intelligent Writing

Executives Hate Reading Plans

Trey Hall, former Chief Marketing Officer, at Quiznos, said:

> *"I hate reading plans. I don't know a single executive who enjoys it. I do it because I can't spend a dime until your plan is rock solid with intelligent writing. I really hate it when writers fill it with fluff. You know when your plan contains genius. It's also obvious when your plan is filled with helium. It looks and feels like a last-minute, desperate attempt to fill paper. If you can't hold my attention with witty, intelligent writing, you'll be sorting my mail tomorrow."*

Make Good Writing a Passion

Good business writing skills are in top demand whether you end up working as a brand manager, media planner, sales rep, account manager, creative director, or most any other career. Make writing your passion. Without strong writing skills it's unlikely you'll get hired into management positions. Even if you do get hired in a top corporation, you won't go far unless you can write. Virtually every important business decision is driven by words, whether on paper or electronically. Invest whatever time it takes to write intelligent, organized media plans.

Quality Writing Can Sell or Kill Your Plan

Resist the temptation to spend too much time with the *Media Flight Plan* software. Tweaking GRPs and dollars gives you a false sense of security when you should be spending more time writing. Fine tuning GRPs is great if you have time, but the written plan is more important than pushing reach or frequency a few points higher. A rule of thumb is to budget one fourth of your time for number crunching, and put the remaining three fourths into strategic planning, writing and editing. A brilliant media strategy is totally wasted unless it is communicated with brilliance. Your client has to "get it."

Kevin Killion, former Media Research Director for DDB Needham Worldwide, Chicago, wrote the memo shown below. Motivated by an intern's "particularly awkward report," he wrote these pointers for new planners and researchers (used by permission). His attitude about written work resonates with many corporate executives.

Memo To: Future interns
From: Kevin Killion
Media Research Director, DDB Needham Worldwide

Subject: **Guidelines For Writing Plans**

Keep It Interesting
No one has to read your business paper (unlike a term paper). Therefore, you must make your paper useful, and, more than that, interesting. An "inverted pyramid" newspaper style works well: give intriguing facts or observations first, and follow with the details.

Outline
Always start the project with a rough outline of your proposed topics. This helps you to cover all the areas you intend. It also helps you to keep your project well organized.

Organization
The paper should be organized clearly into bite-sized sections. Each section (a few paragraphs) should be set off with a header. For any paper of more than a few pages, organize related topics into chapters. Papers of ten or more pages should start with an inviting introduction page, followed by an "executive summary." This helps the readers to glean your key points even if they don't read the whole paper. It also helps them decide if they can benefit by reading further.

Clear organization of your paper has these benefits:

- It keeps your thoughts coherent.
- It lets readers find selected sections easily.
- It builds a better case by flowing logically.
- It looks less makeshift and more professional.

Accuracy
Our lawyers peruse every word written by the copywriters. You should be no less scrupulous. Here are some common problems:

- **Generalization**: "Viewers today prefer the variety on cable." Well, some do, perhaps even many or most, but not all as this sentence suggests. Be specific; what percent of viewers?
- **Unfounded Suppositions**: In many cases, you may not be able to prove a claim with existing data. However, even if the claim seems self-evident, you should qualify any such premise with such words as "perhaps," "we suspect that" or "many researchers believe that." Your arguments must also be *logically* accurate. Conclusions should follow from stated premises. Moreover, you should learn to develop your skills in identifying logic problems in materials you read.

Text and Tables
Some people like pure text. Other people love charts and tables. Make your paper acceptable to both. Give tables when appropriate, showing base numbers, percentages or indexes in detail. A preceding paragraph should take the key or most interesting information from the table and spell it out for the reader in English sentences, preferably with some interpretation.

You should always avoid statements like "Here is a chart of ratings by daypart." This requires readers to analyze the table themselves. It sounds like you are saying "Here's a table. I can't figure it out - - you give it a try!"

Similarly, avoid juicy sentences based on charts which you are not including. This invites readers to either beg for details, or to lose interest in the paper altogether.

Courtesies
It is guaranteed that there will be deletions, additions and revisions. Leave room for notes that will be made on your draft.

If your plan will be edited into final draft by an assistant, it is unlikely he/she will be able to interpret your abbreviations. If you want to say "households," say that, not "HH." Tables should be "assistant-ready" in the form you want them to appear.

Dos and Don'ts for Writing Your Media Plan

Do:
1. Outline all of your objectives and strategies before using Media Flight Plan.
2. Organize your plan into bite-sized sections.
3. Include an executive summary.
4. Use subheads liberally - give them substance so they seduce the reader into the text.
5. Use white space liberally.
6. Leave room for notes with wide margins.
7. Take pity on the reader - keep it interesting or lose me.
8. Number the pages.
9. Avoid generalizations; be specific. Back your work up with hard numbers when possible.
10. Edit, edit, edit for accuracy and clarity.
11. Reduce graphs/charts to smallest size possible and integrate them into the text.
12. Explain tables in English sentences.
13. Label pie charts with words, not legends.
14. Write to the client - use third person.
15. Keep a spare computer ink cartridge in reserve. (Few computer supply stores are open at 1 am).
16. Impress client with primary & secondary research. Cite sources so client can't miss them.
17. Check spelling and grammar. Remember, you're selling yourself as a communicator.
18. Edit the fluff - it's painfully obvious when people fill pages with helium. The corollary: use active voice, not passive. It is direct and requires fewer words.
19. Start early - submit work on time.
20. Expect your computer to crash - make frequent back-ups.
21. Expect print-out problems at the last minute.
22. Allow time to edit, rewrite, and print final drafts.
23. Expect malaria the night before deadline.

Don't:
1. Don't use superlatives like "low cost" or "high reach."
2. Don't write long paragraphs, and don't cram too much on a page. Use white space.
3. Don't expect the client to believe you without adequate backup. Cite secondary and primary sources, not opinion.

4. Don't fill pages to "get the assignment done." Your work will torture the reader if your writing lacks passion, because it will advertise that you threw the stuff together in one day.
5. Seduce the reader with witty headlines and intelligent thinking.
6. Don't isolate huge charts/graphs on single pages. It looks tacky.
7. Appendix is the appendix. Don't put important things the client NEEDS TO KNOW in the back of your plan.
8. Never require the client to perform hard labor to understand your graphics. For example, label pie charts in plain English - never use legends that require translation.
9. Don't throw in tables or graphs without explanation. That says, "Here, you figure it out."
10. Don't forget to number the pages. Attention to detail is assumed by the client.
11. Don't pop a staple in the corner. If you're trying to look professional, bind it.
12. Don't blame computer crashes on anybody but yourself. Saving backups is your responsibility.
13. Don't expect client to gush with sympathy when you're late for most any reason. If you're late, don't make excuses - it reveals too much about you. The best excuse is: "I have no excuse."
14. Don't make last minute excuses. Inform client one or two days ahead if a delay is imminent.

Media Tools for Writing Media Case Studies

Ostrow Model: Theoretical model for estimating effective frequency

The best (really the only) way to determine an appropriate effective frequency level is research. However, many clients either don't have funds or choose not to put resources into doing the necessary research. Nonetheless, clients often expect some idea of what it will take to break through. Many agencies use some form of model or checklist to estimate an appropriate level. Ostrow's approach provides a valuable theoretical base for novice planners by asking you to think about various aspects of your brand situation. It considers a combination of three strategic factors essential for estimating frequency: *Marketing, Copy, and Media*.

Ostrow's model *assumes that 3.0 as a benchmark* or starting point for estimating frequency. To apply this Model, *begin with this 3.0 benchmark*, and add or subtract from it based on the sum of the three parts.

Begin on the accompanying page by "testing" Glacier – use the questions posed in each of the three subheadings in the model. Since 'Glacier' is a new brand, it gets the maximum +0.2 for *Established brand?* under the heading: **Marketing Factors That Affect Frequency**. Positive values increase frequency, while negative values obviously reduce it. Below is a convenient format for reporting your results:

Note: Ostrow Model is important for case studies—use this format to report results.

OSTROW MODEL EXAMPLE: Glacier Spring Water

Part I: Marketing Factors That Affect Frequency	
Established brand? (No, it is a new national brand)	+.2
High market share? (No, Spot markets high, but not nationally)	+.1
Dominant brand? (Yes, in spot markets, but not nationally)	+.1
High brand loyalty? (Yes, in spot markets, but not nationally)	+.1
Long purchase cycle? (No, Short cycle—loyal users buy 2-4 six packs/month)	+.2
Product used occasionally? (No, Product consumed 3-5 times/week)	+.1
Need to beat competition? (Yes, Intense threat from competitors)	+.2
Advertising to older consumers/children? (Yes, Both included)	+.2
	+1.2

Part II: Copy Factors That Affect Frequency	
Simple copy? (Yes, Message will be very simple)	-.2
Copy more unique than competition? (Yes, Better every campaign)	-.1
Continuing campaign? (No, this is a brand new creative concept)	+.2
Product sell copy? (Yes, Combination of image and product sell)	+.1
Single kind of message? (Yes, High continuity creative strategy)	-.2
To avoid wear out: new messages? (Yes, Copy strategy fresh, new)	-.2
Larger ad units? (No, Medium ad units; 15 sec. TV/30 sec. Radio)	-.1
	-.5

Part III: Media Factors That Affect Frequency	
Lower ad clutter? (No, Media selected have high clutter)	+.2
Compatible editorial? (No, Limited opportunity for related editorial)	+.1
Attentiveness high? (No, Low involvement product category)	+.1
Continuous advertising? (No, Limited budget requires flighting)	+.1
Few media used? (No, Moderate media mix)	+.1
Opportunities for media repetition? (Yes, Strong media repetition)	-.2
	+.4

Calculating Freq. Estimate

1. Sum the totals for each of the parts to get three subtotals. See column of numbers on left, with subtotals.

2. Sum the results from the three subtotals. See below:

Summing Results

+1.2
- .5
+ .4
+1.1 + 3.0 Benchmark = 4.1

4.1 is the estimated frequency for Glacier's media plan. The 4.1 estimate is based on strategic consideration of the 3 part model on next page.

Ostrow Model

Once you complete your model, use format on the previous page as a convenient way to report it.

Marketing Factors That Affect Frequency

Established brands	-.2	-.1	+.1	+.2	New brands
High market share	-.2	-.1	+.1	+.2	Low market share
Dominant brand in market	-.2	-.1	+.1	+.2	Smaller, less known brand
High brand loyalty	-.2	-.1	+.1	+.2	Low brand loyalty
Long purchase cycle	-.2	-.1	+.1	+.2	Short purchase cycle, high volume
Product used occasionally	-.2	-.1	+.1	+.2	Product used daily
			+.1	+.2	Need to beat competition
			+.1	+.2	Adv. to older consumers/children

Copy Factors That Affect Frequency

Simple copy	-.2	-.1	+.1	+.2	Complex copy
Copy more unique than competition	-.2	-.1	+.1	+.2	Copy less unique than competition
Continuing [old] campaign	-.2	-.1	+.1	+.2	New copy campaign
Product sell copy	-.2	-.1	+.1	+.2	Image type copy
Single kind of message	-.2	-.1	+.1	+.2	More difficult kinds of messages
To avoid wear out: new messages	-.2	-.1	+.1	+.2	Older messages
Larger ad units	-.2	-.1	+.1	+.2	Small ad units

Media Factors That Affect Frequency

Lower ad clutter in media mix	-.2	-.1	+.1	+.2	Higher ad clutter in media mix
Compatible editorial environment	-.2	-.1	+.1	+.2	Non-compatible environment
Attentiveness (to media) high	-.2	-.1	+.1	+.2	Attentiveness (to media) low
Continuous schedule campaign	-.2	-.1	+.1	+.2	Pulsed or flighted campaign
Few media used in media mix	-.2	-.1	+.1	+.2	Many media used
Opportunities for media repetition	-.2	-.1	+.1	+.2	Fewer opportunities

Source: Ostrow, Joseph W. by personal permission. First published in "Setting Frequency Levels," in Effective Frequency: The State of the Art. Copyright 1982. Note: Model edited by permission for Media Flight Plan.

Reach & Frequency Guidelines

Planners need to ask why on every decision, and provide answers for the client. Two of the most challenging questions in writing media objectives are: How much reach is enough? And, how much frequency is enough? These questions are also related to **Media Strategy**. Media objectives tell *what* the plan will accomplish - e.g., how much reach/frequency is needed? What percent of budget will be spent on TV? Media strategies tell *how* they will be accomplished - that is, which media can best accomplish the reach/frequency goals? Which vehicles? When is the best time to advertise? Is flighting called for? Which markets make sense? etc.

Review of Key Issues is Important. The "Ostrow Model" will help you to estimate frequency levels for your plan. Also review the MFP chapter titled "Organizing a Media Plan" for other important items to include in your plan.

Reach & Frequency Dilemma. As GRPs increase, both reach and frequency increase. But reach follows a law of diminishing returns--it is a curve that flattens as weight increases. Initially reach climbs fastest, then reach takes over and begins to climb more quickly as reach grows ever more slowly. Most marketing situations force the planner to optimize one over the other. Two exhibits shown below are intended to help you deal with the reach/frequency dilemma. These exhibits are simple rules of thumb--most of these rules have exceptions based on the product and marketing situation at hand. Consider these exhibits starting points you can build on to extend your knowledge and experience with reach and frequency.

High vs. Low Reach/Frequency

Highest Reach - 99%

Most computer-based reach curves set 96-99% as the upper limit for reach. In theory, it is impossible to expose 100 percent of a population to any media plan. Some prospects will always be missed either by chance, or because of lifestyle differences. Remember, *Media Flight Plan* was created to play "what if." Experiment to see how high you can build reach while maintaining frequency at acceptable levels, and all inside a given budget.

Moderate Reach - 70 to 75%

Reaching three-fourths of your prospects is considered a respectable goal. Although it is usually desirable to reach as many prospects as possible, the trade-off between reach and frequency may force you to settle for moderate reach.

Lowest Reach - 50 to 60%

The authors suggest that reach not drop much lower than 50% of the target audience. The logic is that if a brand requires advertising, it will probably encounter some level of competition in the market. If the brand is to achieve reasonable exposure, 50% reach may be the minimum for survival. If budget forces your reach to drop below 50%, you may want to employ a flighting strategy to maintain reach levels.

Highest Average Frequency - 12

Most media researchers accept the notion that frequency can hit a point of diminishing returns. This is commonly called the "wearout" . Many studies have been conducted on wear out, which typically occurs somewhere between 6 and 12 exposures per month. Many variables, especially the quality of your creative affect when wearout actually occurs. Since few budgets can support continuous high frequency levels, this may be a moot issue for your brand.

Lowest Average Frequency - 2 to 3

Frequency can drop quite low and still be effective. John Phillip Jones (father of 'recency theory') theorizes that great creative executions have the ability to generate significant response after the first exposure. It is almost a maxim in many media circles, however, that the benchmark frequency for a media plan is three exposures/month. When the average frequency is three, most of the prospects reached are *exposed less than three times* (a small portion of the population, say a fifth, are couch potatoes who are exposed much more heavily than the rest of the population) .

Strategy Decision: Optimize Reach or Frequency?

Use the following guide to think about optimizing reach or frequency. The decision about which to optimize is *primarily a strategic decision based on in-depth intelligence about the marketing situation*. It is not always an either/or decision based on these questions alone. Know your brand, its market, the creative/sales promotion strategy, and the competition. Also, consider all media objectives and how they interact with each other, and how all strategic decisions work together in the plan.

Reach/Frequency Decision Model

The following lists are guidelines--not absolutes. They suggest situations where reach or frequency might be optimized, however, always let the brand objectives guide your decision--they carry far more weight than these general suggestions.

Optimize Reach

Product introduction
In growth phase of life cycle
Few competitors
Strong established brand
Brand leader in category
Brand awareness is higher
Higher market share
High involvement purchase decision
High interest in category
Often higher priced goods and services
Low to moderate competition in category
Infrequent purchase-once a month or less
Continuous advertising schedule
Powerful creative that stands out
Ad message easily understood
Expanding into new markets
Major sales promotion launch
Seasonal peak for sales

Optimize Frequency

Product introduction
Mature well known brand
Many competitors
Less established brand
Among bottom of category
Brand awareness is lower
Lower market share
Low involvement purchase decision
Low interest category
Often lower priced goods and services
Strong to intense competition in category
Frequent purchase-2+ times per month or more
Flighted schedule
Creative on par with other ads
Complex ad message
Status quo geographically
Moderate to low sales promo activity
Beginning new season for brand

Guidelines for Buys with Media Flight Plan

These minimum guidelines will help you make more realistic buys when using *MFP* software. Although ratings shown are for *Adults*, they can be considered rough minimums for any target audience when using MFP. It is recommended that you use or exceed the **Minimum Buy** for a daypart where indicated, and when using multiple dayparts in national television for example, that you meet the Minimum Monthly Buy. These guidelines should not be ignored, however, you may have a need to do something different based on your objectives and strategies. The minimums below are typical 'bare minimums'; you will probably be at somewhat higher levels.

Medium	Minimum Buy	Minimum Monthly Buy
Network Television Avg Rtg: 2.0-5.0 varies by daypart	20 GRPs in a single daypart = about 4 to 10 spots	If used, a minimum of 35-50 GRPs total should be planned across all forms/dayparts of national television, with a minimum of 15 GRPs in any single daypart/form.
Cable Television Avg Rtg: 0.1-2.0 varies by network	20 GRPs in a single daypart = about 10 to 200 spots	
Syndication Avg Rtg: 2.0	20 GRPs in a single daypart = about 10 spots	
Network Radio Avg Rtg: 0.5-2.0 varies by daypart	20 GRPs in a single daypart = about 10-40 spots	If used, 35-50 GRPs total across all dayparts
Internet Avg Rtg: doesn't apply	20 GRPs	20 GRPs
Magazines Avg Rtg: 5.0-12 varies by type	20-25 GRPs = about 2-3 insertions	If used, buy magazines in more than one month—avoid "one time Charlies"—one insertion per magazine over the plan

Medium	Minimum Buy	Minimum Monthly Buy
National Newspapers (USA Today, WSJ, etc) Avg Rtg: 2.0	10-20 GRPs = 5-10 insertions	10 GRPs if run with magazines (national newspapers are often treated as magazines, and can be included in the magazine total) 20 GRPs if alone
Spot Television Avg Rtg: 1.0-6.0 varies by daypart	20 GRPs per daypart = about 5-10 spots	If used, 35-50 GRPs total across all dayparts
Spot Cable Avg Rtg: 0.2	20 GRPs = about 100 spots	If used, 20 GRPs
Spot Radio Avg Rtg: 2.0-3.0	20 GRPs in a single daypart = about 10 spots	If used, 35-50 GRPs total across all dayparts
Local Newspaper-40% coverage* (equivalent to enough papers to equal roughly a 40 rating)	2 insertions = about 80 GRPs	Your ad would appear 2 times in the month for an ongoing campaign. For a "sale" 1 insert may be sufficient.
Outdoor*	25 Showing—this is the rough equivalent of 25 GRPs per day	25 showing
Direct Mail*	10 GRPs	10 GRPs

***Local Newspapers.** In MFP, newspapers are one of the exceptions to buying with GRPs because of complications that come from keeping track of newspapers across 210 markets. To simplify purchasing spot newspapers, MFP assumes you will buy all the papers required to cover 40 percent of the market. Sometimes this would mean buying local weekly papers in addition to major papers in the market. When you buy one insertion in MFP, it means putting one insertion in each of the papers required to meet the 40 percent coverage level.

***Outdoor.** In MFP there are three options for buying newspapers: 25, 50 or 100 showing. Each showing level equates to roughly that number of GRPs per day based on vehicle traffic for the month. In other words, a 25 showing would be estimated to produce 25 GRPs x 30 days = 750 GRPs. The high level of duplication (most boards are stationary, people's travel patterns are repetitive) results in high levels of frequency. More discussion about the characteristics of outdoor can be found in the MFP Tutorial.

* **Direct Mail.** A traditional reach curve doesn't work for direct mail. This is the only medium where one GRP could equal one percent reach among the audience, or that 25 GRPs could equal 25% reach. Theoretically, if you could afford it, 100 GRPs could deliver 100% reach. In reality, it's not that perfect—no direct mail list is completely accurate because of deaths, address changes, name changes, etc. or because people have intentionally omitted information or provided innaccurate information. One major drawback of direct mail is that it probably has the highest cost on a CPM basis when all the production, postage and other mailing costs are counted. Although exceptions do occur, it is rare for direct mail to be used in a national campaign due to prohibitive cost. For this reason, direct mail is only available as a spot option in MFP.

CHAPTER 8

Award-Winning Media Plan
Axe Deodorant

Introduction

The following marketing/media plan for Axe deodorant is excerpted from a case study that won first place in the INTERAD XII Advertising Association competition. It provides an excellent example of relationship marketing with integrated marketing at the core.

Observe the writing style and voice; the writing is crisp and interesting, decisions are thoughtful and the plan doesn't read like a term paper due tomorrow (Note that English is a second language--there may be an unusual turn of phrase here and there). These students understand marketing as both art and science, and they demonstrate the passion and devotion required to succeed at their craft.

The objectives and strategies are very specific with measurable, quantitative goals that Axe can use to evaluate effectiveness throughout the campaign. The plan was written according to the principles in the preceeding chapters of Media Flight Plan—note that syndicated sources are cited, targeted vehicles are named, and budget amounts are identified throughout the plan. Also, subheads are used liberally to draw the reader into the text. Ethnic markets are identified by geographic region along with clearly defined budget amounts.

As you study this plan, keep one important thought in mind: ***Professional marketers are not looking for opinions; they want intelligent, original thinking based on solid, well-documented research***. If you don't have time to do the research before you do the writing, you're in the wrong business. If you don't have time to polish and edit your writing, make time. There are no shortcuts.

Acknowledgement

The authors express appreciation to the American University in Dubai team, Los Maestros IMC, for crafting a strategically driven, well-written marketing/media plan for the Axe brand in the Middle East. Each of these individuals is a winner, and the authors are honored to display their work in this textbook.

Creative: Ahmad M. Issa, Anna Maria Aoun, Boutros G. Karam, Kavitha Kanakar, Lama Helweh, Malda Smadi, and Sara Al Zawqari

Business: Kamelia Bayat, Lina Abou Chaaban, Mustafa Mohammed, Tamara Azab, Vahid Esmaelli

Media: Fatima S. Dockrat, Phoebe E. Youssef, Yogita Manwani, Zeeshan Merchant

Editors: Javeria Pasha, Zenia Mowdawala

The authors also wish to thank their advisors, Dr. Ode Amaize and Dr. Lance De Masi for their help in making this possible (Dr. Amaize is now at Zayed University, Abu Dhabi in the College of Communication and Media Studies).

EXECUTIVE SUMMARY

Ever since AXE was first introduced in the Middle Eastern market in 2003 it has received unprecedented success. According to Unilever, AXE is the most increasingly popular deodorant brand in the world. However, with rising awareness and growing competition, Los Maestros has found that AXE has begun to lose its grip on the extremely brand conscious, young, Arab male population of the UAE. Our target market of *Emiratis*, which consists of local males, aged 18-24 feel AXE is not for them. They enjoy AXE's advertisements but do not feel a connection to the brand. This is the reason for the low market share of AXE in the UAE amongst Emiratis.

Through extensive research, Los Maestros pinpointed the problems and opportunities regarding Emiratis and their connection with AXE, which has built its global brand image around the 'boy gets girl' theme. AXE's sexually explicit ads may be appealing to a more open-minded audience; however, it does not suit a more conservative group such as our proposed target audience. Even though Emiratis represent a small percentage of the total population in the U.A.E., they have a high purchasing power and they exert a sociocultural influence over the rest of the population. Therefore, they prove to be a lucrative target for AXE.

We uncovered two key elements in our research which set the basis for the creative strategy to help bridge the gap between the Emiratis and AXE. These elements consist of two major cultural contradictions that the local community faces.

First, Emiratis have begun to feel less important in their own country due to the rising influx of various cultures. The foreign influence in the UAE has led Emeriti women to accept non-local Arab men for marriage. This makes a typical Emeriti Youth feel less wanted by his own community and therefore less significant in general.

Second, there is a cultural inconsistency resulting in young Middle Eastern men being associated with terrorism, post 9/11. Consequently, our target market feels subjected to prejudice and this gives rise to a acute social anxieties, desires and tension, which they must address. These insights provided Los Maestros with a platform to create a fresh and innovative campaign for AXE. Our strategy of 'AXE: THE MISSING LINK' presents AXE as an exciting brand that specifically speaks to the Emiratis and addresses their social and cultural concerns.

Accordingly we have used a variety of Integrated Marketing Communications (IMC) media and events to convince **our target market of 18-24 year old Emeriti males that AXE, through it's resonating and compelling myths, is a culturally and politically qualified male deodorant brand, designed to enhance the confidence and desirability to the opposite sex by addressing their insecurities and desires that have resulted from economic, social and cultural contradictions.**

AXE must now act as a cultural activist that helps in restoring the Emiratis' identities. Globally, AXE has linked boy and girl successfully with an image that revolves around masculinity, sexuality and confidence. In the U.A.E, our aim is to maintain the same image of AXE but in the Emeriti cultural context. By portraying AXE as 'THE MISSING LINK' in our executions, we will establish a strong relationship between the brand and the target as well as close the gap between western and middle eastern culture, making Emiratis feel that AXE is a brand truly made *for them.*

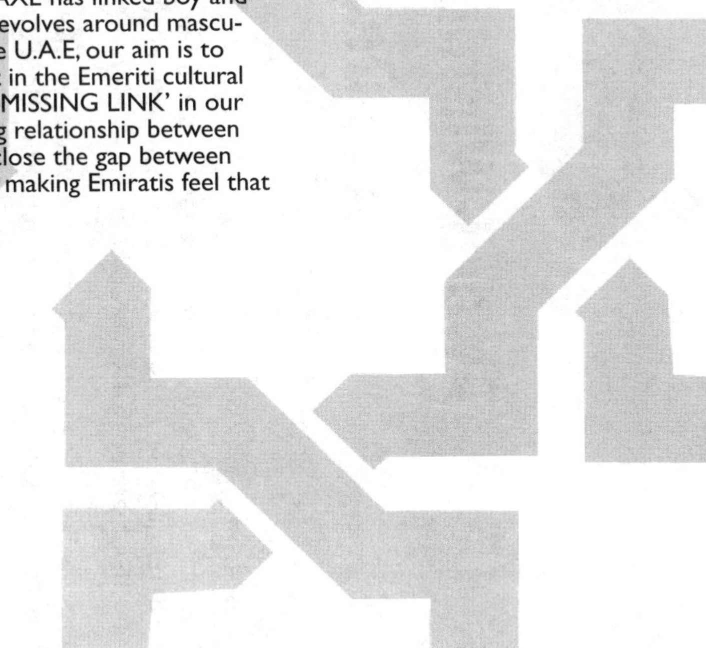

SITUATION ANALYSIS

Los Maestros conducted research to learn and gather insights about 'Emeriti Youth' and the deodorant industry. We established the following objectives:

-To gain insight into the Emeriti Youth culture, lifestyle, interests, values, and beliefs.

-To identify contact point opportunities where we can connect AXE to Emeriti Youth and their daily routine.

-To understand the Emeriti Youth attitude towards AXE, and test whether they identify with the brand.

-To identify AXE's weaknesses by studying what drives Emeriti Youth to favor other competing brands.

-To devise a creative strategy that will be best suited for the Emeriti youth.

-To create a media plan that will communicate with the target market effectively and efficiently.

RESEARCH

United Arab Emirates Culture and Religion

The UAE government provides sponsorship to certain foundations that aim to preserve traditional forms of art and culture such as *The Audhabi Cultural Foundation*. One of the first attempts by the government to preserve Emeriti culture was through *Al Jawaher wal la'li,* the first known manuscript produced in the UAE which discusses the Emirates of the nation.

The population of the United Arab Emirates consists of 76% Muslim, 9% Christian, and 15% other religions. Mosques, Churches and other religious centers are found across the country.

United Arab Emirates Economy

The United Arab Emirates is one of the fastest growing economies, and has a highly industrialized economy that makes the country one of the most developed in the world. As measured by the CIA World Factbook, its GDP per capita ranks 3rd worldwide, and has risen by 35 percent in 2006 to $175 billion, compared with $130 billion in 2005. The UAE owes its growth to petroleum and natural gas exports, the construction boom, an expanding manufacturing base, and the thriving services sector.

Ethnic Groups in the United Arab Emirates
Figure 1: The percentage of major ethnic groups living in the UAE.

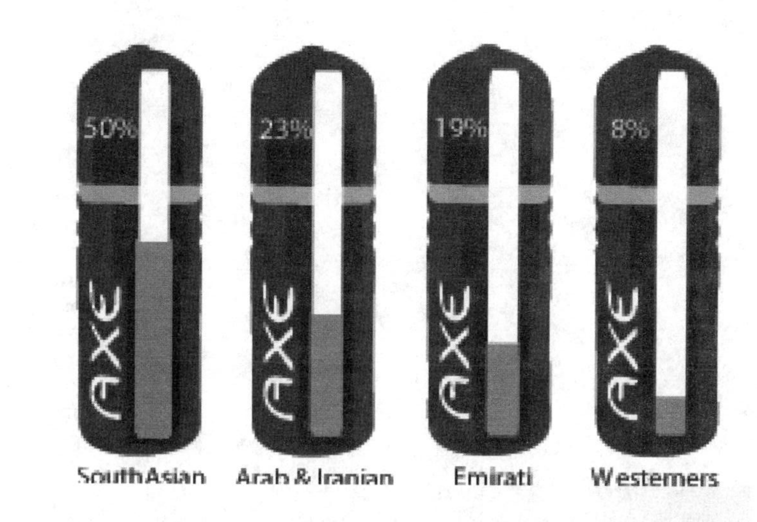

Evidently from the preceding Figure 1, the Emiratis represent a minority (19%) in their own homeland. They have the highest purchasing power among all ethnic groups within the UAE. This is due to constant government support that facilitates Emeriti business transactions, owning and buying land, getting loans, priority in job opportunities and the creation of the localization policy (also known as Emiratization).

Small, But Mighty, And "UNAXED"...

Despite the potential purchasing power of this market, very few brands have targeted them specifically. This was confirmed during interviews when our target market disappointedly mentioned the fact that none of the brand's marketing and advertising messages were directed to them. Los Maestros will customize the entire campaign to cater to the needs and culture of our target market, creating a positive ongoing purchasing cycle. Our creative strategy relies on cultural branding and is based on myths and contradictions that govern Emeriti Youth's daily life. The objective of this is to make our target market feel prioritized and AXED.

Primary Research

Focus Groups
Obtained qualitative data by conducting 6 focus groups of Emerati males aged 18 to 24.

Surveys
Administered 100 surveys to achieve information regarding deodorant consumption, purchasing behavior and lifestyle (habits, attitudes, rituals, interests, etc). Key questions included were:

-How often do you use deodorant per day?
-What brand(s) of deodorant do you use?
-What is your perceived image of AXE?

In-Depth Interviews
Conducted 20 personalized in-depth interviews to gain customer insight, and to develop a 'Day in the life of an Emerati Youth sketch.

Observation and Technology Usage
Observed activities, such as their use of technology (SMS, Bluetooth, and Internet), social behavior (friends, family, and networking) and outdoor activities.

Observation of Retail Outlets
Observed the distribution and shelving of AXE and its competitors in key retail stores (Carrefour, Spinneys, Union Co-op, and Choitram) in the U.A.E. to gather data about AXE's market share.

Interview of Retail Managers
Interviewed four retail and merchandise supervisors in the mentioned retail stores to attain information about the sales, distribution, and turnover of deodorants.

Secondary Research

Demographic and Psychographic Data[2]
Received secondary quantitative data which includes demographic and psychographic data (size, value and deodorant consumption of target market) from consumer research companies such as OMD and PARC.

Media Data[3]
Acquired secondary media data such as reach, frequency, cost and listenership of various mediums (TV, Radio, Internet, Cinemas, Outdoor, etcetera) from Media Edge.

Internet Sources[4]
Referred to a number of credible websites (such as CIA Factbook, official UAE government site, Unilever) to further support the research.

Cultural Industry Analysis
Researched integrated U.A.E. mass culture studies in academics, popular books, and journals to learn about the culture and desires of the Emirati Youth which AXE could help address. Reviewed popular publications on Emirati Culture, such as *Culture Shock by Ginal Crocetti* and *Miseducation of the West by Joe Lokincebe and Shirley Steinberg.* After reviewing cultural resources we observed that the Emirati culture is famous for its television serials and music that represents their society and lifestyle, such as Mohamed Abdo, a respected icon in the Middle East, and the Ramadan television series that bring families together.

Findings

Los Maestros has summarized the main findings of our research, which directed our business strategy, creative execution and media plan.

•Our target is Emirati males aged 18-24.

•They constitute 106,174 of the total population and make up 11.1% of the U.A.E nationals.

• Non Emirati National males of age 18 to 24 constitute 11.8% of the U.A.E population which make up 480,000.

• The Emirati aged 18-24 monetary value is $6,286,341 million, translating into a high potential opportunity for AXE.

• The Non Emirati aged 18-24 monetary value is $11,785,901 million.

2 Pan Arab Research Center, Inc.
3 Media Edge is a global communication planning center and implementation agency
4 www.cia.gov , www.uae.gov, www.unilever.com

CONSUMER INSIGHTS

Lifestyle

Education
Undergraduates or in the process of earning a degree. According to UAE Government statistics:

-Nationals with only high school certificates are 31.5%.
-Nationals with university degrees (Bachelor and above) are 11%
-Nationals with post graduate degrees are 4,185.

Flirting with the Opposite Sex
Emirati Youth bear a passion for the latest gadgets where they depend on Bluetooth and SMS as their major tool of communication with the opposite sex. This medium, being discrete allows them to flirt with one another, in a more private setting.

Outdoor Activities
Young Emirati males enjoy outdoor activities such as Desert Safaris, trips to the beach and lead a relatively laid-back lifestyle.

Leisure and Entertainment
They enjoy going to the cinema and having dinner in the most exclusive restaurants.

Personal Grooming
They are highly conscious of their appearance and scent.

Conspicuous Consumers
Their lifestyle revolves around buying and using brands to distinguish themselves from other social classes and ethnic groups, leading to them being recognised as trendsetters.

Socio Cultural Influence

Cultural Norms
Emirati Youth abide by cultural and religious norms that require them to respect their elders (Grandmother/father) and parents. In addition, there is cultural sensitivity towards expressing attraction or physical interaction with the opposite sex in public. This is why some of AXE's traditional, sexually explicit advertisements appeared to be offensive and culturally insensitive to Emiratis. Los Maestros solved this problem by creating culturally sensitive advertisements that relate to Emiratis and their conservative culture.

Their Grandmother
Friends and family play a major role in their decision making process- particularly the grandmother, who helps in shaping their future path with decisions regarding marriage, children, etc- making her a key figure in our creative strategy and execution.

Cultural Activities
Cultural outdoor activities play a major role in the target's lifestyle such as camel racing, fishing, pearl diving, Arabian horse breeding, falconry, cultural dance and poetry- all of which reminds them of their Bedouin heritage and keeps them in-touch with their traditions in the fast paced modern world. Los Maestros has addressed these needs and created an Emirati Poetry Competition online that relates to Emirati culture and also to AXE's image and positioning in the market. Emirati males like to gather in communal tents (Majlis) to socialize and network with other Emiratis.

Deodorant Usage, Purchase Behaviour and Perception

1. Young Emirati males are heavy deodorant users, purchasing 3 deodorant cans per month.

2. They favor traditional scents such as Musk and Arabian 'Oud.

3. They are brand switchers and non-loyal customers, using up to 3 different deodorant brands at the same time.

4. They spend an average of at least $8 per month on deodorant purchases.

5. 80% of Emirati Youth recognize AXE by its 'boy gets girl' positioning but do not accept it because of sexually oriented ads that are not seen favourably in their culture.

Marketing Objective

1. Increase market share among Emiratis from 14% to 19%, which is a 5% increase.
We want to increase our market share because our competitors have a higher market share than AXE. Therefore, we want AXE to be more visible to our target market.

2. Increase sales figures among Emirati Youth from DHS 4 million ($1.1 million) to DHS 9 million ($2.5 million) .
Increasing sales is our primary objective. We believe that we can achieve and increase sales of AXE by DHS 5,000,000 because Emirati Youth have a high purchasing power. We wish to obtain this through our culturally driven campaign.

$1 = 3.67 DHS

Industry Analysis and Competitive Analysis

Within the UAE, deodorant users constitute 71% of the total 4 million population. This indicates that the sales of the deodorant category are fairly high. This market is not going untapped, as several major corporations are feeding off this large consumer base- namely, Unilever, Procter and Gamble and Biersdorf AG- each of which produce deodorant brands that target different segments of the market. According to the information gathered from OMD and PARC, the current market value of the deodorant category is $120 million.

Competitive Analysis

Figure 2 compares AXE with its competitors in the deodorant market. The following competing brands deliver product specific benefits rather than psychological ones, which is a trait exclusive to AXE. Therefore this characteristic positioning of 'attracting the opposite sex' gives AXE a personality that differs from other brands. This is why Los Maestros decided to keep this image in the mind of Emiratis but execute it in a less sexually explicit way.

Emirati Youth view Nivea, Adidas, Fa as AXE's primary competitors. They believe that deodorants not only make them smell good but provide them with confidence. Unlike AXE, all these three brands provide product benefits instead of psychological ones. Nivea, for example, comes across as a brand that is sensitive to male skin. It is portrayed as a cool, refreshing deodorant that provides gentle care. Integrating Emirati families to speak to the target market through their advertisements is the key to Nivea's popularity among the locals.

Emirati Youth are particularly fond of the brand Fa, since it has the highest market share. Fa comes across a confident, exotic brand and like it's slogan makes the user 'feel good'. Adidias is the only competitor perceived as an athletic brand. It has a large consumer base of sport enthusiasts and perhaps it's strongest asset lies in it's brand name.

Fig.2 Competitive Analysis of 4 Leading Brands of Male Deodorants

Brand	Price DHS	Distribution	Product Line	Target Market	Positioning	End-line	Media
AXE	10.00	All retail & grocery stores, small shelf space	Shower Gel Spray Deo	Males 18-24	Attraction & Sex Appeal	"The AXE Effect"	TV, Cinema, Newspaper, Magazines
NIVEA	8.65	Widely distributed, large shelf space	Lotion, After Shave, Deodorants, Facial and Cosmetic products	Females & Male 18-24	Refreshing & Gentle	"Cool kick, gentle care"	TV, Cinema, Newspaper, Magazines
adidas	10.95	Limited retail, sports outlets, larger shelf space than AXE	Shower Gel Deodorants After Shave & Foam Perfume	Athletic Males & Females	Dynamic & Sporty	"Active Sensation	Not Available
Fa	10.25	Widely distributed	Shower Gel Deodorants Soap	Mainly Females Introduced new line for men	Fresh & Colorful	"Spirit of Freshness"	TV

$1 = 3.67 DHS Price per unit of product

BRAND ANALYSIS

Business Performance

- The following chart illustrates the market share of AXE and its competitors in the UAE market and among Emiratis.

- The chart shows that AXE is performing well and ranks second in the competitive UAE market.

- On the other hand, AXE's market share among Emiratis falls in fifth place.

- AXE is not doing well among Emiratis due to the following reasons:
  - a) AXE's sexually explicit ads are seen as offensive to the UAE culture
  - b) AXE does not specifically target Emirati Youth

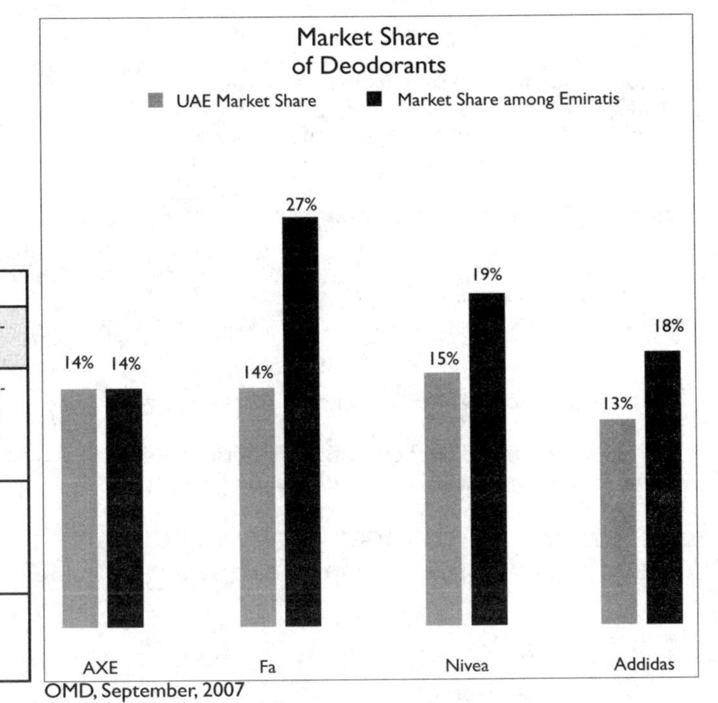

OMD, September, 2007

Based on our research we have developed the following SWOT analysis.

SWOT ANALYSIS

Strengths

- AXE is in second place in the UAE Market, with a market share of 14%
- Males of all cultures identify with AXE's image of attracting the opposite sex.
- It has an established world-wide image.
- It has a variety of scents.

Weaknesses

- 86% of deodorant consumers in the UAE market do not use AXE
- AXE occupies small shelf space in most supermarkets.
- AXE's execution of its sexually explicit ads offend some cultures in the Middle East.

Opportunities

- Emiratis have high purchasing power.
- Consumers in the UAE are heavy deodorant users, due to UAE's hot and humid weather.
- According to TGI, Emiratis are brand driven when buying toiletries and perfumes.
- Emiratis purchase decisions are influenced by TV ads.

Threats

- Emiratis are brand switchers
- UAE advertisement policies hae restrictions that limit the usage of sex appeal.
- Fa is a market leader among Emiratis, while AXE is fifth.
- 12% of Emiratis are non-category users.
- Numerous competitors have similar packinging and sents as AXE

Globally, Axe has linked the Boy & Girl...

successfully with an image that revolves around sexuality, masculinity and confidence. Their image continues to cut through brand parity and advertising clutter to gain maximum brand awareness and a positive attitude, leading to positive behavior from consumers. AXE's positioning has successfully created a badge value where most men purchasing AXE can relate to the brand's built image. Our aim is to maintain the same positioning of AXE while toning down the sexual content of the advertisements.

But Not Quite in the Emirati Youth Market...

where primary research analysis shows that the Emirati Youth are, just like other men, interested in the idea of attracting girls. However, from the individual reactions in focus groups and when asked in the surveys about AXE's image, most confirmed that AXE's presentation and execution through its sexually oriented ads did not consider Emirati cultural factors such as religion, social behavior, traditions, and the role of women in their society. This is because it is not acceptable in the Emirati culture to freely talk about material related to sex in public. Owing to this, most of our target market developed a unfavorable attitude towards the AXE ads.

MEDIA PLAN

The following media plan is a holistic and comprehensive plan covering many different mediums and reaching a significant Emirati population as well as secondary target segments.

The following SOV analysis describes AXE and their major competitors' spending on media in the years 2005, 2006, 2007.

The following SOV analysis describes AXE and their major competitors' spending on media in the years 2005, 2006, 2007.

2005 (in US$)						
Brand	Newspaper	Magazines	Cinema	Outdoor	TV	Total
AXE	20,905	124,356	164,216		93,206	402,683
Adidas						0
Nivea	1,406	67,369	37,877		1,637	108,289
Fa						0
Rexona					147,125	147,125
Total	22,311	191,725	202,093	0	241,968	658,097

2005 (%)						
Brand	Newspaper	Magazines	Cinema	Outdoor	TV	Total
AXE	5	31	41		0	100
Adidas						0
Nivea	1	62	35		2	100
Fa						0
Rexona					100	100
Total						

Year 2005

The dominant brands in the media -in terms of share of voice- were:
AXE, with a spending of $402,683,
Rexona with a spending of $147,125,
Nivea with a spending of $108,289.
Rexona's entire media expense went to TV, while that of AXE and Nivea were distributed to various media classes. AXE had the most varied medium exposure with 94% of the total newspaper expenditure, 67% of the total magazine expenditure, 81% of the total cinema expenditure and 39% of TV's total expenditure.

2006 (in US$)						
Brand	Newspaper	Magazines	Cinema	Outdoor	TV	Total
AXE	2,317	540	31,151		98,241	136,249
Adidas						0
Nivea					1,323	1,323
Fa					2,252	2,252
Rexona		57,063			127,700	184,763
Total	2,317	57,573	35,151	0	229,516	324,587

2006 (%)						
Brand	Newspaper	Magazines	Cinema	Outdoor	TV	Total
AXE	2	0	26	0	72	100
Adidas						0
Nivea					100	100
Fa					100	0
Rexona		31			69	100
Total						

Year 2006

One of the most dominant brands was AXE with an expenditure of $136,249. AXE has successfully been able to achieve the most varied medium exposure by utilizing 100% of the total newspaper expenditure, 1% of the total magazine expenditure, 100% of the total cinema expenditure and 43% of TV's total expenditure. Media not used by AXE in 2006 was outdoors. In 2006, Nivea and Fa's media expense was exclusively spent on TV, while Adidas for the second consecutive year did not advertise.

2007 (in US$)						
Brand	Newspaper	Magazines	Cinema	Outdoor	TV	Total
AXE						0
Adidas						0
Nivea		66,104	20,903		34,736	121,743
Fa						0
Rexona	7,321	76,746	76,312			160,379
Total	7,321	142,850	97,215	0	34,736	282,122

2007 (%)						
Brand	Newspaper	Magazines	Cinema	Outdoor	TV	Total
AXE						
Adidas						
Nivea		54	17	0	29	100
Fa						
Rexona	5	48	48	0		100
Total						

Year 2007

Rexona and Nivea invested heavily in the market during the year 2007, making them the brands with the highest media expenditures. AXE, Adidas and Fa did not advertise. While print ads in newspapers were entirely dominated by the competitor brand Rexona, TV was dominated by Fa. A trend throughout the years was that radio and outdoor were not used. AXE and Rexona have dominated the market in terms of their total media expenditure. Most brands dedicate their media expense to one specific medium, while AXE's strategy has been to penetrate through as many media vehicles as possible to create the most varied media exposure.

MEDIA EXPENDITURE

As can be seen from the graphical illustration above, AXE spent heavily on advertising in 2005, but then reduced their spending in 2006, and it then reduced to null in 2007. Nivea, on the other hand, spent on advertising in all 3 years, but reduced their spending heavily in 2006. Fa only spent on advertising in 2006, but only a minimal amount compared to the other brands. Adidas did not spend at all over the last 3 years, and Rexona has been quite consistent with their spending, with their spending ranging from $147,000 to $ 185,000 in the last 3 years.

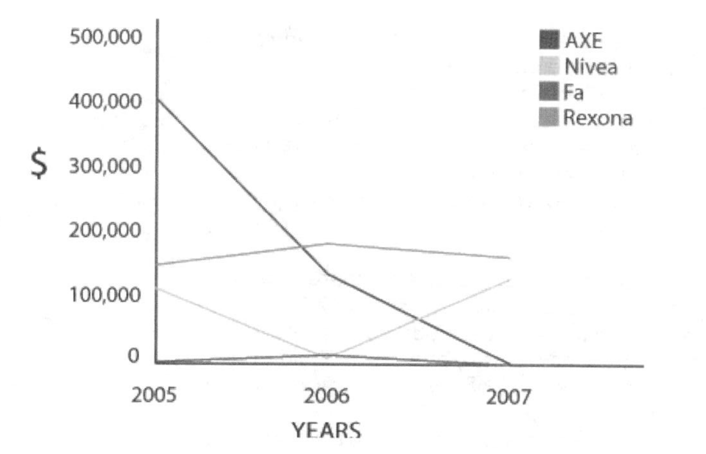

GEOGRAPHY

Geography Objective & Strategy
We are primarily looking to concentrate our advertising efforts more in Dubai and Abu Dhabi, as compared to the other cities in the UAE. These 2 cities are our spot markets. The majority of the population of UAE. is concentrated in these two cities. These cities also have a significant Emirati population as compared to the other cities.

TARGET AUDIENCE & MEDIA MIX OBJECTIVE

Our primary target audience is Emirati men aged between 18-24 years old. The goal is to increase the usage of AXE deodorants among Emirati Youth. The aim is to increase sales by 20.8% and to increase units by 500,000 within this coming year. We will also have a secondary target market, which will be Arabs originating from other Middle-Eastern countries, such as Saudi Arabia, Kuwait, and Qatar. The media mix that will be used for the campaign will be TV, outdoor, radio, magazine, newspapers, cinema, internet, event marketing and sales promotions.

Television

TV has the highest reach of 93% among the Emirati males (obtained from Mediaedge). Because of this high reach and high cost for ad placement, a significant part of the budget will be allocated here. To target Brand Junkies, we will place ads in the following vehicles:

Prison Break (MBC Action): Prison Break is a popular series that is watched by young adults, including the target audience of 18 to 24 years age group. It is a high paced, action TV program that appeals to a lot of young men. Based on the above information, it would be prudent to use the program as a media vehicle, as members of the target audience enjoy watching the show.

Football League (Dubai Sports Channel): Members of our target audience watch a lot of sports channels, especially channels that feature football matches. The Emirates Football League has a huge following from Emirati males who are extremely passionate about the sport, and the team they support.

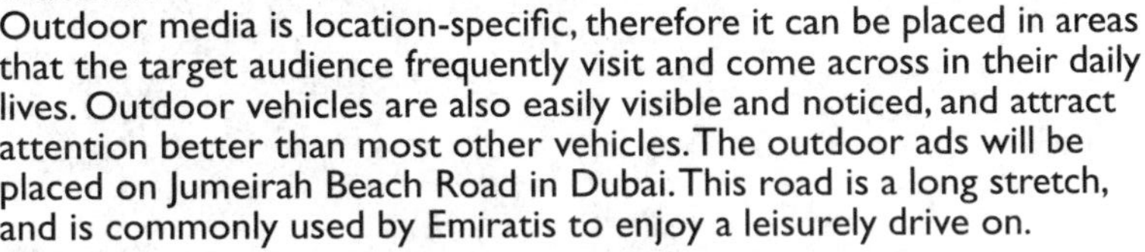

Outdoor

Outdoor media is location-specific, therefore it can be placed in areas that the target audience frequently visit and come across in their daily lives. Outdoor vehicles are also easily visible and noticed, and attract attention better than most other vehicles. The outdoor ads will be placed on Jumeirah Beach Road in Dubai. This road is a long stretch, and is commonly used by Emiratis to enjoy a leisurely drive on.

Radio

Radio is heard quite often in the UAE, since traffic is very common in the country and people use radio as a form of entertainment during the long rush hours. The radio vehicles that are chosen will be Al Khaleejeya 100.9 and Al Rabia 107.8, which have a reach of 14% and 13% respectively (obtained from Mediaedge).

Newspapers

Newspapers reach out to a huge audience and will be an important medium for us to use. The sections that Brand Junkies focus on include international news, sports news and the car section. The newspaper vehicle that will be used is Al Khaleej, since 53% of Emiratis read this newspaper (obtained from Mediaedge).

Magazines

This media ensures segmentation potential, thereby ensuring that it is limited to the target audience. The vehicle chosen is the monthly magazine titled Alam Assayarat, since 76% of its readers are Emiratis, thus ensuring reach to our primary target audience (obtained from Mediaedge).

Cinema

According to the IPSOS statistic, 33% of UAE nationals like to go to the cinemas. The study also indicates that Brand Junkies visit the cinema every two to three weeks. An advantage of this media is the reduced level of distraction, and the possibility that they will pay more attention to advertisements. The chosen cinemas include the cinema in Mall of the Emirates, Grand Cineplex, and Marina Mall (Abu Dhabi). These 3 cinemas are visited regularly by Emiratis.

Internet

Emirati males are tech-savvy and use the internet for educational and entertainment purposes. Internet is highly accessible, and in Dubai, 67% of the population have access to it. Internet usage among Brand Junkies is high.
The websites in which ads will be placed include:
www.dubaimoon.com: Dubai Moon is widely popular with UAE nationals, as a social utility that allows them access to various fun activities. Not only does this website connect them with friends and colleagues through chat rooms, greeting cards and voicemail, it also provides them the opportunity to view the latest gossip, news and weather updates. Furthermore, Emiratis use Dubai Moon to download photos, ring tones, fun text messages and videos for their mobile all for a small fixed fee. Through this website many products including second hand cars are auctioned off and constant bids results in frequent access to the website by those interested. For the businessmen, stock market and real estate updates are available, and as for younger men online games including billiards are accessible free of charge.

www.kooora.com/www.goalzz.com: This is a website frequently visited by Emiratis, and Arabs in general, to obtain current news on many different sports, with emphasis on football/soccer. Advertising on this site will extend our reach beyond Emiratis, to even our secondary target market of other Arab nationalities.

Mobile

Young Emiratis are heavy users of mobile phones. Mobiles are seen as a status symbol within the Emirati target group. It is not uncommon for Emirati men to have more than 1 mobile phone. They use the Bluetooth application frequently as a mode of communication with people of the opposite sex. Therefore, we will use this application as a marketing technique for AXE, in the form of a game.

SCHEDULING OBJECTIVE

Scheduling: Pulsing

Cycle 1: July/August/September

Cycle 2: October/November/December

Cycle 3: January/February/March

Cycle 4: April/May/June

During the campaign, advertising will be relatively light in advertising cycle 1, which consists of the prime summer months, since many Emiratis tend to travel to foreign countries during these months. Advertising will be heavier in advertising cycles 2, 3 and 4.

The following table summarizes the media mix and the costs.

REACH & FREQUENCY

Reach/Frequency & GRP Objective

Achieve 70% reach during the beginning of the campaign. Reach will range from 70-85% over the life of the campaign. The minimum effective frequency per cycle would be 3.4 (refer to Ostrow Model in Appendix). The goal of the events would be to get approximately 2,600 of the target audience to participate.

Months	Medium	Vehicle	Insertions	Message Length/Size	Cost (AED)	GRP's	R/F
July August September	Television	MBC Action Dubai Sports TV	3 times/week 36 in three months	30 Seconds	1,260,000	1080	16/36 14/36
October November December	Magazines	Alam Assayarat	2 times/month 6 in three months	Full Page Color	120,000	456	76/6
	Outdoor	Jumeirah	2 lampposts per month		120,000	100,000 (impressions)	
	Event - Axis of Evil						
January February March	Television	MBC Action Dubai Sports TV	3 times/week 36 in three months	30 Seconds	1,260,000	1080	16/36 14/36
	Cinema	Mall of the Emir. Marina Mall Grand Cineplex	6 times/week 72 in three months	30 seconds	1,944,000	2356	33/72
	Radio	100.9 & 99.0	20 times a week 240 in three months	30 seconds	240,000	3360	14/240
	Event - She'ar Al Imaraty			Feb 1-Feb28			
April May June	Outdoor	Jumeirah	2 lamposts/ Month		120,000	100,000 (impressions)	
	Television	MBC Action Dubai Sports TV	5 times a week/ 60 times in 3 months	Full Page Color	2,100,000	1800	16/60 14/60
	Newspapers	Al Khaleeji	4 times a week/ 48 times in 3 months	Full Page Color	1,200,000	2544	53/48
	Magazines	Alam Assayarat	2 times a week/ 6 in 3 months	Full Page Color	120,000	456	76/6

SCHEDULING STRATEGY

Television
TV will be used in 3 advertising cycles; 1, 3, and 4, but in cycle 4 spending on TV ads will be increased since the ads have the 'Visa for travelling' theme, and cycle 4 is just before the summer months when the Emiratis are likely to travel/try getting a Visa. The ads in cycle 1 will kick-off the campaign and explain the new theme to the Emiratis. Also, the TV ads will not run in advertising cycle 2, mainly because of Ramadan (a holy month for Emiratis) falling in the month of October traditionally.

Cinema
Cinema will be used only in the 3rd advertising cycle of January, February and March since this is the time period when Oscar nominated movies are normally released. Since attendance is very high during this period, reach will be maximized.

Outdoor
Outdoor will be used in the 2nd and 4th advertising cycle. The first cycle will not be used because majority of Emiratis travel during these months. In the second cycle reach will be maximized through other mediums.

Radio
Radio will be used in the 3rd advertising cycle. Radio is a medium that does not have a peak period when it is more effective, and therefore we are going to use it in advertising cycle 3.

Internet
Internet will be used throughout the advertising campaign and a source of information about AXE products and Brand Junkies will be able to access the interactive features that the website provides. Furthermore, we will also have banner ads in the 1st advertising cycle, which will advertise the brand and the website.

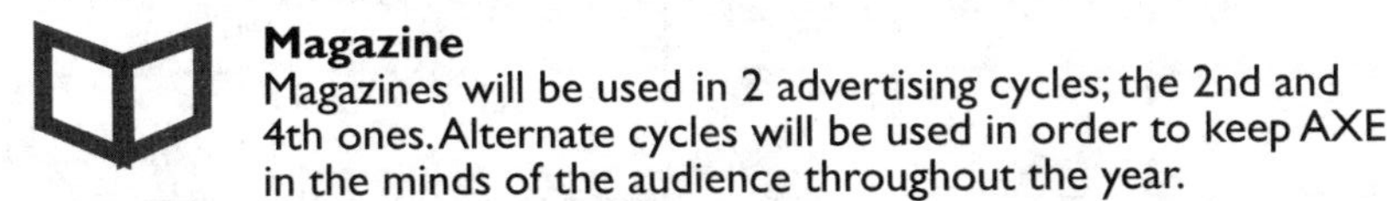

Magazine
Magazines will be used in 2 advertising cycles; the 2nd and 4th ones. Alternate cycles will be used in order to keep AXE in the minds of the audience throughout the year.

Newspaper
Newspaper will be used in the 4th advertising cycle, to ensure that reach is wide and constant amongst Emiratis.

Timeline of Campaign Schedule (1 Year)

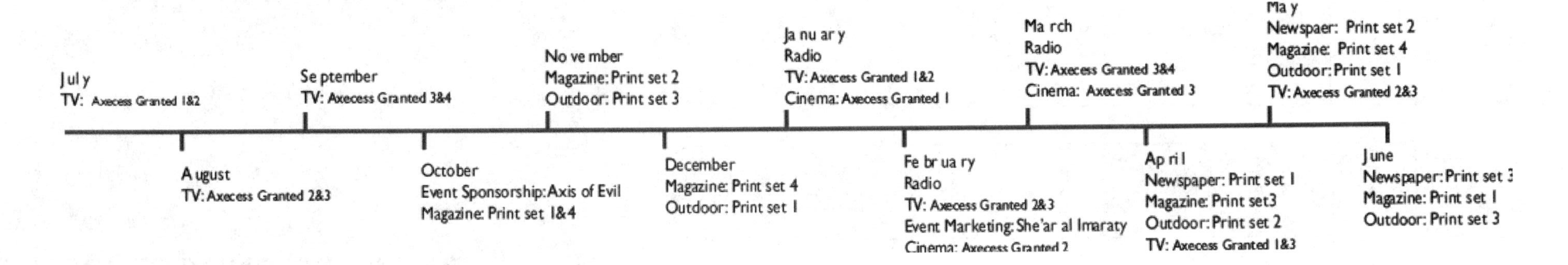

BUDGETING

To achieve a DHS 5 million increase in sales, a media versatile budget is needed. We derived a budget through the percentage of sales; 25% of sales would approximate DHS 7,250,000. However, our campaign warrants an investment of DHS 10,000,000. Our aim is to culturally reposition AXE as an identity brand. For an identity brand to successfully integrate into the target market, frequency of the message needs to be high. For this purpose, the myths need to be retold through the creative execution and this repetition of message justifies the budget of DHS 10,000,000.

As a result, a profitable return on customer investment is expected within 3 years.

Campaign Budget (DHS)	
Media	8,684,000
Events	700,000
Promotion	308,000
Production	308,000
Total	10,000,000
Total in $	2,725,000

1$ = 3.67 DHS

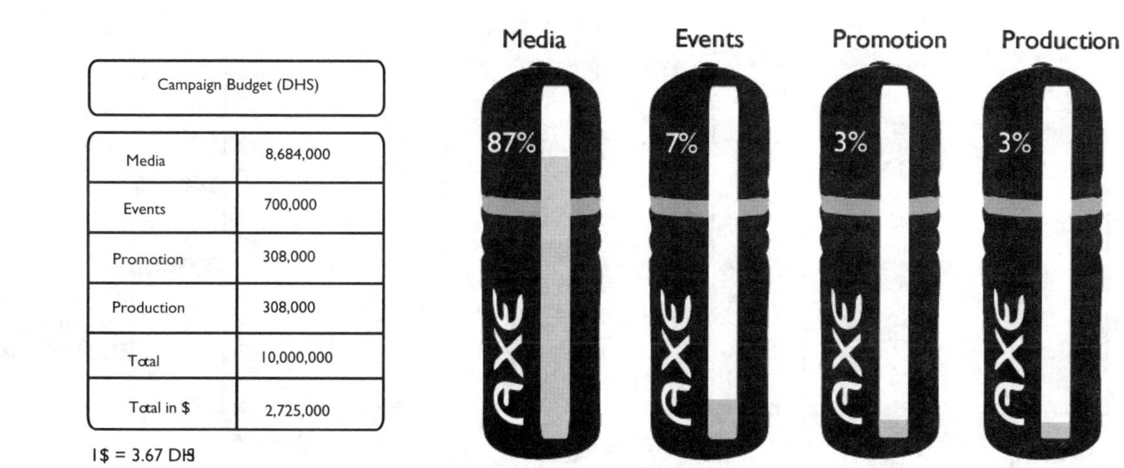

BUDGET STRATEGY

Media Breakdown (DHS)	
Television	4,620,000
Outdoor	240,000
Radio	240,000
Magazines	240,000
Cinema	1,944,000
Newspaper	1,200,000
Internet	200,000
Total	8,684,000
Total in $	2,366,000

1$ = 3.67 DHS

Television 48% 4,620,000
Cinema 21% 1,944,000
Newspaper 13% 1,200,000
Magazine 3% 240,000
Radio 3% 240,000
Outdoor 3% 240,000
Internet 2% 200,000

FLOWCHART

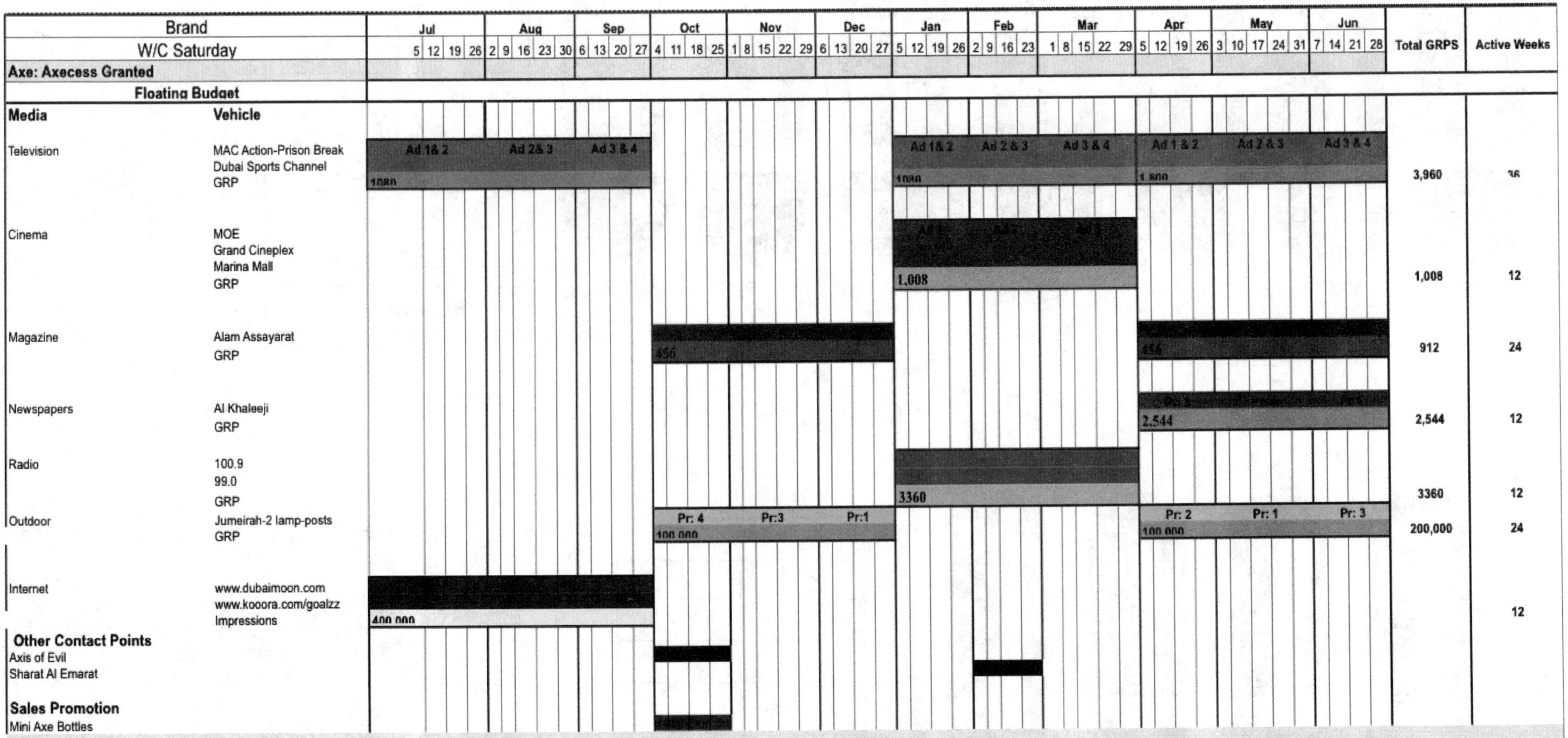

Brand / W/C Saturday		Jul (5, 12, 19, 26)	Aug (2, 9, 16, 23, 30)	Sep (6, 13, 20, 27)	Oct (4, 11, 18, 25)	Nov (1, 8, 15, 22, 29)	Dec (6, 13, 20, 27)	Jan (5, 12, 19, 26)	Feb (2, 9, 16, 23)	Mar (1, 8, 15, 22, 29)	Apr (5, 12, 19, 26)	May (3, 10, 17, 24, 31)	Jun (7, 14, 21, 28)	Total GRPS	Active Weeks
Axe: Axecess Granted															
Floating Budget															
Media	**Vehicle**														
Television	MAC Action-Prison Break Dubai Sports Channel GRP	Ad 1& 2 1080	Ad 2& 3	Ad 3 & 4				Ad 1& 2 1080	Ad 2 & 3	Ad 3 & 4	Ad 1 & 2 1,800	Ad 2 & 3	Ad 3 & 4	3,960	36
Cinema	MOE Grand Cineplex Marina Mall GRP							1,008						1,008	12
Magazine	Alam Assayarat GRP				456						456			912	24
Newspapers	Al Khaleeji GRP										2,544			2,544	12
Radio	100.9 99.0 GRP							3360						3360	12
Outdoor	Jumeirah-2 lamp-posts GRP				Pr: 4 100,000	Pr:3	Pr:1				Pr: 2 100,000	Pr: 1	Pr: 3	200,000	24
Internet	www.dubaimoon.com www.kooora.com/goalzz Impressions	400,000													12
Other Contact Points															
Axis of Evil															
Sharat Al Emarat															
Sales Promotion															
Mini Axe Bottles															

Medium	Budget	Jul	Aug	Sep	Oct	Nov	Dec	Jan	Feb	Mar	Apr	May	Jun
Television	4,620,000	420,000	420,000	420,000				420,000	420,000	420,000	700,000	700,000	700,000
Cinema	1,944,000							648,000	648,000	648,000			
Magazine	240,000				40,000	40,000	40,000	40,000	40,000	40,000			
Newspapers	1,200,000										400,000	400,000	400,000
Radio	240,000							80,000	80,000	80,000			
Outdoor	240,000				40,000	40,000	40,000				40,000	40,000	40,000
Internet	200,000	66,667	66,667	66,667									
Event	700,000				200,000								
Sales Promotion	308,000				308,000				500,000				
Total	**9,692,000**	486,667	486,667	486,667	588,000	80,000	80,000	1,188,000	1,688,000	1,188,000	1,140,000	1,140,000	1,140,000

Section II

Media Flight Plan
Exercises

Impressions and Ratings

Learning Objective:

Impressions and ratings are the most basic measurement tools in media planning, and although both tell us the same thing, each provides a unique way of expressing audience size. Think of ratings and impressions as universal media planning tools that play vital roles in measuring most all media.

We Don't Measure Ad audiences

We don't measure ad audiences– we measure audiences for media vehicles that carry ads. Impressions are commonly thought of as counting "eyeballs on the medium." (e.g., counting the number of people who tune in to *60 Minutes* or buy *People* magazine). It's important to clarify that we are not talking about "eyeballs on advertisements" in *People* or on *60 Minutes*. That's because we don't currently measure ad audience. Instead, we measure the audience for the media vehicles that carry the ads. For example, assume we run an ad for Mercedes Benz C-Class Coupe on Sixty Minutes, and 1.8 million persons tune in to *60 Minutes*. We cannot claim 1.8 million persons saw our ad. In truth, 1.8 million people only had an opportunity to see the ad (were "exposed" as in exposed to a virus – they may or may not "catch" it), because rarely does anyone "catch" all sixty minutes of *60 Minutes*. Keep in mind that "exposure" and "impression" are often used interchangeably. Technically they aren't the same, but in every-day advertising talk, both are used to indicate opportunity to see. We note that many agencies now use "commercial minute ratings" which are an improvement over program ratings, but are still not true exposure. Rather, they are the average of minutes with commercial content, weighted by the number of commercial seconds (e.g. a minute with 3 seconds of commercial content has a weight of 3, while a minute with 56 seconds has a weight of 56).

Table I shows the audiences (in impressions) for several TV programs:

Table I
(Universe for Adults 18-49 = 122.9 million)

Program	Network	Adult 18-49 Imp (000)
Castle	ABC	14140
CBS Evening News	CBS	13650
Monday Night Football	ESPN	7750
Tonight Show	NBC	5900
30 Minute Meals	FOOD	490
White Collar	USA	1360

Note how impressions are shown in thousands (000), the most common way impressions are reported. There are a couple of reasons for this. One is that the precision of measurement for most media requires rounding at this level. Another is that even for programs with small audiences, it's still a big number, and it's unwieldy. When calculating with impressions, be sure all the numbers you work with are expressed on the same scale, i.e., – in the same numeric format. Often it will be necessary to **add the zeros** (i.e. multiply by 1000 if shown in "000") to make sure all numbers are expressed in the same way.

Exercise 1

Example problem: Impressions can be added together to indicate the total "weight" of an advertising schedule. Your client, *Orbit* chewing gum, has agreed to run a schedule consisting of 3 spots on *Castle*, and 12 spots on *Rachael Ray's 30 Minute Meals*. How many impressions – reporting the complete number in thousands – will this schedule generate? Remember: **Complete number = numbers reported with all digits showing, including all zeros.**

Solving for Impressions: Each spot generates the impressions reported for that program. The first step is to figure the **total impressions for each program**. Next, sum the impressions for all programs in the schedule to get the **total impressions for the schedule**. See example in Table II:

Table II

3 spots on *Castle* x	14,140	=	42,420 (000) impressions
+ 12 spots on *30 Minute Meals* x	490	=	5,880 (000) impressions
Total for schedule:			48,300 (000) impressions

Don't forget to multiply by 1000 to get the **complete number**:
48,300 x 1000 = **48,300,000** or 48.3 million impressions

GROSS = Duplication or Multiple Opportunities to See

The total for the ad schedule in Table II would be expressed as 48.3 million *gross* impressions. The term *gross* is applied to situations where there is a chance that a person will have *more than one opportunity to see* an ad. And, since most target audiences get multiple exposures, we call this *duplication*. In our example there was a total of 15 spots – opportunities – for an individual to see an ad running in two TV programs, *Castle* and *30 Minute Meals*. Because a person could see more than one spot in either of these two programs, or could see a spot in both, we must assume duplication and the result is gross impressions. Rule of thumb: The term *gross* infers *duplication*, and duplication infers *multiple exposures*.

Ratings: Easier to Grasp than Impressions

Some media professionals call impressions "boxcar numbers" since they are so unwieldy. Impressions alone don't communicate much information, and using huge numbers verbally or in writing gets awkward. For example, knowing a spot on *Tonight Show* produces 5,900,000 impressions among adults 18-49 doesn't give us a sense of proportion. Knowing what **part or percentage** of the target audience was exposed is much easier to grasp than 5,900,000 impressions. If we factor in the universe of Adults 18-49, then we'll know what **percentage** of the target was exposed (had the "opportunity to see"). Here's the formula for calculating a rating:

$$\text{Rating} = \frac{\text{Impressions (000)}}{\text{Universe (000)}} \times 100$$

Note that both universe and impressions must be expressed in the same numeric format; **often they are NOT** and you must change one or both numbers to get the right answer. This formula will also work if impressions and the universe are in complete numbers. Once again: **Complete number = numbers reported with all digits showing, including all zeros**. For example, in Table III, the **complete number** expression for **Universe Adults 18-49 is 122,900,000**.

Example problem: The *universe* is often reported in *millions*. In the subheading below Table III, note how **Universe for Adults 18-49** is reported as **122.9 million**, but here you also encounter **122,900** when reported in numeric units of thousands (both are common). For example, look carefully at *Castle*. Note how the rating is calculated using Adult 18-49 Imp 000 (**14140**) and universe (**122900**) reported in thousands despite the **122.9** million reported in the heading. This table works because in the math section, *both impressions and universe are expressed in the same numeric units* (in this case NOT adding zeros) when calculated. Pay close attention here – depending on how the data is reported, you may need to add zeros or not add zeros to keep numeric units the same.

Table III
(Universe for Adults 18-49 = 122.9 million)

Program	Network	Adult 18-49 Imp (000)					Rating
Castle	ABC	14140	/	122900	x 100	=	11.5
CBS Evening News	CBS	13650	/	122900	x 100	=	11.1
Monday Night Football	ESPN	7750	/	122900	x 100	=	6.3
Tonight Show	NBC	5900	/	122900	x 100	=	4.8
30 Minute Meals	FOOD	490	/	122900	x 100	=	0.4
White Collar	USA	1360	/	122900	x 100	=	1.1

Gross Impressions vs. Gross Rating

The term *gross impression* indicates the possibility of multiple impressions (duplication) per target member, i.e., - being exposed to an ad more than once in different vehicles, or more than once in the same vehicle. The concept of gross rating is much the same as gross impressions; if duplication is possible, we get *gross ratings*, but as always with ratings, the number is converted to a percentage. If only one opportunity to see is possible, they are just ratings or *net* ratings. Like impressions, **ratings can be added together as long as they are for the same target audience**. When this is done, ratings also become "gross" and are typically called *Gross Rating Points*, or *GRPs* for short. The acronym is pronounced in different ways, "G-R-P's" and "Gurps" are perhaps the most frequent; you'll also hear "Grips." Some ad agencies make a further distinction by reserving the term Gross Rating Points to be used only when measuring households. Moreover, particular targets or demographics are distinguished as "Target Rating Points" or TRPs. This is simply a convention; there is no difference in definition between the two other than one is used for households and other for a specific target audience. You'll see both used interchangeably.

Problems

Table IV provides data for most of the problems in this exercise:

Table IV

Women 25-54 Universe: 116.82 MM [116,820 (000)]

Program	Network	Women 25-54 Imp (000)
Good Morning America	ABC	1520
Regis & Kelly	Syndication	4090
60 Minutes	CBS	12618
The Mentalist	CBS	11683
HBO Movie	HBO	351

1) Report the impressions for *Good Morning America, Regis & Kelly,* and *HBO Movie* as **complete numbers**. What simple math step is necessary to make the conversion?

Exercise 1

2) Your client, *Emeril's Original Essence* and a dozen other labels, (brand licensed by Emeril's Food of Love Productions) has decided to use your recommended TV schedule for the winter season:

Good Morning America	**4 spots**
The Mentalist	**3 spots**
HBO Movie	**12 spots**

Emeril's has decided to report the **total impressions** number – based on the TV schedule in Table IV – as part of a promotional brochure targeted at their sales reps and wholesalers so they know how well Emeril's spices, sauces and marinades will be supported. What number will you give them to place in their brochure? Tip: Create a table above – first calculate impressions for *each* program, and then sum the *total impressions* for the complete TV schedule. Show your math.

3) In preparing your recommendation, you'll need to calculate the rating for each of the programs you considered in Table IV. Calculate the rating for each program and show your math.

Good Morning America

Regis & Kelly

60 Minutes

The Mentalist

HBO Movie

4) How many total Gross Rating Points (GRPs) will be generated by the advertising schedule in problem 2? Tip: You just finished calculating the ratings for these programs, so most of the work is done.

5) You've been working with a new media person who works in the client's corporate headquarters. She recently graduated with from an ivy-league MBA school, but was never exposed to media planning.

A. She noticed that you use the terms "gross rating" and "gross impression," and wants to know the definition for each. Explain each in your own words (Tip: you can refer to the text part of this exercise.)

B. She is also confused on another issue. She thinks *impressions* for an ad in a TV program indicate how many people will actually see the ad. Explain this in your own words.

6) Which will add more gross rating points (GRPs) to a schedule: 6 spots in *Regis & Kelly* or 2 spots in *60 Minutes*? Show math to support your decision.

7. The *Castle* TV program rating for Women 25-54 last month was 12.8. Calculate the impressions for *Castle* and show your math. Tip: impressions(000) = rating/100 * universe(000)

Gross Rating Points, Reach and Frequency

Learning Objective

It's important to understand the direct mathematical relationship between reach, frequency and gross rating points. This relationship allows marketers to determine what proportion of their target audience is being reached and how often the average audience member has an "opportunity to see." Understanding this relationship forms the foundation for media schedule analysis and comparison.

Impressions and Rating Points

Recall that a rating is the number of impressions generated – divided by the universe – and finally multiplied by 100. For example, if you could buy one commercial on a special show that reached each target audience member exactly once, then the rating for that show would be a perfect 100, and the impressions generated would be exactly the same as the universe. In real media life, we have to buy many spots, and reach some target members more than once, and others not at all. So 100 rating points is the same number of impressions as the population, but is not the same as reaching 100 percent of the population. One rating point is equivalent to the number of impressions in one percent of the population (universe):

$$\text{one rating point} = \frac{\text{universe}}{100} = \text{\# impressions equal to one percent of the universe}$$

A gross rating point for **different targets** will equal a different number of impressions, because each target has a different universe or base. Like fractions with different denominators that can't be added, **GRPs for different targets cannot be added either**.

Gross rating points can be converted to impressions and back again with the following formulas:

$$\frac{\text{GRPs}}{100} \times \text{universe} = \text{impressions} \qquad \frac{\text{impressions}}{\text{universe}} \times 100 = \text{GRPs}$$

Solving for impressions

Example Problem: Your latest media planning masterpiece – a magazine schedule – generates 143 GRPs against a target of 11.9 million adults who regularly play board games. How many impressions does this plan generate?

From the discussion above, you know that 100 rating points is the number of impressions equal to the universe. You can use the formula provided above to calculate the number of impressions. Many people find it easier to convert universe figures provided in millions (MM or '0,000) or thousands ('000) to whole numbers before solving the problem. This is done by multiplying the universe by 1,000,000 or 1,000 respectively:

$$11.9 \times 1{,}000{,}000 = 11{,}900{,}000 \text{ impressions}$$

$$\frac{143}{100} \times 11{,}900{,}000 = 17{,}017{,}000 \text{ impressions, or } 17.0 \text{ MM}$$

We round numbers for convenience—the answer would likely be reported as "about 17 million impressions."

Exercise 2

You can calculate how many gross rating points result from a schedule by adding the ratings for each ad. That total can be converted to gross impressions to demonstrate how many total *opportunities to see* occurred. Both of these give us some idea of total weight, but neither tells us how many people were potentially exposed—that is, how many people had *at least one* opportunity to see, regardless of how many opportunities or impressions they received. *The net number of target persons "exposed" at least once is called REACH*. The TV schedule below illustrates the *vital relationship between gross rating points and reach*.

The TV show *Monk* provides 4 impressions to B, D, F, and H. The rating for *Monk* is 40 (4 persons with an opportunity to see out of 10 persons in the universe times 100). *Evening News* "exposes" A, B, and C, and has a rating of 30 (3 persons divided by 10 persons in the universe times 100), and by the same process, Survivor has a rating of 50.

	A	B	C	D	E	F	G	H	I	J
	☺	☺	☺	☺	☺	☺	☺	☺	☺	☺
Monk		■		■		■		■		
Evening News	■	■	■							
Survivor		■			■	■		■		■

Remember: Gross Means Duplication or Multiple Opportunities to See

If the ratings are added together, the schedule produces 120 gross rating points, or 12 gross impressions. Once totaled, the schedule turns gross delivering *gross impressions* and *gross rating points*. For example, persons B, F and H had multiple opportunities to see multiple programs. But if each program is considered alone, ratings and impressions are not gross because each person has only one opportunity to see that program. Example: Survivor gets 50% rating – *and no duplication* – because persons B, E, F, H, and J had *only one opportunity to see* Survivor.

"Impressions" is commonly used as an abbreviation for "Gross Impressions."

As discussed earlier, in theory it is possible for impressions to be UNduplicated. However, in practice impressions are almost always gross (duplicated) when applied to a real world media plan. That's why it is common to see the term "impressions" used without "gross" preceding it.

Reach Formula

Reach = Net number of target persons "exposed" at least once

Notwithstanding all of the media weight in this schedule, we were not able to *reach* (provide an opportunity to see) every person in the target. Count them – only 8 of the 10 received at least one impression. Our schedule, therefore, has a reach of 80. The formula for reach is:

$$\text{reach} = \frac{\text{target audience with opportunities to see ("exposed")}}{\text{target audience}} \times 100$$

Solving for Reach & GRPs

Example Problem: Suppose the client can only afford *Monk* and *Evening News*. What's the reach for this shortened schedule, and how many GRPs are generated? First, note that six persons (A, B, C, D, F, and H) are exposed by *Monk, Evening News* or both.

6 Persons Exposed ÷ Universe of 10 Persons = .06 X 100 = 60 Reach

Rating for Monk = 40 (4 out of 10 exposed); Rating for Evening News = 30

40 + 30 = 70 Gross Rating Points

Calculating both Reach & Frequency (See Pictograph)

While eight of the target population had at least one opportunity for exposure, some had more. B is a heavy viewer—and was exposed to each program. Others, like F and H were exposed twice, and some, like A, only once. We can calculate the average number of times each target member had an opportunity to see by dividing the total number of impressions by the number reached. The result is called "average frequency." In this example:

12 impressions* (total persons exposed) ÷ 8 Persons Reached = 1.5 Average Frequency

** Here's an example where the term "impressions" may be used in practice, but it actually means "gross impressions." Why are the 12 impressions in this equation actually gross?*

This same calculation works with gross rating points and reach, which are impressions expressed as percentages: 120/80=1.5 (recall, from the formula in exercise 1: 12 impressions/10 universe x 100 = 120 gross rating points; and 8 exposed/10 universe x 100 = 80 reach).

Reach, average frequency (often shortened to just 'frequency') and gross rating points are all related this way:

Memorize this formula: Reach x Average Frequency = Gross Rating Points

If you know either of the two values, you can calculate the third. To calculate reach or frequency, you can use these algebraic equivalents:

$$\text{Avg Freq} = \frac{\text{GRPs}}{\text{Reach}} \quad \text{and} \quad \text{Reach} = \frac{\text{GRPs}}{\text{Avg Freq}}$$

This is one of the most important mathematical relationships in media. With it you can estimate the weight needed to achieve goals, and understand the exposure pattern of the average person in the target audiences.

Problems

1. How many impressions are in one gross rating point for each target? First, convert target data to complete numbers, and then divide by 100.

Target	**Universe (MM)**	**X**	**÷**	**= Impressions**
Adults 25-54	116.82	________	________	________
Women 18-49	62.66	________	________	________
Men 65+	13.88	________	________	________

2. Your campaign for Kellogg's Frosted Mini-Wheats, positioned as a "lightly sweetened whole grain wheat alternative" for kids, is primarily targeted to children 6-14. It is hoped kids will request the breakfast "bite size confection" from their parents. The secondary target is mothers of young children. The campaign has elements of fun to attract young children, but health overtones directed at mothers. Your campaign results in 300 GRPs for children 6-14, and 240 GRPs for the secondary target, mothers. The reach for the two targets is 85 and 78 respectively. What is the average frequency for each target?

Exercise 2

3) Your target audience is children age 6-14. Communication objectives for the next media flight call for these minimums:

- Reach: 80%
- Average frequency: 6

Calculate the minimum gross rating points required for this set of objectives.

4. In Question 3, will all children reached (age 6-14) get 6 impressions? You need more than a yes/no answer. Explain the "why" behind your answer.

ALL REMAINING QUESTIONS RELATE TO THE PICTOGRAPH BELOW
Assume your media plan includes magazine schedule targeted to men age 18-34.

	A	B	C	D	E	F	G	H
Car & Driver		■		■	■	■		
GQ		■	■		■			
Bicycling					■	■		■

5. What is the universe for men 18-34 in this magazine schedule? (Tip: Count the smiley faces)

6. Calculate the rating for *each* publication. (Rating = Target Exposed ÷ Universe X 100) Remember, ratings are expressed as percents.

Car & Driver __________

GQ __________

Bicycling __________

7. How many total gross rating points (GRPs) are generated by the whole magazine schedule?

Car & Driver __________

GQ __________

Bicycling __________

Total GRPs: __________

8. How many gross impressions does each magazine generate? Total gross impressions?

Car & Driver ______________

GQ ______________

Bicycling ______________

Total Gross Impressions: ______________

9. Calculate the reach for this magazine schedule, and show your math.

10. Calculate average frequency for this magazine schedule, and show your math.

MFP Online Experiment: GRPs, Reach and Frequency

Logging on with *MFP* Online

Computer display: *Media Flight Plan* is best viewed on a screen with a minimum resolution of 1024 x 768. Most new computers are set to this resolution or higher by default. If your screen resolution is lower (like 800 x 600) you will still be able to use *MFP*, but you'll need to scroll around to see the entire screen.

Recommended browsers: *MFP* has been tested and runs well on a number of browsers. **Firefox is the preferred browser for MFP**. This is one of the quickest, safest browsers available, and best of all, it's free (you can download it at http://www.mozilla.org/products/firefox/). Browsers supported by *MFP6* include the following:

Windows	Macintosh
Firefox 3.5 and higher	Firefox 3.5 and higher
Safari 4.0 and higher	Safari 4.0 and higher
Internet Explorer 7.0 and higher	

Other browsers may work as well, but all of these have been tested. *Note that your screen may vary slightly from the images in the tutorial depending on your browser.*

In all browsers, JavaScript must be enabled. If *MFP* works well for you, you won't need to worry about this. Unless you intentionally turned it off yourself, the JavaScript default is normally in the "on" position, so don't change anything until you try your current browser setup. If you have installed add-ons, like NoScript for Firefox, it will prevent JavaScript from running unless you give the mediaflightplan.com site permission. If you are using a supported browser and are having problems, see the documentation for your respective browser or add-on for further information on enabling JavaScript, or check with computer support at your university. If all else fails, start from scratch by loading the latest version of Firefox.

Performance: A high-speed connection is required (i.e. T1, cable modem, or DSL type connection). *MFP* cannot be run successfully over a dialup connection.

Registration and Logging In . . .Do this before starting Exercise on next page

1. Get your *MFP* Access Code – it's located on the inside front cover of this book. Carefully scratch off the silver coating with the edge of a coin.
2. Open your Internet browser.
3. Go to: www.mediaflightplan.com
4. Click [Login] at top of screen.
5. Follow instructions for new users. You'll need your access code to log in the first time.
6. Turn to the next page and begin the Online Experiment.

Exercise 3

MFP Online Experiment: GRPs, Reach & Frequency

Objective: At this point you should be familiar with the theoretical and mathematical underpinnings of reach, frequency and GRPs. Now it's time to apply your theoretical knowledge with a hands-on experiment. All three experiments use the *Media Flight Plan* program.

Syndicated media measurement services typically measure exposure to specific vehicles—programs for television, average issue audience for magazines, average quarter hour audience for radio, gross impressions for internet, etc. Planners usually don't know which programs or websites they will be using during the planning stages of a campaign, so models must be employed to estimate parameters like reach, GRPs and average frequency. Hopefully, while working through exercises 1 and 2, you discovered that duplication is a major issue in estimating reach. We cannot estimate reach without knowing how much duplication is generated in each media buy. Many millions are spent in measuring media, but measuring the myriad ways duplication happens in every conceivable media schedule is virtually impossible. Reach is usually modeled from GRPs in commercial media programs, and the basic formula (GRPs = Reach x Frequency . . . using the algebraic relationship between these three media pillars) is used to derive the average frequency. Sophisticated formulas allow media planners to estimate the *frequency distribution* which shows how many persons are exposed at each possible frequency level in a schedule.

Fortunately, you don't have to be a statistics genius to be a planning genius—computer programs are much faster at doing such calculations than humans, and good planners can learn how to interpret the results even if they are not the world's greatest mathematicians. A good analogy is the way we use cars. Most of us could not build an engine, let alone explain the internal workings. But we have learned that with the proper input – gasoline and a key – and how to manipulate the input – accelerator, steering wheel, etc., we can transport ourselves from point A to point B. In our journeys, we learn that there is a relationship between speed, time and distance. The same kind of relationship exists with reach, frequency, and gross rating points: If one of the variables is held constant say distance (or GRPs) then as speed (or reach) increases or decreases, time (or frequency) must do the exact opposite to balance the relationship.

To continue this exercise, go to www.mediaflightplan.com and follow the instructions below.

Start *MFP*. Note that your screen might look a bit different depending on your computer or browser, but the information displayed should be the same. If you have difficulty, look at beginning of this exercise to make sure your browser is supported.

On the right side of the screen, you'll see a a row of buttons, starting with one labeled **Target Audience**. Click it, and in the dialog box that appears, click **[Adults]**, then the age groups **25-34**, **35-49**, and **50-54** as shown in the figure below. The "Current Demo" box should be green and read "Adults ages 25-54". Click **[OK]**.

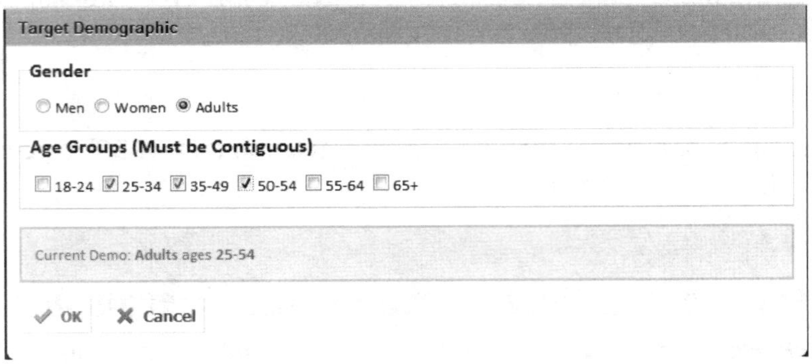

In the **Target Demographic Updated** dialog box that follows, leave the default option selected and click **[OK]**. You should now be back at the main screen.

Now focus on the main screen. Observe the headings—from left to right, Medium, Ad Type, Unit Cost, Units, and Ext Cost. In this exercise, you will be typing only in the Units column. It's circled in the graphic below. (Caution: If your cursor wanders into the Unit Cost column, you'll get wrong answers). The Ad Type column gives the "size" of the unit you're buying. For example, cost of buying Network TV-E Morning is now set at the default Ad Type (:30 seconds). Leave all Ad Types set at the default.

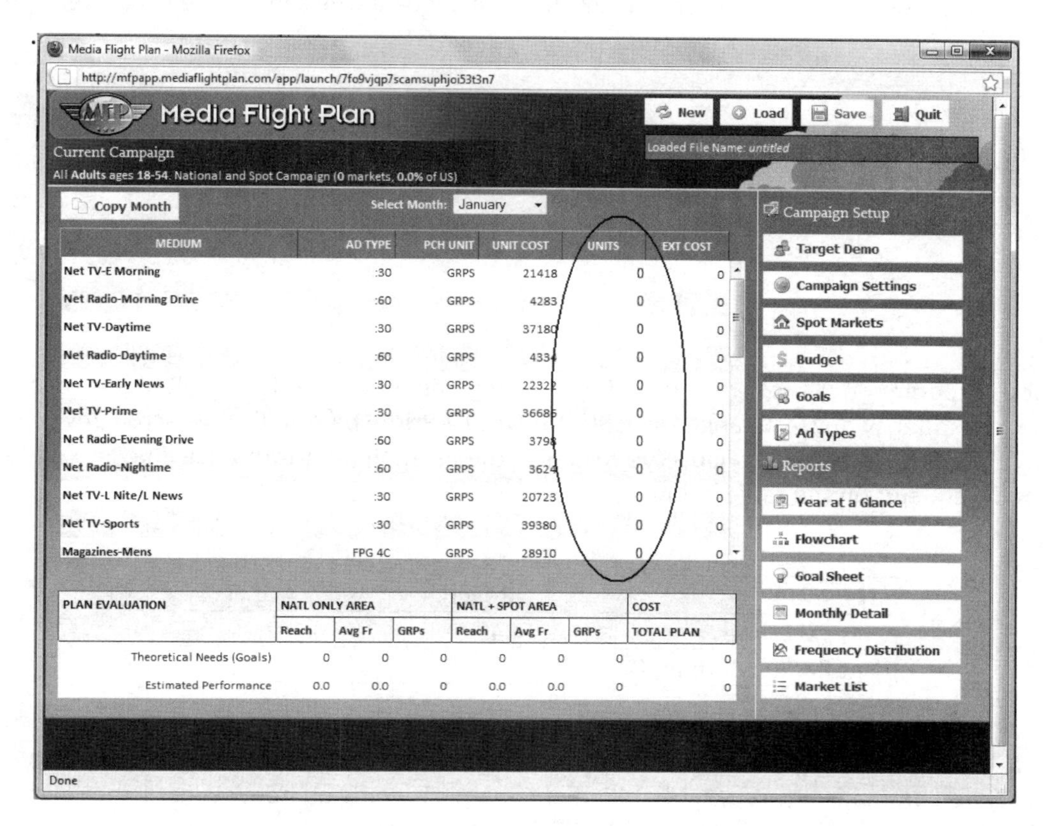

At the bottom of the screen, there is a line labeled Estimated Performance. It's in the **PLAN EVALUATION** section at the bottom of the screen. This is the only line you'll be working with – your answers will appear below the heading **NATIONAL ONLY AREA**.

Experiment 1

With your cursor in the Units column, move to Net TV-Prime and buy 50 GRPs (type 50 in the UNITS column). Observe the Estimated Performance line (bottom of screen) and write your Reach and Frequency in the first line of the table below.

Net TV-Prime	Reach	Avg Fr
50 GRPs		
100 GRPs		

Now double the GRPs – from 50 to 100 – and write your results in the table above.

A) Using the results from above, does Reach x Frequency = GRPS? (After allowance for rounding) Show the math.

Exercise 3

B) Do 100 GRPs equal 100 percent reach? Why not? What does 100 GRPs equal?

C) Did doubling the GRPs double the reach? Why? Tip: Take a look at the sample "reach curve" below.

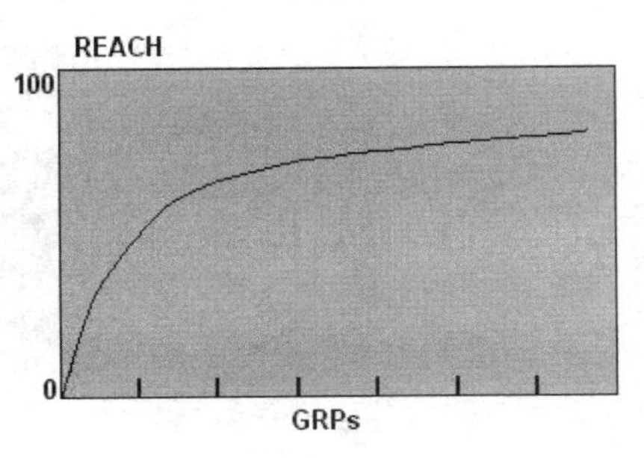

Experiment 2

In the previous experiment, we saw that 100 GRPs in Prime network television resulted in a reach of 45.5 and an average frequency of 2.2. Change the GRPs for Net TV-Prime back to 0. Now scroll down to Net Radio-Morning Drive and type in 100 GRPs. Observe results in the Estimated Performance line, and write down the new reach and frequency in the table below.

100 GRPs	Reach	Avg Fr
Net TV-Prime	45.5	2.2
Net Radio-Morning Drive		

A) Radio and TV perform very differently. After eliminating the TV buy and putting 100 GRPs into radio, Reach/ Frequency changed dramatically. Why? What kind of dynamic is going on here? What's the relationship between the Reach/Frequency in radio compared to TV?

B) If you were to put the same 100 GRPs into a medium that resulted in a 28 reach, what would be the average frequency? (Show the math – remember frequency is rounded to one decimal place).

What if you had a 54 reach?

Experiment 3

Comparing television cultures of different generations, which do you think watches more TV, your generation or your parents/grandparents?

We'll test your hypothesis, but first you'll need to change all the GRPs in Media Flight Plan back to 0. Now click the **Target Demo** button and change the target to Adult 18-24 (Un-check all boxes except 18-24, and click [OK]. Click [OK] in the **Target Demographic Updated** dialog box again.

Buy 100 GRPs in Network TV-Prime and write the new Reach in the table below.

Now test the older generation. Go back into **Target Demo**, uncheck the 18-24 box and check 55-64 and 65+. Write the Reach below and observe the difference.

100 GRPs	**Reach**
Adults 18-24	
Adults 55+	

Did your hypothesis hold?

Cost-Per-Thousand and Cost-Per-Point

Learning Objective

Cost-Per-Thousand (CPM) and Cost-Per-Point (CPP) are basic media evaluation tools. Both democratize media choices by putting all buys on an equal footing—much like calculating cost-per-ounce when comparing Tide with Cheer at your local Super Target. After deciding which laundry brands are worth considering (or media packages in this case), you compare them for value. CPM and CPP let you compare costs even when media is delivered in different packages, e.g., full-page versus half-page, or TV versus print. Both methods let you "weigh" the cost of each medium based on a common denominator--impressions or rating points.

Cost-Per-Thousand

The "M" in CPM originates from the Roman numeral "M" for 1,000. Sometimes expressed "CPM GI," the GI is short for **G**ross **I**mpressions. Besides using gross impressions, CPM can be calculated using other data such as circulation. This would normally be done only if audience is not available - for example, in the case of an unmeasured magazine. The occasional exception aside, CPM almost always refers to gross impressions unless otherwise identified. CPMs can be compared directly, since all CPMs are calculated using the same mathematical base—the cost of delivering 1000 gross impressions to a target audience. The most common formula for CPM is:

$$\text{CPM} = \frac{\text{total cost}}{\text{total impressions}} \times 1000$$

Note that CPMs should be reported in dollars & cents.

Calculating CPM for a Single Vehicle

Example Problem: Your client, Volvic brand water, (a natural, volcanic spring water imported from Europe) is targeted to younger women aged 18-39. The cost for a full-page four-color ad in *Shape* magazine is $106,045. The research department has given you a crosstab where you find that *Shape* reaches 4437 (000) women aged 18-39. What is the CPM?

Solving for CPM:

Cost of 4-Color page in *Shape*: $106,045

Impressions converted to complete numbers: 4,437 X 1000 = 4,437,000

$$\frac{\$106,045}{4,437,000} \times 1000 = \$23.90$$

Cost Per Thousand for Multiple Vehicles (Schedule CPM)

Calculating the CPM for a schedule or media plan is done by summing the gross impressions from all the insertions in all the media vehicles and dividing it into the summed cost for all the ads in the schedule.

Exercise 4

The formula is the same as for a single ad. Assume *Vogue* has a full-page four-color cost of $100,140 and reaches 6911 (000) women 18-49. Let's look at a schedule with 2 insertions in *Vogue* along with 1 insertion in *Shape*. This buy results in the following CPM:

$$\frac{[2\ (\text{Vogue cost } \$100{,}140) + \text{Shape cost } \$106{,}045]}{[2\ (\text{Vogue Impressions } 6{,}911{,}000) + \text{Shape Impressions } 4{,}437{,}000]} \times 1000 = \text{CPM}$$

$$\frac{\$306,\ 325}{18{,}259{,}000} \times 1000 = \$16.78$$

Cost Per Point (CPP)
CPP does essentially the same thing as CPM – it measures efficiency. Similar to CPM, the formula is:

$$\text{CPP} = \frac{\text{Total Cost}}{\text{Total GRPs}}$$

The process for calculating the CPP for a schedule is the same—obtain the total cost by summing the cost of all the adds, and divide by the total GRPs obtained by summing the ratings of all the adds. CPP is usually rounded to the nearest whole dollar.

CPM typically used for print media — CPP preferred for broadcast media

When comparing media options, CPMs and CPPs perform the same function. Each tool makes it possible to see which vehicle or schedule is most cost efficient despite each media plan having a different mix of media, ad sizes or other elements. **Your decision will be the same regardless of which tool you use— the schedule with the lowest CPM will always have the lowest CPP as well**. Ultimately it's a matter of preference, although because of the way syndicated data are reported and used, print is typically compared using cost-per-thousand, while broadcast tends to be compared using cost-per-point.

When planners are in the early stages using rough cost estimates, most use a 'typical cost-per-point' supplied by the broadcast buying group. Because numerous spots are purchased, it's easier to work with CPPs in broadcast to estimate how many Gross Rating Points can be purchased with a given budget.

Efficiency is the rule, but every rule . . .

When one vehicle or plan reaches the target at a lower cost than another, we say it is "more efficient." Efficiency, however, is not always the best strategy. When Saturn launched their new brand, Hal Riney and Partners made a bold print buy. Their media strategy — "full speed ahead and damn the CPMs". They targeted women 18-34 by purchasing magazines that *enjoyed at least 30 minutes reading time*. CPMs took a back seat based on the strategy that quality reading time trumps efficiency.

Calculating Cost Per Point (CPP)
Example Problem: Continuing with *Shape* and *Vogue*, the research tabulation shows that for women 18-49, the ratings for the two magazines are 6.7 and 10.4 respectively. Which has the lowest Cost Per Point? What is the CPP of a schedule consisting of 3 full-page four color insertions in *Vogue* and 4 in *Shape* each publication?

Solving for CPP: First, calculate the CPP for each publication, using the CPP formula:

$$\text{CPP for } Shape = \frac{\$106{,}045}{6.7} = \$15{,}828\ (\$15{,}827.61 \text{ rounded})$$

$$\text{CPP for } Vogue = \frac{\$100{,}140}{10.4} = \$9{,}629\ (\$9{,}628.85 \text{ rounded})$$

For this target, *Vogue* is more efficient (the CPP is $6,000+ lower). As already noted, you may not always use the most efficient cost—editorial environment or value-added packages often trump CPP.

To get the cost of three insertions, calculate total cost and total gross rating points, then use the formula:

$$\frac{[3\ (\textit{Vogue}\text{ cost } \$100{,}140) + 4\ (\textit{Shape}\text{ cost } \$106{,}045)]}{[3\ (\textit{Vogue}\text{ rating } 10.4) + 4\ (\textit{Shape}\text{ rating } 6.7)]} = \text{CPP}$$

$$\frac{\$724{,}600}{58.0\text{ GRPS}} = \$1{,}249\ (\$1{,}249.31\text{ rounded})$$

Problems

1. Calculate **CPM**, **Total Cost**, and **Total Gross Impressions** for each of the magazine titles shown in the table below. As you do the math, FILL IN ALL OF THE EMPTY CELLS. You may wish to use a spreadsheet like Microsoft Excel.

Publication	**Full-Page 4-Color Cost**	**Women Aud (000)**	**CPM**	**Schedule Insertions**	**Total Cost**	**Total Gross Imp (000)**
Parenting	$125,765	9,216		3		
Parent's	129,200	11,633		6		
Prevention	11,300	8,392		2		
Reader's Digest	234,900	23,234		4		
Redbook	121,500	8,537		2		
Time	223,000	11,023		5		
TV Guide	166,100	15,963		2		
Woman's Day	214,750	19,364		3		
Vogue	94,470	8,500		3		
Schedule Totals	----	----		30		

2. Which of the magazines in Exhibit I is the most efficient – has the lowest CPM? Name the magazine and show your math for calculating the CPM.

3. Which has the highest CPM (is *least* efficient) among all magazines on the list? Name the magazine and show your math for calculating CPM.

4. The universe for women is 106,894 (000). What is the rating for *Redbook* and *Woman's Day*? If you've forgotten how to calculate ratings, review the formulas in Exercises 1 & 2. Show your math.

5. Using the information supplied in the following table, fill in the missing values for ALL EMPTY CELLS. Remember to round CPP to the nearest dollar.

Program	:30 Cost	HH Rating	CPP	Schedule Insertions	Total Cost	GRPs
The Mentalist	$330,000	16.9		1		
Sunday Movie	124,200	8.4		2		
Survivor	245,800	11.5		1		
20/20	115,600	6.2		3		
60 Minutes	89,100	8.7		2		
Schedule Totals	----	----		9		

6. What is the **CPP** for *Survivor*? What does it mean?

7. Relating to the TV programs above, Nielsen Media Research estimates that Total TV Homes for the season is 109.6 MM. How many impressions are produced by **one** ad in *20/20*? (If you've forgotten, find the formula in the *Gross Rating Points, Reach & Frequency* exercise that solves for impressions.)

8. What is a Gross Rating Point? Using the universe in question 7, how many impressions are in one **GRP**?

Using Syndicated Consumer Research

Learning Objective

Marketers and agencies use a variety of research to help them understand consumers. One of the principal tools is syndicated research; it gathers comprehensive data from thousands of consumers to help marketers make intelligent, informed decisions. These large studies are done by independent companies and sold to many different clients, including ad agencies and corporations. Generally speaking, syndicated market researchers collect data about magazine readership (often the principal reason for the study), consumer attitudes and purchase behavior, and other media usage. Thousands of data points are collected from individual consumers via personal interviews, phone interviews, and product usage questionnaires.

Syndicated Research

Mediamark Research Inc (MRI) and Simmons are among the major providers of general consumer studies. Other consumer research may be available at many ad agencies depending on client needs. Examples include studies on vehicle owners done by JD Power and Associates, Monroe Mendelsohn's study of the affluent, and MARS, a study for the pharmaceutical industry.

The data compiled by different research companies is distributed through various crosstabbing systems. As a marketer you need to know how to interpret these data formats and tabbing systems – often quite similar among various syndicated providers. This exercise will help you learn to read and understand the tabulations generated by these systems.

How to Interpret Crosstabs

Find **Exhibit I** (after the problems at the end of this exercise) – it shows part of a typical crosstab format. At the very top of the tab, the base is identified as **Adults**. The base of a crosstab can be whatever you wish, but it is the universe within which the tabulation is done. The first row of data and the first column are labeled **Totals**. This row and column contains the total number of base persons in each row or column category. The first cell in the first row, where the two "Totals" intersect, shows the total number of persons contained in the base, and the associated percentages that go with it:

		Totals
Totals	(000)	209373
	Vert%	100.0
	Horz%	100.0
	Index	100

Why is the Data Weighted?

This cell shows that there are **209,373,000** adults in the US. The number in the row labeled **(000)** is called the projection, or count. It's the estimated number of persons in the cell. The reason it's called a "projection" is that the respondents in the cell are reported as "projected" to the universe they represent using weights. Research companies estimate the value of each respondent, then sum the weights of each actual respondent to 'project' the sample up to the universe the cell represents. The vertical and horizontal percentages are 100.0% in this case because the total is everyone in the universe. Indexes represent concentration or potential, and will be discussed in depth in the next exercise.

Although not shown in this example, some tabulations will show the number of respondents in a line that is labeled **UNWTD** (for unweighted). It's tempting to think that there is a linear relationship between the two—but there is not. Each respondent has a different weight, depending on his/her characteristics. Therefore, the two rows are NOT interchangeable in representing the universe. If both Unwgt and (000) are shown, be sure to use the correct row: **(000)**.

Read Rows Horizontally – Read Columns Vertically

Each cell follows the same format—the first number in the block is the raw number of persons who meet the requirements of both the row and the column. Look at the cell (in Exhibit I) where **Men** intersects **Attended Movies Past 6 Months**. You are in the right place if the number on the (000) row is **59851**. The cell should be read, "**59,851,000 men attended a movie in the past 6 months**". Move your finger to the top number in this same column (the "Totals" row). There you will find the **Total** number of persons who went to a movie in the past 6 months: **128,136,000** (remember the numbers in this tab are shown in thousands– mentally add 3 zeros).

The **Vert%** shows that **46.7** percent of adults who went to a movie in the past 6 months were men. You know to use the vertical percentage because the two numbers are **vertically opposed** (one above the other) in the same column. The math is straightforward: **59,851 ÷ 128,136 x 100 = 46.7 percent.**

Move back to the previous cell. Looking across to the totals column on the left, note that total MEN in the survey = **100,457** (000). Because the two cells are **horizontally** opposed in the same row, the horizontal percent represents the ratio of men who attended a movie in the past 6 months as a percent of TOTAL men: **59,851 ÷ 100,457 X 100 = 59.6**, the percentage shown.

Totals are Denominators

The **total** for any column or row is always the **denominator**. Obviously, the other half of the equation must be the numerator – the number in any cell is always the numerator in the ratio. (For examples, see the equations shown at bottom of the **Horiz%** and **Vert%** boxes in Exhibit I). Percentages are extremely helpful and can save a lot of work if you make sure you know which ones to use.

Now find the row **8+ CHILDREN IN HH** and the column labeled **Attend Movies 2x/Month or more**. The cell where they intersect has an asterisk (*) next to it. Look at the bottom of the tab sheet; there's a footnote indicating that this cell has insufficient sample size to reliably project, and that caution should be used in interpreting the data. The cutoff for flagging data is different for each data source, but is typically around 50 respondents. If your crosstab has a lot of asterisks, it is an indication that the columns are too narrowly defined, and you should consider making the group larger, even if it doesn't define the target as precisely as you'd like. It's better to have good data for a reasonable likeness of your desired target than to have useless data for exactly what you want.

The last label in each row's data set is **Index**. (Find the **Index** box). For now it is sufficient to know that they indicate the likelihood or potential of an activity or characteristic in the cell. A 100 Index indicates the "average", and indexes above 100 indicate greater than average propensity, while indexes below 100 indicate below average – less likelihood that a behavior or condition exists.

Crosstabs can be quite lengthy; it's not unusual to run tabs many columns across and up to hundreds of pages long. For example, MRI, Simmons, and others query respondents on hundreds of product categories, and several thousands of brands within those categories. Audiences are collected for well over 200 magazines, and many network and syndicated television programs, cable networks, newspapers, radio and other items!

Problems

Data needed for these problems is available online: www.mediaflightplan.com

You can look at the data on-screen, or download it and print. It's an Excel file about 10 pages long, and will be used for the next exercise, so hold on to it if you print it out.

If you haven't downloaded it yet, go to **mediaflightplan.com** and click on **Student.** Next, click **Ground School**. Then, click on the link to download MRI data. It's titled: *Exercises 5 & 6 – MRI Movie Cross Tab*

VERY IMPORTANT TIP: Is it a Horizontal or Vertical problem? First look for the two projections (raw base numbers) referred to in the problem. If the two base numbers are horizontally opposed, it is a horizontal problem, and the percentage you need is in the row labeled HORZ%. If the two projections (raw base numbers) are vertically opposed – one above the other – it is a vertical problem, and the percentage you need is in the row labeled VERT%. Always find both raw numbers first, then divide to make sure you've got the right percentage.

NOTE: Round all of your percentages to one place – e.g., 24.07 = 24.1

1. How many **Adults** say they **Attended Movies Past 6 Months**? (See page 1 of MRI data). Tip: This tab shows **Unwgt** respondents; use the projection row labeled **(000)**.

2. Referring back to question number 1, all of the projections in this cross tab are displayed in a common, numerical way. All projections are expressed numerically in ______________________.

3. Among all Adults who GRADUATED HIGH SCHOOL, what percent **Prefer to See Movie On Opening Weekend**? (We're still on pg. 1) Is this a horizontal or vertical problem? Show math used to get the percentage. Tip: Break each problem into bite-size units, and *always begin by finding the two base numbers*. In this problem, first find the projected number of Adults who GRADUATED HIGH SCHOOL in the **Totals** column. Start at top of the **Totals** column and follow it *down* to the projection row (000). Next, follow this row *across* and find the projected number who **Prefer to See Movie On Opening Weekend**. Last, divide the two numbers, and then multiply by 100 to verify that you have the correct percentage. (Note that it's reported as either **Vert%** or **Horz%**; your job is to decide which is correct.) Show complete equation below:

4. Targeting adults who **Attend Movies Once a Month**, list the seven marketing regions. Start with PACIFIC—MKTG REGN on Page 8 and follow through on page 9. Rank these seven markets from high to low based on the *percentage* of adults who **Attend Movies Once a Month** in each geographic region. Is this a vertical or horizontal problem? Tip: Begin by calculating the PACIFIC-MKTG REGN. The numerator for this equation is found on pg. 8 in the **Attend Movies Once a Month** column. The denominator for all seven markets is in the projected **Totals** row on page 1. Be sure to use the correct total – the projected total below the column **Attend Movies Once a Month**. List all seven markets, show the equation for each, and rank them 1-7.

Exercise 5

*** * From here on you'll need to find the correct MRI pages on your own. * ***

5. Of all **Adults** with CHILDREN 6-11 YEARS, what percent **Prefer to See Movie On Opening Weekend**? Is this horizontal or vertical? Show the math.

6. Among adults who **Prefer to See Movie on Opening Weekend**, what percent have CHILDREN 6-11 YEARS? Horizontal or vertical? Show your math.

7. Find the set of data for WORKING WOMEN. Among the three groups listed below, which has the highest percentage of movie goers that are WORKING WOMEN? Tip: Although focusing on working women, you still need to consider them as part of the total number of movie goers.

- **Prefer to See Movie On Opening Weekend**
- **Prefer to See Within 1st 2 Wks After Open Wknd**
- **Prefer to See After Second Week**

Is this a Horizontal or Vertical problem? Show Math.

8. Of all MEN who **Attended Movies Past 6 Months**, what percentage **Prefer to See Movie On Opening Weekend**? Tip: This is a bit of a brainteaser because the percentage **(Vert%** or **Horz%)** is **NOT** reported for you on the tab.

EXHIBIT I

Note: Exhibit I corresponds with the first two pages of this exercise. It may be easier to follow along if you tear this sheet out.

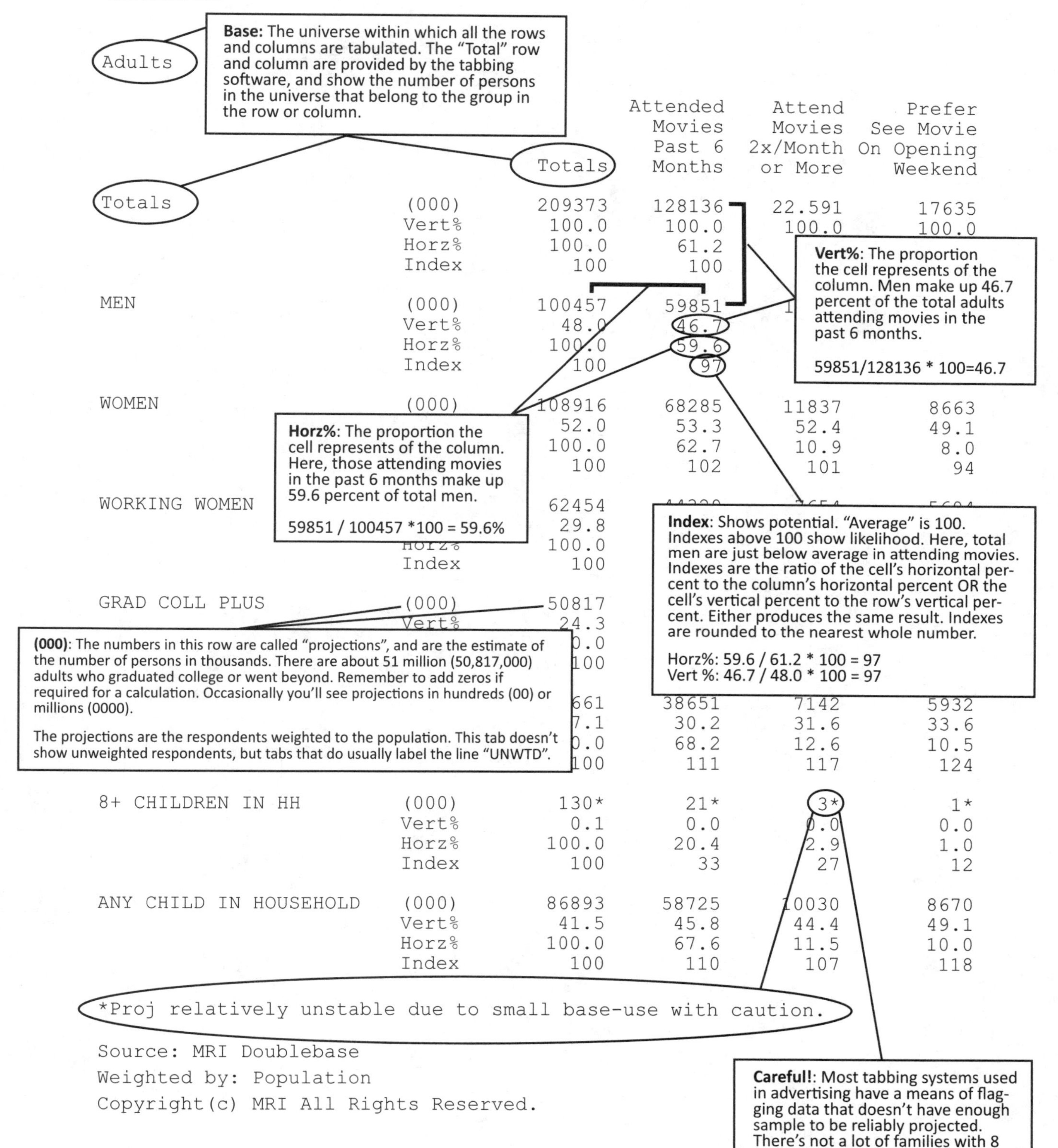

Adults

		Totals	Attended Movies Past 6 Months	Attend Movies 2x/Month or More	Prefer See Movie On Opening Weekend
Totals	(000)	209373	128136	22.591	17635
	Vert%	100.0	100.0	100.0	100.0
	Horz%	100.0	61.2	[illegible]	[illegible]
	Index	100	100	[illegible]	[illegible]
MEN	(000)	100457	59851	[illegible]	[illegible]
	Vert%	48.0	46.7	[illegible]	[illegible]
	Horz%	100.0	59.6	[illegible]	[illegible]
	Index	100	97	[illegible]	[illegible]
WOMEN	(000)	108916	68285	11837	8663
	Vert%	52.0	53.3	52.4	49.1
	Horz%	100.0	62.7	10.9	8.0
	Index	100	102	101	94
WORKING WOMEN	(000)	62454	[illegible]	[illegible]	[illegible]
	Vert%	29.8	[illegible]	[illegible]	[illegible]
	Horz%	100.0	[illegible]	[illegible]	[illegible]
	Index	100	[illegible]	[illegible]	[illegible]
GRAD COLL PLUS	(000)	50817	[illegible]	[illegible]	[illegible]
	Vert%	24.3	[illegible]	[illegible]	[illegible]
	[illegible]	[illegible]	[illegible]	[illegible]	[illegible]
	[illegible]	[illegible]	[illegible]	[illegible]	[illegible]
[illegible]	[illegible]	[illegible]	38651	7142	5932
	[illegible]	[illegible]	30.2	31.6	33.6
	[illegible]	[illegible]	68.2	12.6	10.5
	[illegible]	[illegible]	111	117	124
8+ CHILDREN IN HH	(000)	130*	21*	3*	1*
	Vert%	0.1	0.0	[illegible]	0.0
	Horz%	100.0	20.4	[illegible]	1.0
	Index	100	33	27	12
ANY CHILD IN HOUSEHOLD	(000)	86893	58725	[illegible]	8670
	Vert%	41.5	45.8	44.4	49.1
	Horz%	100.0	67.6	11.5	10.0
	Index	100	110	107	118

*Proj relatively unstable due to small base-use with caution.

Source: MRI Doublebase
Weighted by: Population

Base: The universe within which all the rows and columns are tabulated. The "Total" row and column are provided by the tabbing software, and show the number of persons in the universe that belong to the group in the row or column.

Vert%: The proportion the cell represents of the column. Men make up 46.7 percent of the total adults attending movies in the past 6 months.

59851/128136 * 100=46.7

Horz%: The proportion the cell represents of the column. Here, those attending movies in the past 6 months make up 59.6 percent of total men.

59851 / 100457 *100 = 59.6%

Index: Shows potential. "Average" is 100. Indexes above 100 show likelihood. Here, total men are just below average in attending movies. Indexes are the ratio of the cell's horizontal percent to the column's horizontal percent OR the cell's vertical percent to the row's vertical percent. Either produces the same result. Indexes are rounded to the nearest whole number.

Horz%: 59.6 / 61.2 * 100 = 97
Vert %: 46.7 / 48.0 * 100 = 97

(000): The numbers in this row are called "projections", and are the estimate of the number of persons in thousands. There are about 51 million (50,817,000) adults who graduated college or went beyond. Remember to add zeros if required for a calculation. Occasionally you'll see projections in hundreds (00) or millions (0000).

The projections are the respondents weighted to the population. This tab doesn't show unweighted respondents, but tabs that do usually label the line "UNWTD".

Careful!: Most tabbing systems used in advertising have a means of flagging data that doesn't have enough sample to be reliably projected. There's not a lot of families with 8 or more children and the flag is a warning to be careful when using the data.

Using Indexes to Identify Target Audiences

Learning Objective

Learn to calculate and understand fundamental usage of index numbers. Index numbers allow planners to compare potential for usage of a product/brand across demographic groups or across media users.

Offensive and Defensive Marketing Strategies

A defensive marketing posture protects the marketing franchise that a brand has already built up. Often the best strategic decision is to spend media dollars wherever current sales are highest. In contrast, an offensive approach is one of conquest where you would spend in markets where your brand has the highest potential, not necessarily highest sales. Both offense and defense have their place in marketing strategy, and one is not necessarily better than the other. Indices help marketers see areas of strength and weakness.

Indexes

An index compares a product's usage within a demographic group relative to usage within the total population. It helps marketers to discover whether a particular demographic group is more or less likely to consume a product/brand compared to the total population. For example, if professional/managerial people are much more likely to buy imported cars, index numbers would be significantly higher for this group. If you were a brand manager for BMW, you might concentrate media pressure on a professional/managerial target because of their higher potential for purchasing a BMW.

Index numbers provide a way of putting two different numbers on the same "base" or "scale" so that they can be compared easily. In crosstabs, indexes are usually of composition that corresponds to vertical percents. For example, if we only had the vertical percents in EXHIBIT I, we might assume that the 12.8% shown for HEAVY USERS OF PACKAGED DINNERS Age 45-54 is better than the 10.1% shown for Age 18-24. That's because we don't have these percentages in context, compared to the groups from which they come. If we take those percents and compare them to the corresponding proportions in the population we would find that the 10.1 vertical percent for Age 18-24 represents a higher concentration of heavy users. And, that is exactly how indexes are calculated.

Calculating Indexes

To compute the index for Age 18-24, divide the proportion that Age 18-24 represents among HEAVY USERS by the proportion that Age 18-24 represents in the population, and multiply by 100. *Index numbers are always rounded to the nearest whole number.*

$$\text{index} = \frac{\text{\% demo in target group}}{\text{\% demo in base population}} \times 100$$

Age 18-24 Heavy User of Packaged Dinners Index: 10.1 ÷ 8.8 X 100 = 115 Index
Age 45-54 Heavy User of Packaged Dinners Index: 12.8 ÷ 15.3 X 100 = 84 Index

Index numbers are constructed so that *100* represents the average potential for usage—in other words, the proportion of usage for a group is exactly the same as its proportion of the population. An index greater than 100 is above average, and an index below 100 represents a group with lower than average potential. In this example, if you were to "grab a handful" of 18-24 year olds, you'd be 15 percent (115 Index) *more likely* than average to find a heavy user of packaged dinners than if you grabbed a handful of the population. Conversely, you'd be 16 percent *less likely* (see 84 Index) to find a heavy user among 45-54 year olds (100-84=16).

Exercise 6

While we've shown how one way indexes are calculated to provide some understanding, the focus of this exercise is *using* indexes. More discussion on different kinds of indexes comes in a later exercise.

Using Indexes

While comparing demographic groups, you should initially highlight groups with index numbers over 100. Think of high index numbers as "flags." They save time by identifying important demographic factors, but high index numbers are not to be trusted without careful scrutiny. Low indexes are also important because they tend to show activities or products that are less popular among the target group. Index numbers are helpful, but do not reveal the whole picture. Planners must take care to use them intelligently. *Never trust an index number until you have examined the projections (the "000" row) for all the demos in a group.*

Look at the set of age groupings in EXHIBIT I. Among all age groups who are HEAVY USERS OF PACKAGED DINNERS, 128 is the highest index number. If you selected your target audience based on this index alone, you would choose the 35-44 age group. However, the younger 25-34 age group also offers high sales potential, with an index of 124. Despite a slightly lower index, this group is still well above average, and represents nearly a third of all heavy users (Vert%=29.5). Reasoning: Age 25-34 is actually bigger (2.3 million bigger) than Age 35-44, and includes more heavy users (251,000 more). Despite the lower index number for Age 25-34 (4 points lower), it would be smart to combine both groups into one target audience.

Whenever the spread between index numbers in a grouping is not significant (10 points or less), it often makes sense to combine or collapse the groups into a single target audience.

EXHIBIT I

		Total Shoppers	Hvy Users Pkgd Dinners
Totals	(000)	112018	15518
	Vert%	100.0	100.0
	Horz%	100.0	13.9
	Index	100	100
Age 18-24	(000)	9907	1559
	Vert%	8.8	10.1
	Horz%	100.0	15.7
	Index	100	115
Age 25-34	(000)	26761	4585
	Vert%	23.9	29.5
	Horz%	100.0	17.1
	Index	100	124
Age 35-44	(000)	24489	4334
	Vert%	21.9	27.9
	Horz%	100.0	17.8
	Index	100	128
Age 45-54	(000)	17156	1990
	Vert%	15.3	12.8
	Horz%	100.0	11.6
	Index	100	84
Age 55+	(000)	33706	3050
	Vert%	30.1	19.7
	Horz%	100	9.0
	Index	100	65

Begin by highlighting all demo groups with index numbers greater than 100. Next, within a demo set, if adjoining demos are significantly above average, combine them into a single target if they are a good "fit."

Problems

If an index is above 100 and higher than other indexes in the same group (age, income, etc.) by 10 points or more, use the index as the initial criterion for target selection. However, if the spread between the index numbers is less than 10 points, consider the size of each group (the projection (000) or vertical percent) as the best way to pick the winner. Also keep in mind that index numbers somewhat below 100 should not be ignored if the projections are promising. It is common to include multiple target demos in a media strategy, but still give priority a group representing a significant proportion of the population when the spread between the indices is not significant. *Be sure to use the projections, not the UNWTD counts when doing the problems.*

If you haven't downloaded it yet, go to **mediaflightplan.com** and click on **MFP Ground School**. Then click on the link to download MRI data: *Exercises 5 & 6 – MRI Movie Cross Tab*

1. Assume your target is **Adults** who **Prefer to See Movie on Opening Weekend**. Based solely on index numbers, which AGE group has greater potential? (See AGE groups in MRI data pg. 2)

2. As noted, *it often makes sense to combine or collapse multiple target groups into a single target audience.* Continuing with **Adults** who **Prefer to See Movie on Opening Weekend**, which is the "next best" demo group that makes the most sense to combine with the demo you selected in question 1?

   a) Cite both index numbers.
   b) What is the new projected **Total (000)** users who would be in this combined target audience?

3. Stay with **Prefer to See Movie On Opening Weekend**, and evaluate occupation as a demo set – set begins with demos titled: NON EMPLOYED, PROFESSIONAL/MANAGERIAL, etc.

   a) Based on index numbers alone for all five occupations, *name the two occupation demo groups* offering the greatest potential and list their index numbers.
   b) A third demo group could be included, even though it has a lower index. Which one? Explain why.

Exercise 6

4. Go to the page with a set of **HHI index numbers**. In the column **Attended Movies Past 6 Months**, highlight all eight of the index numbers.

a) Plot the indexes and draw a line through them to make a line chart below. Analyze the trend you see.

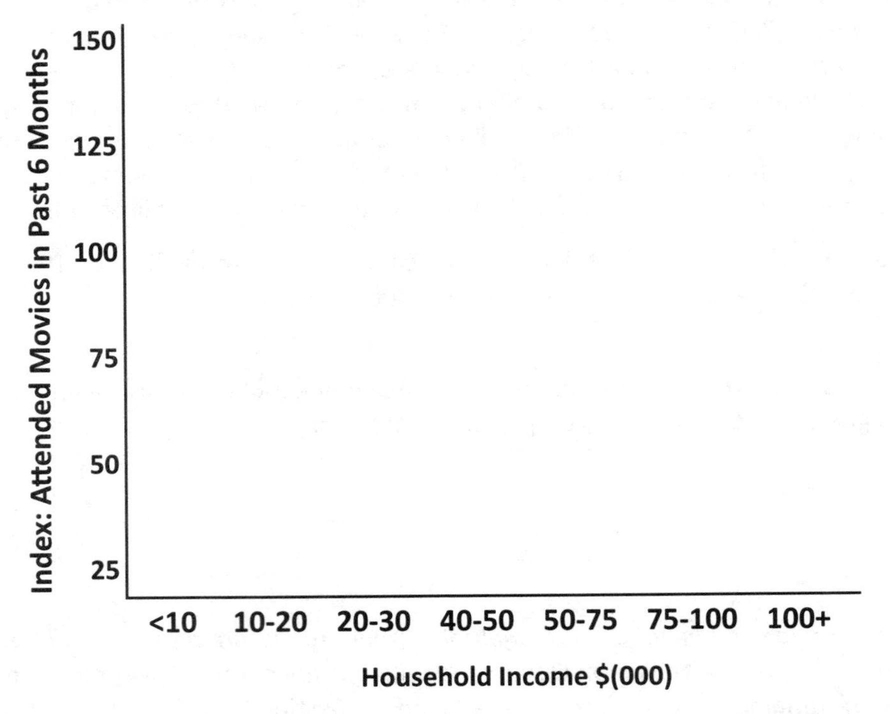

b) Speculate on *why* this pattern exists – give several reasons why this pattern emerges. Check MRI for relevance of education and income, and cite the data in your answer.

5. Your client, the owner a national Drive-In movie chain, has noticed resurgence in attendance and she wants to expand into new locations. Knowing she cannot compete with the multiplex cinemas in the metro cities, she is conducting marketing analysis in rural areas – known locations where drive-ins are still popular. MRI provides three levels of movie attendance: **Attend Movies 2x Month or More, Attend Movies Once a Month**, and **Attend Movies Less than 1x/Month**. You have this data for COUNTY SIZE C and COUNTY SIZE D – both more rural and farming areas. Though both C and D counties contain roughly the same population, your client needs to know if there is any significant difference in attendance and if she should focus on one or the other. Use the population projections (000) together with attendance groups (see box below) to calculate the monthly gross movie attendance for C and D counties:

Attendance Group	Weight
2 x A Month or More	3
Once a Month	1
Less Than Once A Month	0.5

The concept of "weighting" is covered in depth in Exercise 10. For now, consider "weighting" a tool used to assign added value to target groups, target markets and other marketing variables. Here, the marketer has decided that 2 x A Month movie goers are 3 times more valuable than once a month movie goers. Weighting allows the marketer to manipulate the value of both counties based on movie attendance.

Follow these seven steps to weight the attendance groups and calculate the index.

(1) Consult the MRI data for COUNTY SIZE C and COUNTY SIZE D projections based on *Attendance Groups* shown in the table below.

(2) Write these Projections (000) into the corresponding cells in the table below.

3) Multiply Est.Weight x Proj (000) to get Gross Movies for each county size.

4) Sum each of the Gross Movies columns to get Total Gross Movies (000) for each county size.

5) Consulting MRI data, write the Total Adults Proj (000) for each county size. (Careful - use Total Adults, NOT Total County Size movie attenders).

6) Compute the average number of movies per person ("Per Capita Movies") for both county sizes by dividing Total Gross Movies (000) by the Total Adults Proj (000).

7) Calculate the index number to discover relative movie attendance rates based on County Size. To calculate the index, divide the "Per Capita" movie attendance for County C by the Per Capita attendance for County D, and multiply by 100. Calculating the index is NOT enough. Your client wants you to articulate what this index number means. Review calculating index numbers on the first page of this exercise to properly explain your answer.

	County Size C			County Size D		
Attendance Groups	**Est. Weight**	**Proj (000)**	**Gross Movies**	**Est. Weight**	**Proj (000)**	**Gross Movies**
2x/Month or More	3	X	=	3	X	=
Once a Month	1	X	=	1	X	=
Less Than 1x/Month	0.5	X	=	0.5	X	=
Total Gross Movies (000)			Sum			Sum
Total Adults Proj (000)						
Per Capita Movies (Total Gross Movies ÷ Total Adults Proj)						
* Index C to D Counties (C Cnty Per Capita ÷ D Cnty Per Capita X 100)						

Write **index** number (final answer) here:

***A different kind of index**: This may be one of the simplest applications of indexing. Unlike the example on the first page of this exercise, here we are simply comparing two types of movie goers based on projected attendance. It's an index number based on a ratio of two market behaviors in two geographic locations, county size C and county size D.

Exercise 7

Category and Brand Development Indexes (CDI & BDI)

Learning Objective

Category and brand development indexes can help you decide if a market deserves extra advertising/marketing dollars or any dollars at all. You'll also learn how to calculate both indexes and get a basic understanding of what they mean and how they can be used.

Background on CDI/BDI Usage

Often planners have to make decisions about placement of additional advertising weight in a market. While the index numbers in the syndicated data might inform you about the relative importance of different regions with respect to the potential for usage of the product/brand, these regional breakdowns are very broad in scope. Clients often have sales data for individual markets. When available, planners prefer using objective, market specific data. This is where the Category Development Index (CDI) and the Brand Development Index (BDI) are used.

The CDI and BDI compare the sales of a product category or a brand with the potential for sales of that category or brand based on the population in each market. If a market accounted for two percent of the U.S. population, the assumption is that it should account for two percent of the product or brand's sales. This would reflect an average level of consumption and would be seen in an index of 100, the average. In reality, markets account for varying levels of sales that often are not in direct proportion to the population that market represents. The CDI and BDI identify specific markets that account for heavy usage of a product/brand, and if the advertiser intends to target the campaign toward the heavy user, these index numbers help identify those markets for the advertiser. BDI and CDI can also be used to identify areas of opportunity or weakness which a marketer may want or need to address.

Calculating Development Indexes

BDI and CDI can be calculated for any geographic area, although you will probably see media markets most frequently. Sometimes clients cannot provide the data on a media market basis, and you will have to use your best judgment in applying county or state level data to the specific situation. While BDI and CDI are generally calculated using sales or revenue, other items may occasionally be used as surrogates, such as store count or vehicle registrations. The CDI is calculated like this:

$$\text{Category Development Index (CDI)} = \frac{\text{\% of category sales in area}}{\text{\% of population in area}} \times 100$$

Calculation of Brand Development Index is identical, except that brand sales are substituted for category sales:

$$\text{Brand Development Index (BDI)} = \frac{\text{\% of brand sales in area}}{\text{\% of population in area}} \times 100$$

By convention, both CDI and BDI are rounded to whole numbers.

Jacuzzi spa Example: 5.25% of all sales of whirlpool spas take place in the Los Angeles metro market, and your company, Jacuzzi, sells 6.0% of its product in the LA market. If the Los Angeles metro has 4.2% of U.S. population, calculate the category and brand development indexes and explain what they mean.

Exercise 7

Calculating CDI and BDI for Jacuzzi:

$$\text{CDI} = \frac{\text{\% of category sales in area}}{\text{\% of population in area}} \times 100 = \frac{5.25}{4.2} \times 100 = 125$$

$$\text{BDI} = \frac{\text{\% of brand sales in area}}{\text{\% of population in area}} \times 100 = \frac{6.0}{4.2} \times 100 = 143 \text{ (142.8 rounded)}$$

The Los Angeles metro is a great market for whirlpool spas—both the category (CDI) and brand (BDI) development indexes are greater than 100, indicating above average sales for the category and especially for the Jacuzzi brand.

Using CDI and BDI to evaluate markets

CDI and BDI should not be the only marketing data used in making a media decision. However, if we assume all other marketing criteria are equal, then CDI and BDI would likely take on added importance. The relative weight that is given to the CDI or BDI varies, depending on the situation. Sometimes a marketer may choose to give added weight to CDI over BDI; at other times the reverse might hold true. One way of assessing markets is to compare the BDI and CDI based on one of the following four scenarios:

Scenario 1. High CDI and High BDI

Scenario 2. High CDI and Low BDI

Scenario 3. Low CDI and High BDI

Scenario 4. Low CDI and Low BDI

Scenario 1 represents a market where both the category and the brand are doing very well and, therefore, is a promising market. Often these markets are singled out for added media emphasis.

Scenario 2 is a market where the brand is doing poorly compared to the category. This market might be seen as one where there is room for the brand to grow. However, some research must be done to find out the reasons for the poor showing of the brand and subsequently, marketing or advertising must address the problem.

Scenario 3 is a market where even though the brand is doing well, the product category is showing lower potential. This is a situation where reasons for the poor showing of the category must be investigated. If the category has been showing continuous decline, then it might not be worth the added investment to advertise the brand even though it might be doing well. However, if a category will remain constant or can be rejuvenated, then advertising for the brand may well be worth the investment. The advertising message might need to encourage product category usage rather than brand usage exclusively.

Scenario 4 on first glance is a no-win situation. When both the product category and brand are languishing, additional advertising investment must be based on compelling reasons.

CDI and BDI are only one set of criteria that are used in making decisions about which markets deserve additional advertising weight. The strength of index numbers is that they are based on sales data and are, therefore, objective data. It makes sense for a marketer to concentrate media pressure in markets where brands are already doing well or are likely to do well because the product category shows promise.

Problems

1. If San Francisco accounts for 1.24 percent of total U.S. population, and has 1.43 percent of total U.S. laundry detergent sales, what is the CDI for this market? Also, what does this index mean? **The convention for CDIs and BDIs is to express them as whole numbers**. Use the formulas shown at the beginning of this exercise, and show your math below.

2. You are marketing Red Baron frozen pizza, and you are looking for some place to spend $50,000 in surplus advertising budget. You have narrowed the choice down to two markets: Seattle and San Francisco. Calculate the BDI/CDI for both markets. If the surplus can only be spent in one market, based on BDI/CDI ONLY, which market should you choose?

Market	%US	%Red Baron	%Frozen Pizza
Seattle	0.9	1.6	1.9
San Francisco	1.7	2.8	3.0

Exercise 7

3. You are the Marketing Director for *Great Lakes'* brand *Cherry Treats*, a regional company headquartered in Traverse City, MI. You distribute cherry-based snack products made from Michigan cherries exclusively, and you sell to the markets that surround Lake Michigan. Competition comes from all other brands in the category, referred to by Great Lakes as *Fruited Snacks*.

TIPS: To simplify this problem, assume that these seven markets comprise the **total universe** for your brand. Likewise, the 6,308.5 (000) Households in the table below represent 100% of the population. The $3 million in sales for Great Lakes and the $27 million for Fruited Snacks also represent totals for the "universe".

Using data provided in the table below, calculate the BDI and CDI for each market. Begin by converting the data to percentages; then calculate the BDIs and CDIs using the formulas illustrated in the examples above.

Market	HHs (000)	%HHs	Great Lakes Sales $(000)	% Great Lakes Sales	Fruited Snack Sales $(000)	% Fruited Snack Sales	BDI	CDI
Chicago	3,449.3		1,350		14,040			
Grand Rapids	727.1		390		2,160			
Green Bay	424.2		180		1,890			
Lansing	256.2		180		1,350			
Milwaukee	872.7		450		3,510			
South Bend	332.3		150		1,890			
Traverse City	246.7		300		2,160			
TOTALS	6,308.5		3,000		27,000			

Tip for answering all of the following questions: Index numbers have value but they may fall short of a complete answer; consider other data from this table to add substance.

4. Name the markets with both high BDI and high CDI, and advise your client on the best advertising/marketing action in light of your brand, the category, and potential competitive threats.

5. Name the markets with high BDI and low CDI, and advise your client on the best advertising/marketing action in light of your brand, the category, and potential competitive threats.

6. Name the markets with low BDI and high CDI, and advise your client on the best advertising/marketing action in light of your brand, the category, and potential competitive threats.

7. Name the markets with both low BDI and low CDI, and advise your client on the best advertising/marketing action in light of your brand, the category, and potential competitive threats.

Using Quintiles to Evaluate Media Potential

Learning Objective

Learn to define "tiles" (quintiles, quartiles, terciles, etc.) and how they are constructed. This exercise will also show one of the ways tiles are used – to evaluate media consumption.

Background

Quintiles are a specific case of "tiling"--a technique that breaks a population into roughly equal groups to highlight differences in product or media consumption. There is nothing magic about quintiles, terciles or quartiles (other tilings are also used). They are simply a convenient way to group people. Organizing people into "quintiles" is simply dividing an ordered population into five roughly equal groups. Likewise, quartiles would be groups containing one-fourth of a population, etc.

To construct tiles, the respondent group or population is ranked from high to low on a particular characteristic, for example, "bars of soap used in the last 30 days." Then starting from the heaviest user, persons are counted off until there are sufficient to complete the first tile. In a universe of 100 persons, twenty would be placed into each quintile. If using terciles, there would be 33 in each group. The completed tile groups can be used to analyze demographic characteristics or media usage.

Application

Media quintiles can be used to determine what media affinities exist for various consumer products and categories. Note that once a person's quintile for a medium is determined, it does not change based on product usage. This makes it possible to find concentrations of heavy or light users of a medium regardless of the product beign analyzed.

In Exhibit I, the heaviest viewers of TV – in Quintile 1 – make up 20% of the population (by definition, since adults were the basis for the quintile), but 35 percent of all Gum Users are in the heaviest TV usage group. **The Heavy TV – Quintile 1 – index for Gum Users is 175 (35 ÷ 20 X 100 = 175 Index)** indicating TV is a good way to reach Gum Users because a disproportionate number of Gum Users (75% above average 100 index) are Heavy TV Users.

Exhibit I
Gum Users by TV Viewing Quintiles

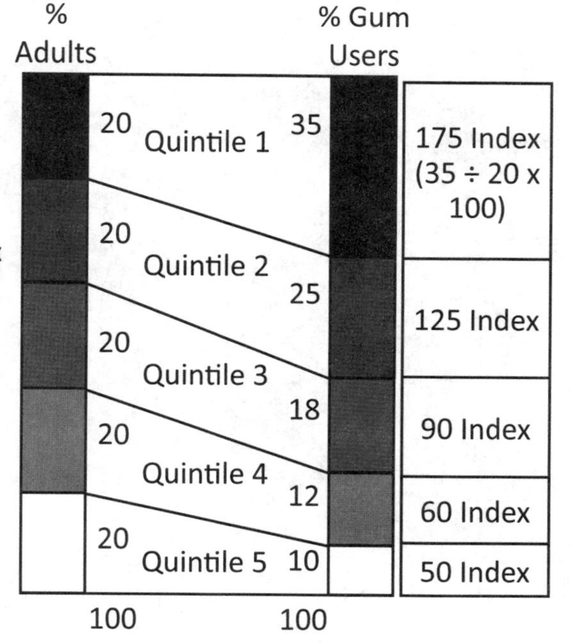

Twisted? Higher Index Numbers in Quintiles IV and V = Lighter Usage

In many media surveys, Quintile I represents the heaviest usage group, Quintile II next heaviest, and so forth until Quintile V, lightest usage group. **Heads up**: If a high index number shows up in Quintile IV or V for television (e.g. the index is above 100 for the low usage quintiles), it means the group is *above average for low usage* (twisted, but true)—in other words, the medium is not used as heavily. Even so, you may need to use the medium—while overall television usage may be lower, there will likely be some programs that do a good job reaching the target.

Exercise 8

When using real data, it's important to note that human beings rarely have the courtesy to form perfect, equal size groups of media usage. Most all frequency distributions have "lumps"-- cells that are unusually large in size. In theory, each quintile should contain exactly 20% of the total sample. But when using survey data, persons at a particular frequency level are often kept together, because logically they belong together (e.g., if most of the people in the "5"level would fall into the 3-5 group in a perfect split, it usually makes more sense to keep all "5" level persons together in the 3-5 group rather than splitting them up and putting part of them with a 6-10 group). Because of this, you will occasionally see slight variations in tiles depending on the data source—a quintile might not contain exactly 20% of the population, but it will be very close.

With 5 or more tiles, it is a good idea to look at both quintiles I and II, rather than to focus only on quintile I.

Quintiles show relative usage, an important fact to remember. High indexes in the low usage quintiles mean that the target is less likely to use that medium, not that they are non-users of the medium. Even if a target is a relatively light user of magazines or television as a category, there will be specific magazines or TV programs that reach them well. Generally, media usage quintiles help planners in determining media mix, rather than the sole arbiter of whether to use a medium. An upscale professional/managerial type target for example, might be a very light user of television in general, but could be reached well using specific sports or financial programs.

EXHIBIT II

Frequent Flyer Program Members
Pop(000): 36378

		Mags	Nwsp	Radio	TV	Intrnt	Outdr
Quintile I(Heavy)							
	(000)	8904	10790	6260	4151	12826	9193
	Vert%	24.48	29.66	17.21	11.41	35.26	25.27
	Horz%	21.01	25.46	14.78	9.80	30.31	21.69
	Index	122	148	86	57	176	126
Quintile II							
	(000)	8739	7854	7488	6053	10352	8839
	Vert%	24.02	21.59	20.58	16.64	28.46	24.30
	Horz%	20.63	18.54	17.67	14.28	24.43	20.87
	Index	120	108	103	83	142	122
Quintile III							
	(000)	7688	6932	8609	8424	7041	7628
	Vert%	21.13	19.06	23.67	23.16	19.36	20.97
	Horz%	18.14	16.35	20.32	19.88	16.61	18.00
	Index	106	95	118	116	97	105
Quintile IV							
	(000)	6718	6112	8017	8651	3339	6452
	Vert%	18.47	16.80	22.04	23.78	9.18	17.74
	Horz%	15.86	14.44	18.92	20.42	7.88	15.23
	Index	92	84	110	119	46	89
Quintile V (Light)							
	(000)	4329	4688	6004	9098	2819	4265
	Vert%	11.90	12.89	16.50	25.01	7.75	11.72
	Horz%	10.22	11.06	14.17	21.48	6.65	10.07
	Index	60	64	83	125	39	59

Problems (See Exhibit II for all problems.)

1. How many Frequent Flyer Program Members are reported in *Newspaper Quintile V*?

2. Out of all Freq Flyers reported in the *Newspaper* column, what proportion (percentage) is made up of *Newspaper Quintile V* readers? Based on your experience with index numbers in previous exercises, you can calculate this percentage yourself. It's the ratio between the number of Freq Flyers reported at the intersection of Quintile V and Newspapers, and the sum of all the quintiles for the newspaper column. Show the math to prove you have chosen the the correct percentage from the crosstab.

3. You're media director working on the Motorola mobile phone business, and you need to evaluate magazines for your target audience, Frequent Flyer Program Members. After evaluating Exhibit II, what conclusion would you draw about magazine readership? Report index numbers to support your answer, and report the percentage of Freq Flyers in the *heaviest* magazine user quintile.

4. How is the index for Freq Flyers in the *heaviest* Magazine user Quintile calculated? Show your math. Tip: What percentage of adults are in the heaviest magazine user quintile? Review Exhibit I – see Gum Users graphic – and the *Application* section of this exercise.

Exercise 8

5. Focusing exclusively on Quintile I, highlight the index numbers across all five media for your Freq Flyer target. Based on index numbers, rank all five media from high to low, and list the Quintile I index number for each medium.

6. Relatively speaking, which medium is used the *least* by Freq Flyers based on the indexes in the *bottom two quintiles*? (Report the numbers.) Tip: Review the text under the heading, "Twisted?"

7. Based on your answer to question 6, can Frequent Flyer Program Members still be reached by using this medium? There are two significant sections in the text that are relevant to light user Quintiles – cite both and provide complete answers.

Competitive Spending Analysis and SOV

Learning Objective

One of the first steps in developing a good media plan is to analyze the way your clients and their competitors allocate dollars to various media. Two major sources of competitive expenditures are TNS *Competitive Media Reporting* (CMR) and Nielsen's *Monitor Plus*. Most agencies have one of these sources for competitive reporting.

Once the competitive set for a brand has been determined, dollar expenditures in the various media classes can be used to evaluate both your own and your competitors' media mix, share of voice (SOV), and changes in annual expenditure. This helps provide a better understanding of your client's media environment.

Calculating Media Mix for Your Brand

The way media dollars are allocated is called the media mix. It is determined by calculating the proportion of ad dollars spent on your brand in each media category. As marketing director, assume you allocated your brand's annual advertising dollars in these four media:

Expenditures in $(000)				
Total	**Magazines**	**Network TV**	**Spot TV**	**Cable**
13,000	3,000	7,000	2,000	1,000

Media mix is calculated by dividing expenditure in a given media category by total expenditure. For example, here's how you would calculate the magazine part of the mix:

$$\text{Media Mix} = \frac{\text{brand medium expenditure}}{\text{brand total expenditure}} \times 100 = \frac{3000}{13000} \times 100 = 23\%\ (23.08\ \text{rounded})$$

Using this formula, the complete media mix showing the proportion of advertising dollars spent in each media class is calculated as shown below:

Total	Magazines	Network TV	Spot TV	Cable
100%	23%	54%	15%	8%

Calculating Share of Voice

Share of voice (SOV) is a common tool for competitive analysis. It shows a brand's strengths and weaknesses using individual media as well as overall position in the media marketplace. SOV is defined as a brand's percentage of total advertising dollars spent within a category. Share of voice can be applied to total expenditures or to a particular medium. The formula for share of voice is similar to the media mix formula, but the denominator of the equation is the spending total for the entire media category rather than total spending for the brand:

$$\text{Share of Voice} = \frac{\text{brand medium expenditure}}{\text{category medium expenditure}} \times 100$$

Exercise 9

Example: Your client, *MetroWerks* markets a specialized piece of software for developing video games. You have two competitors, *Borland*, and *Intel*. You have been provided with the following advertising expenditures, and have been asked to calculate each brand's share of voice for each media category. The equation in the box at right shows how the expenditures in Table I were used to calculate the Spot TV SOVs in Table II.

Table I

ADVERTISING EXPENDITURES $(000)					
Brand	**Total**	**Magazines**	**Net TV**	**Spot TV**	**Cable**
Borland	13,000	3,000	7,000	2,000	1,000
MetroWerks	17,000	5,000	9,000	**1,000**	2,000
Intel	18,000	1,000	14,000	3,000	0
Total Category	48,000	9,000	30,000	**6,000**	3,000

Table II

SHARE OF VOICE					
Brand	**Total**	**Magazines**	**Net TV**	**Spot TV**	**Cable**
Borland	27	33	23	33	33
MetroWerks	35	56	30	**17**	67
Intel	38	11	47	50	0
Total Category	100	100	100	100	100

MetroWerks Spot TV SOV:

$$\frac{1000}{6000} \times 100 = 17 \text{ (16.67 rounded)}$$

MetroWerks is responsible for about 17 percent of the activity in spot television, and about a third of overall category spending with a 35% Share of Voice. One cannot overestimate the value of data like this – SOV gives a brutally honest picture of your brand's advertising environment.

Exhibit I: Competitive Spending Problems

Exhibit I applies to the questions below. If you prefer working in Excel, this table is available as a spreadsheet on **mediaflightplan.com**. Click on **MFP Ground School**, and then look for Exercise 9.

EXHIBIT I

COPIER CATEGORY EXPENDITURES $(000)							
	Magazines	**Natl Nwsp**	**Outdoor**	**Net TV**	**Spot TV**	**Cable TV**	**Net Radio**
Canon Inc	7095.0	1011.2	212.1	4914.2	51.2	763.9	0.0
Compaq	374.1	545.9	0.0	0.0	0.0	0.0	0.0
Harris Corp	1116.2	124.0	0.0	0.0	11.6	357.0	0.0
Konica Corp	2558.8	129.8	11.1	0.0	30.3	878.2	0.0
Matsushita	172.1	0.0	0.0	0.0	4.6	0.0	0.0
Minolta	3902.2	0.0	3.3	0.0	43.2	0.0	0.0
Mita Co	1829.2	716.3	506.6	3222.7	134.0	405.1	778.8
Pitney Bowes	0.0	0.0	0.0	1128.9	0.8	411.1	595.1
Ricoh Co	1164.2	1471.9	0.0	1265.7	226.4	1345.9	0.0
Sharp Corp	2862.5	311.0	37.0	3525.7	1189.8	859.0	0.0
Toshiba Corp	0.0	0.0	0.0	0.0	24.6	0.0	0.0
Xerox Corp	37.2	635.6	2.4	547.2	0.7	0.0	0.0

Problems

1. Five copiers, Canon, Mita, Ricoh, Sharp, and Xerox, are targeted to the same market. Using Exhibit I, fill in media expenditure data and complete this "Big Five" table for the five brands listed.

"Big Five" Table: Media Expenditures

	Magazines	Natl Nwsp	Outdoor	Net TV	Spot TV	Cable TV	Net Radio	Total
Canon								
Mita								
Ricoh								
Sharp								
Xerox								
TOTAL								

2. Which of the five copier brands is the biggest media spender - i.e., which had the highest total advertising expenditures across all media? Name the brand and give the total amount below.

3. Which brand spent the most ad dollars in cable TV? Name the brand and the total amount.

4. Which brand spent the most ad dollars in Network TV? Name the brand and the total amount.

5. Using the figures you copied into the "Big Five" Table, calculate **Media Mix** (as percentages) for each copier brand. Enter proportions into the table below, rounded to one decimal place.

Media Mix								
	Magazines	Natl Nwsp	Outdoor	Net TV	Spot TV	Cable TV	Net Radio	Total
Canon								100.0
Mita								100.0
Ricoh								100.0
Sharp								100.0
Xerox								100.0

Exercise 9

6. Using the figures in the "Big Five" Table, calculate *Share of Voice* for each copier brand. Enter SOV data into the table below. Round percentages to the nearest tenth.

Share of Voice (SOV)								
	Magazines	**Natl Nwsp**	**Outdoor**	**Net TV**	**Spot TV**	**Cable TV**	**Net Radio**	**Total**
Canon								
Mita								
Ricoh								
Sharp								
Xerox								
Total	100.0	100.0	100.0	100.0	100.0	100.0	100.0	100.0

7. The *Media Mix* table reveals percent of total budget that each brand allocates to each medium. In contrast, the *Share of Voice* table reveals which brand's "voice" dominates each medium, and which brand has less voice in each medium. Be sure to consult the correct table for questions below.

a) Xerox invested over 95 percent of total budget into two media. Relative to Xerox's media mix, name the two media and their respective percent of total budget.

b) What's significant about Xerox's SOV in these 2 media? Prove this with hard data.

c) Based on this SOV scenario, what is Xerox's best move? As media director, other than raising the budget, what advice would you give Xerox to help fix their problem?

8. Which brand has the highest share of voice in network TV? Lowest share in network TV? Give the specific shares for each:

9. Which brand has the highest share of voice in magazines? The lowest in magazines? Give specific shares for each:

10. Assume you are marketing director representing a totally new brand in the copy machine category, with a $6 million budget.

a) Do you see any opportunities here to use unexploited media? Why or why not use them?

b) Plan your own media strategy. Where would you spend the most, and why?

Factor "Spreadsheeting" With a Pocket Calculator

The easiest way to grasp the concept of ranking markets is to create your first factor "spreadsheet" using a hand-held calculator. After mastering this skill, you'll build on it using a spreadsheet, such as *Excel* with market weighting.

Learning Objective

This exercise demonstrates how spreadsheets can help evaluate and rank a group of markets, ranging from a handful to a hundred. Besides evaluating markets, factor spreadsheets are equally useful for evaluating media choices, media vehicles, etc. This is the first of three spreadsheet exercises; the next two focus on market weighting strategy.

Sharpen Your Media Math

The goal in this exercise is to sharpen your math skills, and help you think through the process as you design a simple market-ranking spreadsheet. Research published in academic journals indicates that professors and media planning professionals are concerned about weak math skills among entry-level planners. In one published study, Professor Sandra Utt, University of Memphis, said, "I was disappointed that a few of my students didn't even know how to get a percentage – I had to tell them to divide the big number into the little number." Dale Coons, Campbell-Ewald, lamented: "When interviewing interns, I'm often disappointed how some seem to tense up when I ask a few basic math questions. Students need to know that most marketing careers require a modest level of math and spreadsheet skill."

You can learn to use a spreadsheet and build confidence in your own math skills by designing a spreadsheet for every case study you write. Keep these case studies in your portfolio – they make good "show and tell" when the interviwer asks, "Do you have any experience?", or "Tell me about a major project in school."

How Factor Spreadsheets Work

Rhodes Bake 'n Serve Products markets a regional brand distributed in super stores. As marketing manager, you need to rank four cities based on their food sales potential in super stores. Data are available for four factors:

1. Total Population
2. Total Food Sales
3. Discretionary HH Income
4. Total Number of Super Stores

A factor spreadsheet reduces many pieces of data into a single "score" which can easily be compared across the markets.

Step 1: The first step is to build the factor spreadsheet, and calculate the ESTIMATED VALUE% of each city.

Calculating Estimated Value (EV%): The EV% is a ratio between the Total Across and the Total for that column. Look at the EV% for Reno in Exhibit I (10%). It is calculated like this:

405,011 ÷ 3,996,077 = .101 X 100 = 10% (10.1 rounded)

Factor spreadsheets must be customized to fit each marketing problem. If you were marketing cosmetics instead of baked goods in super stores, which of the columns in Exhibit I would you replace? With what? An obvious replacement for cosmetics would be to replace "Total Food Sales" with "Total Cosmetic Sales". You might also want to replace "Total Pop" with "Female Teens".

Exhibit I

Raw Number Factor Spreadsheet: Rhodes Bake 'n Serve Products						
	Total Pop (000)	**Total Food $ Sales (000)**	**Discretionary $ HH Income (000)**	**Number of Stores**	**Total Across**	**Est. Value %**
Reno	190.0	170,000	45,000	11	215,201	8.8
Salt Lake	230.0	564,000	46,000	17	610,247	25.0
Portland	540.0	697,000	48,000	20	745,560	30.5
Seattle	596.0	821,000	49,000	29	870,625	35.7
Totals	1,556.0	2,252,000	188,000	77	2,441,633	100.0

Note: Est. Value % has been rounded for ease of discussion

This is a very small spreadsheet. Most spreadsheets contain multiple marketing factors across the top (columns) and run 50 to 100 markets (rows) deep.

Problem: Raw numbers in factor spreadsheets lead to unintentional weighting due to differences in scale. For example, in Reno, 11 stores will have very little impact because store count is overwhelmed by population. Population is reported in (000), but even so, the 190 figure is a factor of ten larger than the number of stores (hundreds vs tens). So the figures for population have an unintentional "weight" of 10 (10x10=100) compared to stores.

Solution: "Democratize" all raw numbers by converting them to percents. Note how data shown above for Pop, Food, HH Income and Number of Stores differ widely as numbers. Since the Number of Stores column has comparatively small numbers with only 2 digits, **Est. Value%** – the end result – would not change at all if you eliminated this entire column from the sheet.

Step 2: To create a more useful analysis, convert the raw number spreadsheet to percentages. For example, the Total Pop% for Reno is calculated using the numbers for Reno and the Total from Exhibit I:

190 ÷ 1,556 x 100 = 12% (rounded)

Exhibit II

Percentage Factor Spreadsheet: Rhodes Bake 'n Serve Products						
	% Total Pop (000)	**% Total Food $ Sales (000)**	**% Discretionary $ HH Income (000)**	**% Number of Stores**	**% Total Across**	**Est. Value %**
Reno	12	8	24	14	58	14
Salt Lake	15	25	24	22	86	22
Portland	35	31	26	26	117	29
Seattle	38	36	26	38	138	35
Total	100	100	100	100	400	100

Note: All percents have been rounded to the nearest whole number for ease of discussion

The Estimated Values here (compared with the Raw Number Factor Spreadsheet) have changed significantly for all four markets, and especially for Reno. Reno increased 4 percentage points compared with the raw number spreadsheet. By using percentages in the Raw Number Factor Spreadsheet, all of the "boxcar" numbers have been put on the same scale, giving all the factors equal weight. For example, Seattle's **Food Sales** originally has six digits (821,000), and the Number of Stores column is expressed with only two digits: 29. When adding across, Seattle's Pop, Food Sales, and HH Income literally drown out the number of Grocery/Super stores. Once converted to percentages, both Food Sales and Number of Stores have the same scale and are placed on equal footing. Converting to percentages gives all the factors the same relative weight by washing out differences in scale.

Estimating Ad Budgets: Although the markets still happen to be ranked in the same order, the new Est. Value% changed each market's relative worth. In addition to ranking markets, EV% can also be used to help allocate budgets. With a total budget of $200,000, a planner could allocate the funds for Rhodes using the Est. Value% from Exhibit II by converting the percentages to decimals this way:

Reno estimated ad budget:	$200,000 X .14 = $28,000
Salt Lake estimated ad budget:	$200,000 X .22 = $44,000
Portland estimated ad budget:	$200,000 X .29 = $58,000
Seattle estimated ad budget:	$200,000 X .35 = $70,000

Chili's Niche Marketing Mini-Case

Niche marketing is an excellent strategy for building brand share in the Eating & Drinking/Restaurant category. Research conducted by Chili's discovered the Hispanic market niche (respondents of Mexican heritage = 42%) has the potential to increase national sales by 5% within two years. Research also suggests that the strongest appeal for this ethnic target audience would be one of Chili's most successful menu items – "Baby Back Ribs." Multi-ethnic, non-traditional promotions, combined with radio advertising, have been prepared to test Hispanic responses to Chili's ribs. Chili's will test in seven southwestern and southeastern markets.

To prepare for the test, your job is to analyze the syndicated data in Exhibit III. Using a calculator, create a simple factor spreadsheet to rank seven designated test markets: San Antonio, Jacksonville, Tucson, Albuquerque, Corpus Christi, St. Petersburg, and Orlando.

Follow the math models explained above (Exhibits I and II) to create your own factor spreadsheets for Chili's test market. Using the blank tables provided below, do the following:

1. Create a Raw Number Factor Spreadsheet for all 7 METRO AREAS. Use the blank table on the next page.

2. Fill in the factor spreadsheet using data provided in Exhibit III (last page of exercise). Follow these important instructions as you consult the three tables:

Population Table: Use **Total (000)** from the **Population** table. Remember numbers represent population in thousands (000). It is not necessary to convert the numbers before using them in a factor spreadsheet (and we won't), however, *it is absolutely necessary that you are consistent in recording data for a factor*. Don't use 1244.7 to record San Antonio and 291,300 for Corpus Christi. Use the same format for both. For this exercise, record the figures in (000) as reported in Figure III (e.g. 1,244.7 and 291.3, etc.)

- **Retail Sales & Store Count**: There are eight columns of data in the **Retail Sales & Store Count** table. Look at all eight columns carefully. Choose *only one* of the eight columns in addition to the # of Chili's stores that best represents Chili's business.
- **Discretionary HH Income**: Use Discretionary HH Income. Again, record the numbers as reported in (000). For example, Discretionary HH Income San Antonio: 28,601
- Now, fill in the Total Across and calculate the Estimated Value % as shown above. Round EV%s to one decimal place

Raw Number Factor Spreadsheet

Markets	Pop (000)	Choice from Retail Sales:	Store Count	Discretionary HH Income (000)	Total Across	Estimated Value %
San Antonio						
Jacksonville						
Tucson						
Albuquerque						
Corpus Christi						
St Petersburg						
Orlando						
Total						

3. Create a **Percent Conversion Spreadsheet**. Convert all raw data from step 1 to the spreadsheet below. Round to one decimal place – for example: 24.9% or 3.6%.

Percent Conversion Factor Spreadsheet

Markets	% Pop (000)	%Choice from Retail Sales:	% Store Count	% Discretionary HH Income (000)	% Total Across	Estimated Value %
San Antonio						
Jacksonville						
Tucson						
Albuquerque						
Corpus Christi						
St Petersburg						
Orlando						
Total						

4. Based on the **Estimated Value %** column, rank order all seven markets from strongest to weakest. This list of markets will be based on your answers to question 3 above.

5. a) After the percent conversion, only San Antonio stays in the same position-second. All the remaining markets changed their ranking in the percent conversion. List them showing the old EV% ranking (based on raw numbers) and their new EV% ranking after percent conversions.

Market	**Old EV% Rank**	**New EV% Rank**

b) Why did this happen? (Tip: Review the text below Exhibit II.)

6. Total advertising budget for the seven metro markets is $1,500,000. Based on the Estimated Values (**EV%**) from the Percent Conversion Factor Spreadsheet, calculate the total advertising budget allocated to each of the seven markets, and rank them from 1 to 7. For example, if one market had 11.7% EV, then multiply .117 X $1,500,000 in order to find that market's budget ($175,500).

Exhibit III

Population

Metro Market	Total (000)	% U.S	Median Age Of Pop.	% of Pop. by Age Group 18-24 Years	25-34 Years	35-49 Years	50 & Over	HHs (000)
San Antonio	1,244.7	0.410	40.1	8.3	14.2	17.8	38.9	53.9
Jacksonville	798.1	0.270	38.3	8.1	14.0	18.2	36.1	70.5
Tucson	521.7	0.170	33.0	11.6	17.3	20.0	26.1	365.9
Albuquerque	488.6	0.160	32.1	11.4	17.1	21.0	24.0	49.3
Corpus Christi	291.3	0.097	31.2	12.3	17.5	20.7	22.7	128.6
St. Petersburg	274.5	0.091	51.1	6.7	11.7	15.1	51.1	115.7
Orlando	215.0	0.072	40.5	8.7	14.4	17.3	39.6	838.9

Retail Sales $(000) and Stores

Metro Market	Elec & Cons Prods	Grocery & Super store	Eating/ Drinking & Restrnt	General Mdse.	Furniture & Appliance	Auto Parts & Access	Phar macy	# Chili's Stores
San Antonio	1,170.0	257.0	152.3	899.0	117.7	250.7	40.0	17
Jacksonville	123.8	261.5	109.4	150.8	71.3	249.8	49.3	12
Tucson	7,210.4	1,385.9	1,046.9	838.7	321.6	1,996.0	190.1	12
Albuquerque	848.3	129.3	143.7	113.7	44.7	231.3	28.6	14
Corpus Christi	2,009.4	408.6	249.4	332.5	109.3	497.3	57.1	9
St. Petersburg	2,200.9	418.7	285.0	245.5	204.2	517.1	95.5	12
Orlando	13,442.9	2,903.6	1,742.0	1,760.5	874.1	3,132.8	461.2	10

Income

Metro Market	Total HHI (000)	Discretionary HH Income $ (000)	% of Households By Income Group (A) $10,000-$19,999 (B) $20,000-$34,999 (C) $35,000-$49,999 (D) $50,000 & Over: A	B	C	D	Household Buying Power Index
San Antonio	28,702.3	28,601	25.8	26.4	12.0	15.4	0.0602
Jacksonville	27,238.6	28,300	31.4	25.9	9.4	7.9	0.0652
Tucson	28,542.2	26,188	23.4	27.0	16.7	17.1	0.4085
Albuquerque	26,686.1	22,702	29.8	25.8	11.6	7.6	0.0456
Corpus Christi	23,889.2	23,420	22.8	26.3	16.6	15.0	0.1301
St. Petersburg	31,164.5	33,818	23.3	23.6	14.4	15.9	0.0847
Orlando	25,703.9	24,469	26.5	26.8	14.6	14.4	0.8236

Weighting Factor Spreadsheets

This tutorial requires a spreadsheet (like Microsoft Excel 2007). Those who are familiar with Excel will find they know other methods to copy and format. This tutorial is written so that someone less familiar with Excel can complete the exercise successfully.

Now that you've learned the basics of factor spreadsheets using a calculator, this exercise introduces two new concepts: (1) How to design a marketing factor spreadsheet using a program like Excel. (2) How to apply "weight," and how it can be used as a tool to manipulate the outcome of a marketing factor spreadsheet.

Since you are familiar with the data from the previous exercise, you'll use the same data here. The first part of the exercise will be familiar; you'll create a raw number spreadsheet, then convert it to percentages. *The EV%s you obtain using a program like Excel may vary slightly from the results you obtained on your calculator.*

Learning Objective

Learn the concept of "weighting" and ranking markets. Based on evaluation of marketing/media columns in a factor spreadsheet, marketers may want to give added value to exceptional columns of data. The objective in this exercise is to learn how to give extra weight to a column of data that is considered more important than the rest of the columns.

Understanding Weighting

Its a good bet that some marketing factors in your spreadsheet are more important than others. If one or two of the variables are judged to be exceptional in value, they can be "loaded" with extra weight. Weighting of variables will affect the Estimated Value percents once the spreadsheet is calculated, giving those variables the emphasis their importance demands. Emphasis can be controlled in two ways—by weighting only those variables considered to have exceptional value, and by varying the amount of weight applied to a variable. It might be tempting to weight every factor, but avoid this line of thinking. Weighting everything is like weighting nothing. If a spreadsheet has five or six variables, typically one or two variables should be singled out for extra weight.

Frequently Asked Questions about Weighting

Some questions frequently come up as factor spreadsheets are put together. The guidance that follows will help you as you think about the strategies and objectives you are trying to accomplish as you build your factor spreadsheet.

Why is it necessary to weight in the first place? It is not always necessary, but weighting is often helpful in ranking markets. A seasoned marketer once remarked, "I have never met a marketing spreadsheet that could not be improved by weighting." What he means is that we can usually assume that all columns in a spreadsheet do not have equal value in helping us rank markets. Once we understand that a spreadsheet is a *strategic tool,* we can use it to manipulate the output (the EV%s or Estimated Value % Column) to help us make some kind of marketing decision.

Weighting can be useful by putting extra emphasis on the most important column (or columns) of data in a spreadsheet. Of course, the "most important column" is a judgment call.

How do I know which column to weight? In most all spreadsheets, at least one of the columns is more valuable than the others. To discover that column, consider "trashing" all the columns in the spreadsheet except one. In other words, if you were forced to live with only one column of data to rank your markets, *which* *column can you NOT live without*? Decide which column is indispensable, and you'll know which column to weight.

Why use exponential weighting? There are many ways to weight data and calculate estimated value. Some of these have mathematical drawbacks and are best avoided. Using exponentiation (raising numbers to a power) and summing across factors avoids several issues.

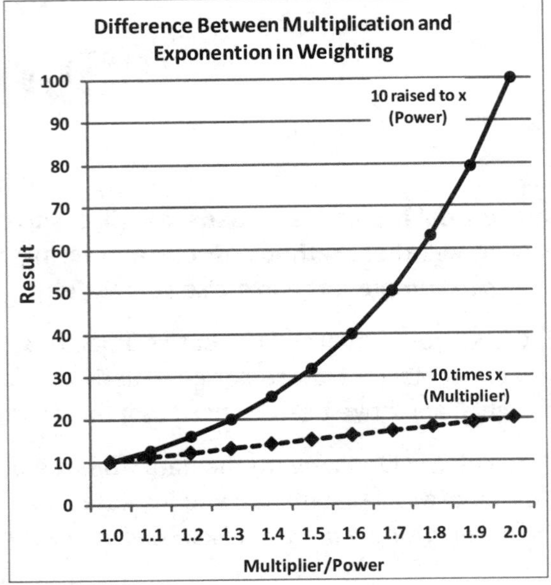

While this isn't a math exercise, a couple of quick points will illustrate some of the reasons we prefer exponents for weighting and summing for EVs.

Thinking about weighting for a moment, and you will realize if a single factor is simply doubled or tripled, the new value will still get lost when it is summed with several other factors—and testing has shown that there is little movement when using simple multiplication. The chart to the right shows how exponentiation overcomes this problem. In a sense, the two lines could represent two different factors, each with the same value, 10. You can see the difference in separation as one is weighted with multiplication (lower, dotted line) and one is weighted with exponentiaion (upper, solid line) with the same weights. The factor that is exponentially weighted by squaring (raising to a power of 2) is significantly higher than the one that was simply doubled. Exponentiation allows weighting that survives the summing of many factors to compute EV values.

The factor spreadsheets we'll build use summing to combine the factors for EV calculation. Some advocate multiplication, but this has a serious flaw. Can you think of what it might be? What would happen to a market that had five high value factors and a single factor that was zero if they were multiplied together? The result would be zero, implying the market had no value at all.

Building a Factor Spreadsheet using a Spreadsheet Program

These instructions were designed for Microsoft Excel 2007. Commands for Excel 2003 may be in a different location than indicated here. You can use another spreadsheet you prefer, but you will have to find the equivalent commands yourself. As you work this factor spreadsheet, be aware that errors can easily creep in through typos or misplacement of formulas. To help monitor your progress, you may want to double-check each input and mark each step as you complete it, and save your work frequently.

This tuturial makes use of several Excel features. The image below shows where the "Menu" and "Ribbon" areas of Excel are. Your screen may be somewhat different depending on how it was set up. Though some commands are available in other places, everything we will use is available in the ribbon when the Home menu tab is selected as shown. Commands are organized into "Groups" on the ribbon, like "Alignment".

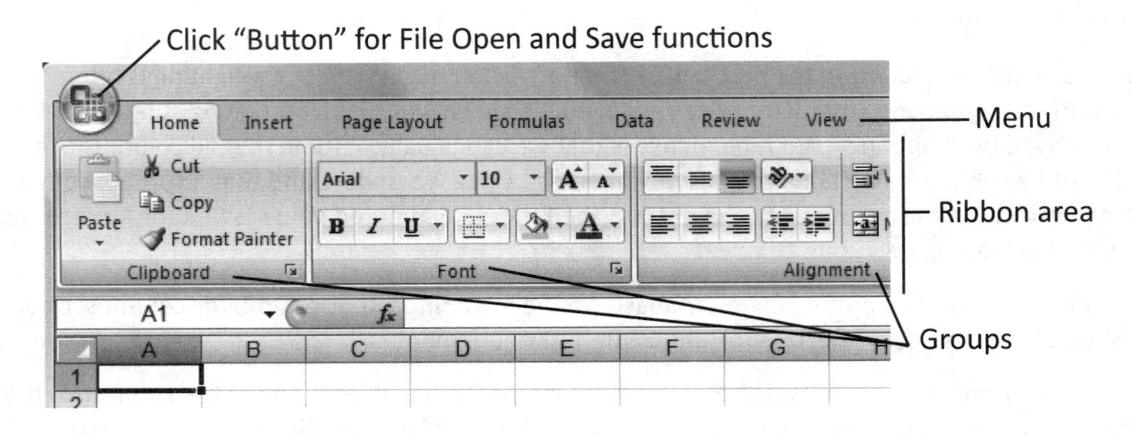

Before you start, make a weighting decision: Which column should be weighted in the Chili's spreadsheet? Look over the four columns of data you used in the previous exercise and decide which one you think is the most important.

Write your answer here:____

Part I: Begin with Raw Number Spreadsheet

• **Step 1**: Open a new spreadsheet. In cell A1, type "**Chili's Raw Number Data**" to title this area of the spreadsheet. Click A1 again, and on the Home menu tab, click the **B** (bold) button to bold the heading. Be sure you title each new area of your factor spreadsheet as this will help clarify what you are doing.

To help monitor your progress, USE THE EXACT COLUMNS AND ROWS OUTLINED IN THIS TUTORIAL. If you make a mistake, staying with the "system" will save time and grief by helping you pinpoint where the error occurred instead of starting all over.

• **Step 2**: In spreadsheet programs, rows are horizontal – columns are vertical. Individual cells are found at the intersection of the row and column indicated. For example, A3 is at the intersection of column A and row 3. Starting at column A on the far left, in row 3, type the following headings in the cells indicated. The complete heading won't show, but we'll fix that in a moment.

Cell	Column Heading
A3	Markets
B3	Population
C3	Eat&Drink Rest Sales
D3	# of Chili's Stores
E3	Discretionary HH Income
F3	Total Across
G3	EV%

To make the entire text of the headings show, first highlight the cells A3 to G3 by clicking in the middle of A3 and dragging across to G3. Now find the "Wrap Text" command in the Alignment group on the ribbon and click it. Your headings will now take several lines, but all the text should be showing. Also click the **B** (bold) command to bold the headings.

Now, widen the columns where necessary to make the text fit better. At the top of each column is a title letter (A,B,C, etc) with boundary lines on either side. Move the cursor over the boundary line until it turns into a vertical bar with a double headed arrow. Click the boundary to grab it, and move it until you are satisfied, then release the mouse button. You will probably want to widen the *Population* column until the heading fits on a single line, and the other headings until they fit comfortably on two lines.

The weighting variable chosen for this example is "# of Chili's Stores". Eating/Drinking & Restaurant Sales (this would be the category sales data for Chili's) could also be justified. To keep us all on the same page, follow the directions here and weight *# of Chili's Stores* even if you chose another factor. Chili's has research on store vs. brand sales in each market, and knows that number of stores is related to Chili's brand sales.

• **Step 3**: Using Exhibit III from the previous exercise, enter all seven markets under the *Markets* heading, beginning with cell **A4**.

- San Antonio should be in cell A4, Jacksonville in cell A5, etc. Cell A10 should be Orlando.
- Type *Total* in cell **A11**
- If necessary, widen column A by grabbing its boundary and moving it so that the market names fit comfortably in the column.

• **Step 4**: Using Exhibit III from the previous exercise, enter the data into the appropriate cells. For example, in cell **B5**, type *1,244.7* for San Antonio's population. Reminder: the heading of the table indicates that the units are (000), so that the 1244.7 represents 1,244,700. As you create your own factor spreadsheets, you can use whatever format you wish, as long as you are consistent within a factor. As long as you are consistent, the results of the factor spreadsheet will be the same. For purposes of this exercise, type in the numbers from Exhibit III as you see them. You may have to widen some of the columns, see the box below.

- Type in the data for all columns. Here's an easy guide; double-check entries for accuracy:

For this factor...	Use this column of data from Exhibit III
Population	Total Population
Eat/Drink & Rest Sales	Eating/Drinking & Restrnt
# of Chili's Stores	# of Chili's Stores
Disc HH Income	Discretionary HH Income

What to do when you get something like 1.2E+11 or ####
At times you may enter values or get calculated results that are too big to display in the cell. When this happens, Excel will first try to represent the number in scientific notation (something like 1.23E+11). If that won't fit, you'll get #####. In either case, you can get the numbers to display by making the column wider.

Part II: Using Excel's Summation Tool

The **Σ Auto Sum** button is found on the Home tab ribbon at the far right in the Editing group (It is also on the Formulas tab). The Σ button will automatically sum a row or column.

• **Step 5**: Click on cell **F4**. Now click on the **Σ button**, and then press [Enter]. Cell F4 should now read 30,015.0. (Widen the column if necessary.)

To show commas in all the numbers, highlight the entire block of data from **B4 to F11** (not all of those cells currently contain data). On the Home menu tab, click the **Format** button in the Cells group, and select *Format Cells* from the dropdown menu (very last item). Click the *Number* tab, check the *Use 1000 seperator (,) box*, and enter 1 in the *Decimal Places* box. Then click OK.

• **Step 6**: **Shortcut for summing remaining rows**: Click on cell **F4**. In the dark outline around F4 in the lower right corner is a tiny square box. We'll call it **CB** – short for "copy box". Position the mouse over the CB – once you have the mouse positioned over the bottom right hand corner of the cell, the cursor changes from a hollow cross into a solid "plus sign". Click on the CB, (don't release the mouse,) and drag down to cell **F10.** Release the mouse. Rows 5 through 10 should now be totaled. You may need to widen the column a bit.

• **Step 7**: **To sum columns**: Click on cell **B11**, click **Σ** and hit [Enter]. Cell B11 should now read 3,833.9.

Shortcut: Clicking the Auto Sum button automatically puts the formula =SUM(B4:B10) into A11. Since we need to do the exact same sum in the other cells in the Total row, we can copy A11 to the other columns, and Excel will adjust the formula to sum the correct data for us automatically. Highlight cell **B11**, click on CB and drag across to cell **F11**. Release the mouse button. Now, TOTAL figures appear for all columns.

Part III: Calculating Estimated Value % (EV %)

EV% is a ratio between the row's *Total Across* number and the sum of all the rows' Total Across number (in F11). EV%s represent the relative value of each market.

• **Step 8**: To get the EV%, divide cell F4 by cell F11 and multiply by 100. Put cursor in cell **G4** and type the following:

- **=F4/$F$11*100** then press [Enter]. You just divided cell F5 by cell F11, and multiplied by 100 to convert to a percentage. The $ signs are important. They make the demonimator of the formula "absolute" so that it always refers to F12 when it is copied. If you leave them out, you will get errors when you copy the formula down.

- Click on cell **G4**
- Click on **CB** (Tiny bottom "copy box")
- Drag down to cell **G11**
- Now format your percentages with one decimal place. Begin by highlighting all the cells in column G, from **G4 to G11**. Click *Format*, and in the dropdown box, select Format Cells. Click the Number tab, then select the category *Number*. Choose 1 decimal place in the box to the right. The sample box should show your result with one decimal place (e.g. 15.4)
- Now all of the EV% data should expressed as a percentage with one decimal place. Cell **G11** should read 100.0
- **Save your work!**

Part IV: Converting Raw Numbers (Columns B, C, D and E) into Percentages

• **Step 9**: In cell **A16**, type "Chili's Percentage Data". Bold it using the B button in the Font group.

• **Step 10**: Go to first table "Chili's Raw Data," highlight all column headings (A3-G3)

• **Step 11**: With the headings highlighted, click *Copy* from the Clipboard group on the ribbon (first group on left)

• **Step 12:** Click on cell **A18.** Now find the *Paste* command in the Clipboard group on the ribbon, just to the left of the Copy command, and click it. Excel will copy the headings from the previous table, including formatting.

- Now highlight the markets and Total label in cells **A4 to A11**. Click *Copy* again.
- Click on cell **A19**, then click the *Paste* command.
- DO NOT copy or paste any of the numbered data.

• **Step 13**: To convert to percentages, start by dividing San Antonio's pop (1,244.7) by the Total (3,833.9) and multiplying by 100 to get a percentage.

- In cell **B19**, type this division formula: **=B4/$B$11*100** then hit Enter (remember the $ signs!)
- Click cell **B19**, then click and hold on **CB**, then drag to **B26**
- Cells B20 through B27 should still be highlighted. If not, highlight them
- Click *Format*, and select *Format Cells* as before
- Make sure you are in the Number tab
- Click *Number*
- Choose 1 decimal place and click OK
- Total Down for column B should now be 100.0

• **Step 14**: Columns C, D, and E must also be expressed as percents. Follow the procedure in Step 13, but remember to change the formula to match the column. For example, the formula in cell **C19** will be **=C5/$C$12*100**. Don't forget the $ signs!

Part V: Summing the Total Across Column

• **Step 15**:

- Highlight cell **F19**
- Hit the **Σ button** and hit [Enter]
- Select cell **F19**, click on CB, and drag down to total all rows

Part VI: Calculating the ESTIMATED VALUE % (EV %)

- **Step 16**: Put cursor in cell **G19** and type: **=F19/$F$26*100 then hit Enter**
- **Step 17**: Click on cell **F19**; click on CB and drag down to **F26** to get EV% for all rows

Part VII: Exponential weighting

You will be weighting the same data two times, but each time you will use a different weight.

- **Step 18**: In cell **A30**, enter **"Chili's Weighted Data"**. Click A30 again and bold it with the bold button.
- **Step 19**: In cell **A31**, enter **"Column Weight:"** and bold it. In B31, C31, D31 and E31, enter the number 1. Highlight these four cells and format to one decimal place (Click on **Format** in Cells group, select *Format Cells* on drop down, then click on *Number* for Category and enter 1 for *Decimal Places*, then click OK.)
- **Step 20**: Now copy and paste all column and row headings . . .
  - Copy **A18** through **G18** (**Markets**, **Population**, etc.) and paste at cell **A32**.
  - Copy the markets – **San Antonio** through **Total** from cells **A19** to **A26** into **A33**.
- **Step 21**: This step will set up weighting. Go to cell **B33**.
  - Enter the formula **=B19^B$31** *There is only one $ in this formula!*

The ^ symbol (shift-6 on most keyboards) is the exponentiation operator in Excel.

  - Select **B33**, click the **CB**, and drag the formula *across* to **E33**. Let go of the mouse.
  - Grab the **CB** again (four cells should be outlined) and drag it *down* to **E39**.
  - All of the rows except *Total* should have a formula in the four data columns.
- **Step 22**: Insert the formulas for Total Across. Select **F33**, then click the **Σ button** and [Enter]. This time, click on **F33** and use the **CB** to drag the formula down to Orlando (**F39**), and stop. Do not copy down to the *Total* line. Now, highlight cell **F40** and click the **Σ button** again. This will give you a TOTAL in the Total Across column of 400. There won't be totals in any other column.
- **Step 23**: Calculate EV% again. Click on cell **G33**. Type the formula **=F33/$F$40*100** and [Enter].
  - Click on **G33** and format to one decimal place.
  - Now, click on **G33**, grab **CB**, and drag down to **G40**. The Total for the EV% column should be 100.0
- **Step 24**: Now you can play "what-if". Change the weight above # Chili's Stores (in cell **D31**) from 1.0 to 1.5 and watch what happens to the EV%'s. Did you notice the EV% for San Antonio changed from 17.8 to 20.4?

Part VIII: Saving Scenarios and Sorting

The *Chili's Weighted Data* table we just created is handy because we can try different weighting scenarios without creating a new table each time. It is only necessary to change the weights at the top of the columns.

However, it has a large drawback—Excel cannot properly sort it. If you try, the market labels will be sorted in the correct order according to EV%, but the EV%s do not move along with the labels. This is because there is no way to tell Excel to modify the formula structure during a sort.

We need a way to save different scenarios in a manner that allows us to sort them. We will need the original *Chili's Raw Number Data* (which we already have), and the *Chili's Weighted Data* table with *# of Chili's Stores* weighted at 1.5 and 2.0 for the next exercise.

The next steps will show you how to save and sort scenarios.

• Step 25: Saving Different Scenarios of the Chili's Weighted Data
There are many ways to do things in Excel. You may know some shortcuts which you can use later. For now, follow along so that you see exactly what is happening.

Each time we save a scenario, the first paste will copy the labels and their formatting, the second will copy numeric values and their formats.

- Change your weights to match these if they don't already— B31: 1.0; C31: 1.0; D31: 1.5; and E31: 1.0
- Highlight the entire table, including titles, headings and weights (**A45 to G55**).
- On the home menu ribbon, click *Copy*
- Click on cell A60. That is where we will save the 1.5 weight scenario.
- Click *Paste*. This copies the labels, but the formulas are all wrong.
- Immediately, click the little arrow underneath the Paste Clipboard icon
- Select *Paste Special* (near the bottom) from the dropdown.
- In the dialog box, select *Values and number formats* on the right hand side and click [OK].

Your scenario is saved, formatted, and is now sortable, since there are no more formulas. That (obviously) means you can't change it anymore. But you still have your original live copy of the table to make changes with.

• **Step 26**: Create the 2.0 weight scenario, and save it:

- Change the weight in **D31** to 2.0
- Highlight the entire table again, including titles, headings and weights (**A45 to G55**).
- On the home menu ribbon, click *Copy*
- Click on cell A73.
- Click *Paste*.
- Immediately, click the little arrow underneath the Paste Clipboard icon
- Select *Paste Special* (near the bottom) from the dropdown.
- In the dialog box, select *Values and number formats* on the right hand side and click [OK].

Now that you know how to save a scenario, you can create as many as you wish, saving them following this pattern.

• Step 27: Sorting Markets Into Rank Order
It would be nice to have our scenarios sorted in rank order, with the highest EV% markets at the top. *Only do this on a saved scenario, **never** on your live table!*

- Highlight the column headings and data, but not the Total row in your 1.5 weight scenario (**A47 to G54**).
- On the home menu ribbon, click the little down arrow under *Sort and Filter* (under funnel icon)
- Select *Custom Sort*, the third option.
- Make sure the *My data has headers* checkbox in the upper right is checked.
- In the *Column Sort by* dropdown, pick *EV%*. In the *Order* dropdown, pick *Largest to smallest*
- Click [OK]
- Your data should now be sorted in the proper order, with San Antonio first and Corpus Christi last.

• **Step 28**: Sort the 2.0 weighted scenario following the same directions, but highlighting cells **A62 to G69**

• **Step 30**: Print and Save

- Click the round "Windows Button" and select Print. This exercise will print on two sheets.
- Save your printouts for the next exercise.
- **Save your work!**

Interpreting Weighting Results

You will need the printouts of your factor spreadsheet results from the previous exercise to answer these questions.

Learning Objective

The purpose of weighting a spreadsheet is to manipulate the ranking of markets thereby changing the outcome of the spreadsheet. This exercise tests your understanding of exponential weighting theory.

1. What are the differences in the relative value between the three spreadsheets after exponential weighting was applied? Focus on the EVs for these two markets:

Market	Chili's Percentage Data EV%	1.5 Weight Scenario EV%	2.0 Weight Scenario EV%
San Antonio			
Orlando			

2. If advertising budgets were allocated based on the results of **# of Chili's Stores** weighted at 1.5 (*1.5 Weight Scenario*), which markets gain ad dollars compared to the unweighted EVs (*Chili's Percentage Data*), and by how much? (Your answer should be expressed in EV% points gained.)

3. If advertising budgets were allocated based on the results of **# of Chili's Stores** weighted at 1.5, which markets lose ad dollars compared to the unweighted EV%? (Look for markets whose EV% declined)

Exercise 12

Exhibit I
Original Unweighted Budget

Previously, you calculated ad budgets for all seven markets based on unweighted EV%s, shown below.

Market	EV%	EV% Decimal		$ Ad Budget		$ Budget Allocation
San Antonio	17.9	.179	X	1,500,000	=	$ 268,394
Jacksonville	13.2	.132	X	1,500,000	=	197,992
Tucson	17.4	.174	X	1,500,000	=	261,019
Albequerque	11.2	.112	X	1,500,000	=	168,694
Corpus Christi	9.3	.093	X	1,500,000	=	139,660
St Petersburg	11.7	11.7	X	1,500,000	=	175,474
Orlando	19.3	.193	X	1,500,000	=	288,768
Total						$1,500,000

4. Using the original $1.5 million total budget shown in Exhibit I, calculate a new ad budget for each of the 7 markets using EV% resulting from the 2.0 weight you applied.

Market	Weight 2.0 Scenario EV%	EV% Decimal	Total Ad Budget	Budget Allocation
San Antonio			1,500,000	$
Jacksonville			1,500,000	
Tucson			1,500,000	
Albuquerque			1,500,000	
Corpus Christi			1,500,000	
St. Petersburg			1,500,000	
Orlando			1,500,000	
				Total $1,500,000

5. Using the budget results from your calculations above, how much ad budget did San Antonio, Albuquerque, and St. Petersburg gain compared with the original unweighted ad budget in Exhibit I?

San Antonio: Albuquerque: St Petersburg:

6. Based on exponential weighting, some markets sacrifice a portion of their ad budget to benefit stronger markets. In this case, how much did the 3 gaining markets obtain at the expense of four other markets? Calculate the difference for all sacrificing markets compared to unweighted EV allocations in Exhibit I.

Sacrificing Market	$ Difference From Exhibit I
Jacksonville	
Tucson	
Corpus Christi	
Orlando	
Total Given to Gaining Mkts	

MFP
Gem Car NEV Tutorial

The MFP software simulation will run on computers with Windows or Mac operating systems Read carefully to assure a successful setup.

Computer display

Media Flight Plan is best viewed on a screen with a minimum resolution of 1024 x 768. Most newer computers are set to this resolution or higher. If your screen resolution is lower (like 800 x 600) you will still be able to use MFP, but you'll need to scroll around to see the entire screen.

Recommended browsers

MFP has been tested and will run on a number of browsers. The preferred browser for *MFP* is Firefox. This is one of the quickest, safest browsers available, and best of all, it's free (you can download it at http://www.mozilla.org/products/firefox/). Browsers supported by MFP include the following:

Windows	Macintosh
Firefox 3.5 and higher	Firefox 3.6 and higher
Safari 4.0 and higher	Safari 4.0 and higher
Internet Explorer 7.0 and higher	

Other browsers may work as well, but only these have been tested. *Note that your screen may vary slightly from the images in the tutorial depending on your browser.*

JavaScript must be enabled in all browsers

If *MFP* works well for you, don't mess with JavaScript. Unless you intentionally turned it off yourself, the JavaScript default is normally in the "on" position. Don't change anything until you try your current browser setup. Browser add-ons like NoScript for Firefox, will prevent JavaScript from running unless you give the mediaflightplan.com website permission. If you are using a supported browser and are having problems, see the documentation for your respective browser or add-on for further information on enabling JavaScript, or check with computer support at your university. **If all else fails, start from scratch by loading the latest version of Firefox or Netscape.**

Performance: We recommend a high-speed connection whenever possible (i.e. T1, cable modem, or DSL type connection). MFP will not run over a dial-up connection.

Registration instructions on next page.

Exercise 13

Registration and Logging In: You must do this before you start the tutorial.

1. Get your *MFP* Access Code – it's located on the inside front cover of this book. Carefully scratch off the silver coating. If you scratch off part of your code, send the characters you can read to support@mediaflightplan.com and we will look up the rest of your code.
2. Open your browser
3. Go to: www.mediaflightplan.com
4. Click [Login] at top of screen.
5. Follow instructions for new users. You'll need your access code to log in the first time.

Getting the tutorial

Click on **Students**, then click on **Ground School** and download or print the Gem Car Tutorial. If you like, you may also print the instructions for loading and saving with your Browser and Operating System.

Why is the MFP Tutorial online?

To keep *MFP* software current, our media cost database needs to remain flexible. For example, media costs change significantly each year, and posting the Tutorial online gives us the flexibility to upgrade data more frequently.

To provide the best support possible, instructions for saving and opening files are provided online for each browser/operating system supported by the *MFP* website. If and when browsers update their software, we can also update our instructions with them.

If you will be using *MFP* in more than one place with different browsers, you may want to download the directions for each browser now. Both the Tutorial and File Save/Open instructions are available on the *MFP* web site.

National + Spot Heavy Up Media Buys

Learning Objective

To grasp the dynamic relationship between national and spot media, and how they impact each other when combined. Used alone, spot market buying gives marketers the freedom to concentrate media weight in specific geographic regions. In contrast to national buys that cover the entire US, spot buys range from one market to dozens. However, a more dynamic media force can be created when the two are combined intelligently and strategically.

Examples for strategic uses of spot market media planning

Regional Brands: If your brand is marketed in only one or two cities, spot market planning lets you buy media market-by-market, and add markets as you grow. Many well-known brands started out very small, marketing in only a few cities, adding markets as they grew. Red Lobster is a classic example; founder Bill Darden originated the concept of casual seafood dining with a single store in Lakeland, Florida and by the early 70s had expanded into the southeast. As he expanded his store count from coast to coast, his spot advertising campaign grew one market at a time until he was into over 50 markets. That's when he went national, and now has over 400 stores.

Test Markets: It is much cheaper to "test the waters" in a few isolated markets to discover a new brand's potential for success. Spot buying allows you to limit your test market to one or two cities.

National With Spot Heavy-Up: Due to regional differences in culture, lifestyle, climate, etc., national brands are rarely consumed equally in all metro markets. For example, if you are assigned to create a national marketing plan for Snickers Frozen Ice Cream Bars, a common marketing practice is to add heavy-up weight in markets with above average category or brand potential. Houston, Texas, has a high CDI (186) and strong BDI (157) for frozen confections. (See Exhibit I) In addition to the national media weight (300 GRPs); the Snickers brand manager might give Houston a heavy-up dose of media weight—say, an extra 100 GRPs. Spot markets with high potential often get an advertising boost.

Exhibit 1

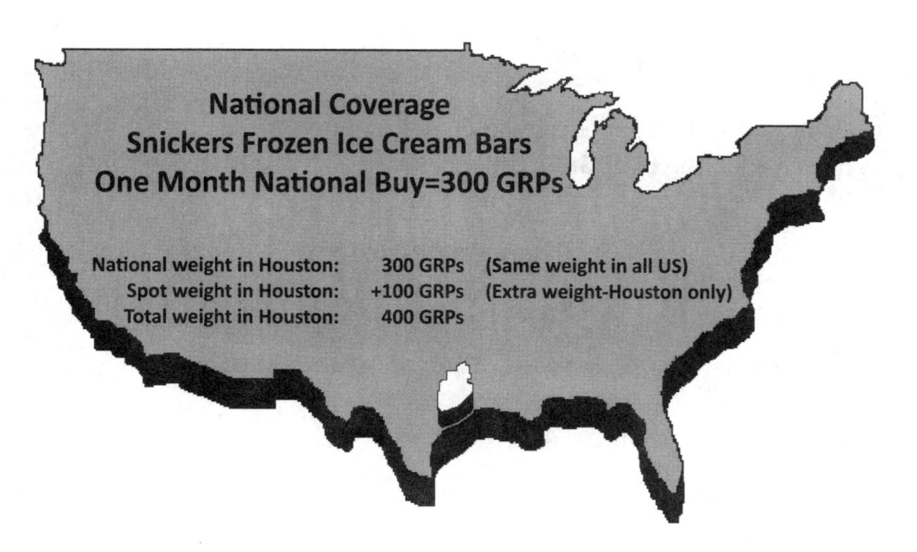

National Coverage
Snickers Frozen Ice Cream Bars
One Month National Buy=300 GRPs
National weight in Houston: 300 GRPs (Same weight in all US)
Spot weight in Houston: +100 GRPs (Extra weight-Houston only)
Total weight in Houston: 400 GRPs

Exercise 14

You can think of a spot buy as a second media plan integrated into the national plan. Heavy-up markets are endowed with extra media weight in addition to the national weight that already covers them. The effect is that reach/frequency will be higher in the spot markets than in the rest of the US. *Media Flight Plan* will help you see this more clearly as you complete this exercise.

Problems

Your assignment is to create a national media plan integrated with a spot plan for PF Chang's China Bistro. PF Chang's sales are strong nationally, but 12 markets in the Northwest and Mountain West regions demonstrate excellent growth potential.

Step 1: Campaign Basics

Go to mediaflightplan.com, launch Media Flight Plan and enter the following data:

- *Target Demo:* For Gender, select **[Adults]**, then **Age Groups 18 through 49**. To exit, click **[OK]**.
- *Campaign Settings:* For Campaign Scope, click **[Both National and Spot]**. For your Starting Month, select **[June]**. This campaign will run for only three months (June, July, and August) as a test bed for PF Chang's market research team. To exit, click **[OK]**.
- *Spot Markets:* Click **[Spot Markets]** and select the 12 markets listed in the box below.

Bend, Or	Grand Junction, CO	Salt Lake City, UT
Colorado Springs, CO	Las Vegas, NV	Seattle-Tacoma, WA
Denver, CO	Medford, OR	Spokane, WA
Eugene, OR	Portland, OR	Yakima, WA

- *Budget:* Click on the **[Budget]** tab and type **8000000** into **Total Budget Amount**, and hit **[Enter.]** Make sure 8000000 (with 6 zeros) shows on the bottom line, **Total Media Budget**. Click **[OK]** to exit.

Step 2: National Goals

Click on **[Goals]** tab. Beginning in June, enter the Reach/Freq goals for all 3 months (see table below). Take note that *MFP* automatically calculates GRPs and Share for you. Write down the GRPs in the table below.

National Goals Table

Month	Reach	Freq	GRPs
June	70	4	________
July	75	5	________
August	80	5	________

Step 3: Spot Goals

You should still be in Goals. Enter the Spot Goals shown below – be sure to begin with June. When done, take note of the numbers displayed in the **[AD] GRPs** column. Write all three **[AD] GRPs** into the table below. [AD] GRPs=ADDITIONAL GRPs needed to achieve the higher Reach/Frequency goals in your 12 spot markets.

Spot Goals Table

Month	Reach	Freq	[AD] GRPs
June	80	6	__________
July	85	7	__________
August	90	8	__________

Step 4: National & Spot Dynamic – A Key Concept

Complete the math below to learn how Media Flight Plan calculates [AD] GRPs. You can verify your answers here – NATL GRPs and [AD] GRPs should agree with the GRPs in both tables above.

Month	Spot Reach	X	Spot Freq	=	Spot GRPs	-	Natl GRPs	=	[AD] GRPs
June	80	X		=		-		=	
July	85	X		=		-		=	
August	90	X		=		-		=	

Step 5: Total GRP weight delivered to the Spot Markets is higher than shown in the [AD] GRPs column. When you "heavy-up" in spot markets, MFP combines the [AD] Spot GRP weights with pre-existing National GRP weights to produce the required weight. To prove this mathematically, you can calculate the total GRP weights actually delivered to the 12 spot markets each month. Look at Exhibit I to see how Total Weight is calculated using Houston as an example, and complete the following table with the GRPs from steps 2 and 3.

	Nat'l GRPs		Spot [AD] GRPs		Total GRP weight in 12 Spot Markets
June	____________	+	____________	=	____________
July	____________	+	____________	=	____________
August	____________	+	____________	=	____________

Step 6: GRP Experiment

Click on the **[Goals]** tab. On the Spot Goals side of the screen, find June and make these changes:

Reach = 70
Frequency = 4

A) Did you notice what changed? Write the new [AD] GRPs for June below.

New [AD] GRP for June: ____________

B) What happened? If you compare both National and Spot goals, note that June has identical Reach/ Frequency goals in both screens. Explain why spot goals must exceed national goals. Prove your answer using an example with numbers. (Tip: See Exhibit 1)

Step 7: Change your Spot Goals in June back to the original spot goals.

Reach = 80
Frequency = 6

Save your work now. Data from this exercise will be used in the next exercise. (Click the SAVE button displayed in upper right corner of screen).

Step 8: How MFP Calculates BUDGET SHARE for each month

Monthly budget Share is a simple calculation done automatically by Media Flight Plan at the moment you enter your Reach/Frequency goals. Each month's budget share is a percentage displayed for both National and Spot buys.

Exercise 14

Focus on the National Goals Budget Share for the month of June. It is a ratio between two figures. Here's the formula:

$$\frac{\text{National GRPs for June}}{\text{Sum of all National Goals GRPs + all Spot Goals [AD]GRPs}} \times 100 = \text{June Share}$$

The share calculated by MFP is used to estimate the dollars available to meet your goal in June. You may actually need to spend more or less to accomplish your reach/frequency goal in any given month.

Step 9: Applying the formula to calculate budget Share for June:

National GRPs

Calculate the SUM of all **National Goals GRPs** below: June ______________

July ______________

Aug ______________

Sum ______________

Spot [AD] GRPs

Calculate the SUM of all **Spot Goals [AD] GRPs** below: June ______________

July ______________

Aug ______________

Sum ______________

Apply the formula shown above to calculate National budget Share for June.

Using the same logic, calculate Spot budget Share for June and show your math.

Stretching Your Media Budget

Learning Objective

This exercise will help you discover creative ways to stretch your ad budget. You will have a stronger working knowledge about theoretical goal setting, and how to think creatively when faced with real-world marketing challenges.

Reach/Frequency goals provide a good starting point

As you may recall from the MFP tutorial, the reach/frequency goals you type into the goals screens are very rough estimates, and can always be adjusted up or down as needed. After reach/frequency goals are converted to GRPs, you can begin buying GRPs in the various media. Remember, however, that these estimated GRPs may or may not achieve your reach/frequency goal after the buy is made. Every buy is an experiment.

Problem Setup

This exercise builds on the *PF Chang's* mini-case you started previously. If you saved it, load the file and go directly to Step 1. (Click **[LOAD]** at top of MFP screen). If not, go back to Exercise 14 and enter the following data into *MFP*:

1. All the Campaign Basics for *PF Chang's China Bistro*
2. Goals: Enter all National and Spot Reach/Frequency goals for *PF Chang's*

Step 1: National and Spot Shares

Click on the **[Goals]** tab. Write shares below for both National and Spot Goals:

	National Goals Share	Spot Goals Share
June	____________________	________________
July	____________________	________________
August	____________________	________________

Step 2: Tweaking the Budget

- Click on **[Budget]**. On the bottom line, Total Media Budget should be $8 million.
- Change the Total Budget to $10.00. (Ten dollars is obviously absurd, but go along for now).

Step 3: Nothing Changes

Click on **Goals.** Compare the budget shares (both National and Spot) with the percents you reported above. Has anything changed? It should *not* have. Why do budget Shares remain constant even after your total budget drops to ten dollars? *MFP* is indifferent to whatever number you type into the Budget, from a penny to a million dollars.

Goals are not absolutes. Since *MFP* doesn't know if your budget is realistic or not, it's also indifferent to how high or low you set the reach/frequency goals. Once you set the goals for national or spot buys, you don't have to go back and change them to continue buying. Goals are planning guidelines, not absolutes.

Reach/Frequency: Although higher reach/frequency may be desirable, avoid jacking up GRPs simply for the sake of higher reach/frequency. What marketers want is brilliant thinking behind the GRPs. Mindless media buying is myopic; corporations will only hire and promote people who learn to create ingenious, strategically driven media plans.

Step 4: National and Spot Contingency
If you have a generous budget, it's a good idea to hold some money back for marketing emergencies. Open the **Budget** screen and change your budget to the amounts shown below:

Total Budget Amount:	$8,000,000	***This $1 million contingency can be used anytime. If you run short, take it out and spend it.**
National Contingency:	**500,000***	
Spot Contingency:	**500,000***	
Effective Budget:	$7,000,000	

Step 5: Make National media buys for June
Click **[Campaign Settings]** tab and make sure starting month is set for June. At bottom of the screen, your Theoretical National GRPs should read 280. This is simply a "theoretical" goal – an educated "guess" made after MFP multiplies R times F. Put your cursor in the UNITS column. Begin buying the media of your choice for *PF Chang's* – buy until you accumulate 280 GRPs. Normally, you would do a lot of research before choosing media, but for now, make buys that you consider reasonable for your client. Also, as a rule of thumb, *buy a minimum of 20 GRPs in a medium or daypart.*

Avoid chasing reach/frequency with every buy you make. Focus more on strategy and less on pushing reach/frequency higher. Clients (and professors) care most about why you buy and less about cranking GRPs higher. Be true to your strategy and avoid playing the numbers game for games sake.

Step 6: Make Spot buys for June
Check out the Natl + Spot area near the bottom of your screen – note that your total GRP goal for June is 480. You've already bought 280 GRPs in National media. This leaves you with a "theoretical" 200 [AD] Spot GRPs to spend. Buy 200 more GRPs in spot media. Remember that spot market newspapers are different than national. *Newspapers (40% HH Cvg)* is *not* purchased using GRP units. Each unit in this medium equals one insertion. For example, if you type the number 4, you are buying four newspaper insertions that month in all of your spot markets.

Step 7: Monitoring the Budget in June
By now you should have bought a total of 480 GRPs: Your buy includes 280 GRPs in national media and 200 GRPs in spot media for June. Report total dollars you've spent thus far for June in the box below:

Budget Update for June		
Natl + Spot GRP Goal (From Est. Perf. Section)	Total $ Spent-June (From Est. Perf. Section)	Balance Remaining (from $8 Million)

Step 8: Money Goes Fast
You've probably spent about half of your $8 million budget (perhaps over half), and you've only bought June. Actually, $8 million is a very generous budget for a single quarter, and with experience you'll learn ways to stretch the money. Recall that the main objective in this exercise is to challenge you to discover strategies for conserving budget. *Keep in mind that all goals are theoretical, and there is no rule that says you must achieve all goals, or that you must achieve all goals in all months.*

Step 9: News Bulletin! Budget Downsized
You just received a memo from the marketing director. Competitive pressures in *PF Chang's* northeastern region require budget cuts in all other regions. To assist your sister stores, your budget has been cut by 50%. Instead of $8,000,000, your advertising budget is now $4,000,000.

Step 10: Click on Budget and change Total Budget to $4,000,000
There are no absolute "rules" when it comes to strategy, so start thinking creatively.

Your task is to start over in June, and not exceed the $4 million. To conserve budget, you are free to change anything in the case except the Target Demo and the Total Budget, and you cannot advertise longer than three months: June, July and August. There are no other rules – review the case thoroughly, and experiment with different media options.

Step 11: A few tips to get you thinking

- Review the *PF Chang's* case in Exercise 13. Evaluate your client's marketing situation, and consider extreme measures as well as moderate cuts.
- Consider each item in *MFP* and evaluate how you could change it to conserve budget. What about using less expensive dayparts? Would less expensive Ad Types work for this brand? Experiment and find creative ways to save money.

Step 12: Finish up your campaign in July and August
After June, develop your strategy for July and August. You need to address all three months and yet remain inside the $4 million total budget.

Step 13: Print out a Flowchart, your Goals, and staple both print outs to this exercise.

Step 14: Reveal your strategic genius
Alas, few companies will pay you to throw money at marketing problems. There are infinite ways to stretch the budget. List at least eight strategies that you employed.

1.____
2.____
3.____
4.____
5.____
6.____
7.____
8.____

Introduction to the Nielsen NAD

Learning Objective

Nielsen generates many reports to help marketers and media planners make the best TV buys for their target audiences. A commonly used report is "National Audience Demographics," typically called "The NAD". The objective in this exercise is to help familiarize you with the kinds of data in the NAD. It is published monthly, but follows "broadcast months." Broadcast weeks (and months) always start on Monday and end on Sunday.

NAD reports include multiple sections covering dayparts, program types, and individual listings for each program. It is published for network, syndication and cable television. This exercise focuses on one individual program section, but data produced for the other sections follows the same format.

NAD universes are estimated for each calendar year. Universes are used for a "broadcast year," which starts in mid-September with the new fall season. An example of a universe page is shown in Figure 1.

Note: Gender and age breaks run across the top, while market sections (geographic, household, race, etc.) run down the side. Nielsen estimates TV households and persons in TV households in this table, not total populations.

Nielsen uses the term "composite" to represent "Total U.S." in the universe table (Top left, Figure 1). You can locate the universe of any group in the NAD by finding the age/gender column (across the top), then you find the intersection by cross referencing this column with the demographic groups listed on the far left. For example, to find the universe of "teens 12-17 living in the Southwest," look on the upper far right for a column labeled *TEENS-TOTAL 12-17*. Move down six rows of data to find 2.87 million. Note how this row intersects horizontally with *SOUTHWEST* on the far left. The top of Figure 1 indicates all data in the table are actually in millions; write answers in millions where appropriate.

Problems

1. What is the total number of women age 25-54 in homes with $75,000+ income?

2. What is the total number of children age 6-11 (hint: Composite)?

3. Observe data for both men and women age 18-34. Are there more in the northeast or in the pacific?

	NORTHEAST	PACIFIC
WOMEN 18-34		
MEN 18-34		

Exercise 16

Now look at Figure 2, the NAD report for a comedy, *Whose Line is it Anyway?* At the top-left of the page, note WEEKS 12345. This tells us it ran all five weeks in the month of this report. Some broadcast months have 4 weeks, others have five. If the program skips a week, you'll find a blank spot in the WEEK line - for example, 1 345 means the program skipped the 2nd week. On the same line with WEEK you can see the total number of minutes (MINS) this show was telecast during the month (150). The next line down reports the day of the week, WED. Broadcast time runs 9:30PM - 10:00PM, a thirty minute program. GV means "General Variety," and ABC is the network. Note that on both upper and lower tables the following symbols may appear: ^ <. These indicate reliability of the estimates. IFR indicates "Insufficient for Reporting." Still on Figure 2, observe the middle of the page where it reads: VIEWERS PER 1000 TOTAL US VIEWING HOUSEHOLDS -- hereafter called VPVH. All figures below this middle line report VPVH.

4. Go to Figure 3 and look for *Will & Grace* at top left of the page.

   a) How many weeks was it broadcast this month?

   b) Which week(s) did not have a broadcast of *Will & Grace*?

5. If you tuned in *Will & Grace*, what time does it start? How long does it last?

6. Return to Figure 2, *Whose Line is it Anyway?* The top half of the table reports ratings for households, age and gender. Demographic information is listed at the far left. The upper half of the table reports average ratings for the current month. The ratings report the percentage of a population that viewed the average minute of this program.

   (a) What's the rating for *Whose Line is it Anyway?* for total US Households?

   (b) What's the rating for Men 18-34 in households with $40-59,999 income?

7. Compare *Whose Line is it Anyway?* with *Will & Grace*. Which one reached more total Men 55+?

   Rating for *Whose Line is it Anyway?*

   Rating for *Will & Grace*

8. Look the text in the middle of Figure 3: VIEWERS PER 1000 TOTAL US VIEWING HOUSEHOLDS -- All data is REFERENCED TO 7.88 MILLION HOUSEHOLDS TUNED TO THIS PROGRAM on average during current month.

How many households tuned into the average telecast of *Will & Grace*?

9. Ratings tell what percentage of a universe saw the program; VPVH helps us to understand the composition of the audience. All VPVH in the network NAD have a base of 1000 households. It is calculated by taking the total viewers in a group, dividing by the number of households from the reference line in the middle of the page and multiplying by 1000. Because they all have the same base, VPVH can be added and subtracted,

whereas ratings cannot. VPVH also tells which groups have the highest concentration of viewers--something not readily visible from ratings, because ratings have different population bases. Since households are the basis of VPVH, there are no VPVH figures in the households column of the table.

Using data from VPVH table, circle which of the two demo groups is strongest for *Whose Line is it Anyway?*

Women 18-34 VPVH:

Women 25-54 VPVH:

10. (a) List the RATINGS% and VPVH for TOTAL US WOMEN 18+ viewing *Whose Line is it Anyway?* and *Will & Grace*? Both do a good job reaching women, but assume you can buy only one.

Program	**RATING**	**VPVH**
WHOSE LINE IS IT ANYWAY?		
WILL & GRACE		

(b) Which would you choose, and why?

FIGURE 1

Estimates of U.S. TV Households and Persons in TV Households (Millions)#

	HOUSE-HOLDS	WRK WOM 18+	WOMEN 18+	WOMEN 18-34	WOMEN 18-49	WOMEN 25-54	WOMEN 35-64	WOMEN 55+	MEN 18+	MEN 18-34	MEN 18-49	MEN 25-54	MEN 35-64	MEN 55+	TEENS TOTAL 12-17	TEENS FEMALE 12-17	CHILDREN 2-11	CHILDREN 6-11
COMPOSITE	99.40	47.80	101.70	30.72	62.66	59.33	52.31	30.64	93.36	30.63	61.24	57.49	49.45	24.17	22.14	10.87	39.43	23.89
TERRITORY																		
NORTHEAST	20.67	10.60	21.96	6.53	13.41	12.72	11.32	6.74	19.72	6.42	12.88	12.12	10.52	5.15	4.22	2.07	7.45	4.45
EAST CENTRAL	13.35	6.11	13.41	3.94	8.08	7.67	6.93	4.19	12.12	3.83	7.78	7.33	6.51	3.27	3.00	1.47	5.09	3.13
WEST CENTRAL	15.69	7.57	15.49	4.63	9.47	9.02	7.93	4.74	14.35	4.62	9.35	8.85	7.65	3.77	3.48	1.70	6.33	3.88
SOUTHEAST	19.61	9.36	19.90	5.82	11.88	11.28	10.15	6.36	17.86	5.67	11.38	10.73	9.39	4.95	4.18	2.06	7.14	4.33
SOUTHWEST	11.39	5.24	11.47	3.67	7.31	6.83	5.90	3.21	10.57	3.64	7.12	6.61	5.57	2.56	2.87	1.41	5.12	3.13
PACIFIC	18.69	8.92	19.47	6.15	12.51	11.81	10.08	5.40	18.73	6.45	12.73	11.85	9.81	4.47	4.40	2.15	8.30	4.96
COUNTY SIZE																		
A	39.24	20.08	41.52	13.00	26.35	24.92	21.42	11.77	38.22	13.15	25.85	24.19	20.18	9.15	8.45	4.15	15.37	9.14
B	30.48	14.61	30.68	9.42	19.12	18.02	15.77	9.06	27.97	9.26	18.53	17.36	14.84	7.10	6.63	3.27	12.01	7.26
C& D	29.68	13.11	29.50	8.30	17.19	16.39	15.11	9.81	27.17	8.22	16.86	15.95	14.44	7.92	7.06	3.46	12.05	7.49
CABLE/VCR STATUS																		
CABLE PLUS ADS	75.16	37.91	77.82	23.21	47.62	45.65	40.57	23.40	71.66	23.20	46.82	44.52	38.42	18.44	16.19	7.95	28.18	17.18
CABLE PLUS WITH PAY	47.53	25.98	50.66	16.11	33.07	31.79	27.54	12.79	47.75	16.07	32.67	30.79	26.50	10.73	11.58	5.69	19.98	12.30
BROADCAST ONLY	24.24	9.89	23.88	7.51	15.04	13.68	11.74	7.24	21.70	7.43	14.42	12.97	11.03	5.73	5.95	2.92	11.25	6.71
VCR OWNERSHIP	84.20	43.64	88.13	27.52	56.74	54.20	47.60	23.51	82.43	27.30	55.35	52.16	45.08	19.87	20.35	9.99	35.35	21.69
HHLD SIZE																		
1	24.43	5.08	14.35	1.61	3.90	4.49	5.36	9.43	10.08	2.55	5.71	6.06	5.18	3.50	0.00	0.00	0.00	0.00
2	31.81	15.33	32.69	7.04	14.23	15.30	17.37	14.81	28.50	6.61	11.81	12.52	13.49	14.08	0.99	0.49	1.23	0.71
3+	43.16	27.40	54.66	22.07	44.53	39.53	29.58	6.40	54.79	21.47	43.72	38.91	30.78	6.59	21.15	10.38	38.20	23.18
4+	26.06	16.46	34.57	14.68	29.80	25.65	18.48	2.96	35.53	14.00	30.11	26.32	20.48	2.95	17.30	8.49	32.07	19.84
PRESENCE OF NON-ADULTS																		
ANY UNDER 18	37.12	21.81	42.32	18.43	38.28	33.99	22.93	2.29	36.50	13.74	32.04	29.59	22.07	2.15	22.14	10.87	39.43	23.89
ANY UNDER 12	28.19	15.72	31.77	16.23	29.43	25.83	14.90	1.52	26.67	11.28	24.32	22.67	14.94	1.27	10.47	5.14	39.43	23.89
ANY UNDER 6	16.98	8.98	19.46	12.50	18.24	15.07	6.68	0.78	16.20	8.69	15.12	13.73	7.30	0.63	3.65	1.79	24.48	8.94
ANY 6-11	18.16	10.04	20.16	8.32	18.59	17.60	11.36	1.07	17.01	5.51	15.39	14.88	11.19	0.85	8.77	4.31	30.83	23.89
ANY 12-17	17.16	10.87	20.19	5.19	17.84	16.33	14.48	1.18	17.82	4.40	14.94	13.69	13.06	1.21	22.14	10.87	11.32	8.63
HOUSEHOLD INCOME																		
$30-39,999	12.18	5.90	11.97	4.12	7.67	7.05	5.85	3.43	11.43	4.29	7.72	7.03	5.32	3.01	2.76	1.35	5.11	3.13
$40-59,999	19.60	11.62	20.35	6.90	14.11	13.43	11.30	4.53	20.85	7.31	14.74	13.96	11.48	4.47	4.98	2.44	8.47	5.21
$60-74,999	10.00	6.75	11.04	3.50	8.02	7.94	6.71	1.93	11.79	4.02	8.52	8.17	6.94	2.14	3.05	1.49	4.46	2.73
$75,000+	18.78	13.36	22.00	5.98	14.98	15.32	14.37	4.26	23.44	6.51	15.63	15.59	15.25	4.85	5.12	2.51	7.74	4.80
SELECTED UPPER DEMOS																		
$50,000+ WITH NON-ADULTS	16.53	11.54	19.47	6.83	17.65	16.42	12.25	0.89	19.48	5.80	16.89	16.14	13.37	1.08	10.51	5.14	16.09	9.95
$50,000+ & HOH POM	16.08	11.49	17.38	5.34	13.00	13.30	11.37	2.37	18.35	5.65	13.43	13.49	12.05	2.74	4.46	2.18	7.22	4.57
$50,000+ & HOH 1+ YRS. COLLEGE	25.97	17.21	28.29	8.63	20.31	20.48	17.70	4.92	29.87	9.13	21.14	20.96	18.68	5.46	7.00	3.43	11.24	6.97
EDUCATION OF HEAD OF HOUSE																		
NO COLLEGE	49.04	20.40	51.23	14.30	28.29	26.12	24.75	18.99	45.17	14.28	27.61	25.19	22.75	14.01	11.23	5.51	19.68	12.00
4+ YEARS OF COLLEGE	24.84	13.69	24.79	7.71	16.73	16.81	14.05	5.68	24.66	7.78	16.69	16.68	14.16	5.52	4.85	2.38	9.12	5.48
RACE																		
BLACK	11.75	6.30	12.48	4.56	8.69	7.76	6.33	2.90	9.76	3.79	7.10	6.23	4.99	1.96	3.42	1.68	6.25	3.79

Including Alaska and Hawaii

NOTE: Cable and VCR Estimates are updated quarterly. All other market divisions are updated annually.

For explanation of procedures used to derive the above household and persons estimates, see UNIVERSE ESTIMATES REFERENCES.

FIGURE 2

WHOSE LINE IS IT ANYWAY?
WEEKS 12345 MINS 150
WED 9:30PM - 10:00PM GV ABC

NTI NAD REPORT -- JANUARY
TABLE 10A -- EVENING
AUDIENCE BY MARKET SECTION
INDIVIDUAL NETWORK PROGRAMS (TOTAL DURATION)

RATINGS(%)	HOUSE-HOLDS	WRK WOM 18+	WOMEN 18+	18-34	18-49	25-54	35-64	55+	MEN 18+	18-34	18-49	25-54	35-64	55+	TEENS TOTAL 12-17	FEMALE 12-17	CHILDREN 2-11	6-11
TOTAL U.S.	8.7	7.2	6.0	7.1	7.6	7.7	6.5	3.2	5.5	6.7	6.6	6.8	5.7	2.9	6.4	5.3	2.6	2.9
TERRITORY																		
NORTHEAST	9.3	7.8	6.6	6.6	8.9	9.1	7.9	2.8	6.0	6.9	7.2	7.2	8.5	3.0	7.2	IFR	2.6	3.5
EAST CENTRAL	9.9	8.3	6.8	9.4	8.7	9.1	7.2	3.4	5.5	7.0	6.5	6.8	5.6	3.2^	8.6	IFR	2.8	2.6^
WEST CENTRAL	9.6	8.6	6.8	8.7	8.7	8.4	7.4	4.1	6.3	8.1	8.1	7.7	6.5	2.9^	9.6	IFR	3.6	3.9
SOUTHEAST	7.3	6.3	5.0	5.8	6.3	6.5	5.5	2.7	5.2	6.6	6.2	6.8	4.9	3.1	4.3	IFR	1.7	1.9^
SOUTHWEST	7.6	5.5	4.7	5.8	5.3	5.8	4.7	3.1^	5.4	6.3	6.2	6.4	5.7	2.5^	5.2	IFR	2.5	2.9^
PACIFIC	8.7	6.3	5.8	7.0	7.0	6.9	5.8	3.4	4.9	5.7	5.8	6.0	5.2	2.7	4.2	2.9^	2.3	2.8
COUNTY SIZE																		
A	8.8	6.7	5.8	6.0	7.2	7.5	6.7	3.1	5.4	6.0	6.1	6.4	5.9	2.9	5.5	4.1	2.2	3.1
B	8.7	7.3	6.3	7.2	7.9	7.9	7.2	3.1	5.4	6.4	6.4	6.5	5.6	3.1	6.8	4.8	2.4	2.8
C&D	8.7	7.7	6.0	8.8	7.8	7.6	5.5	3.4	5.9	8.2	7.7	7.6	5.6	2.8	7.0	7.2	3.1	2.9
CABLE/VCR STATUS																		
CABLE PLUS ADS	8.6	7.0	6.0	7.6	7.7	7.7	6.3	3.0	5.6	7.1	6.9	6.9	5.7	2.6	5.9	5.0	2.4	2.9
CABLE PLUS WITH PAY	8.8	6.8	6.0	7.6	7.4	7.5	6.2	2.8	5.4	6.4	6.4	6.5	5.7	2.7	5.0	5.1	1.8	2.1
BROADCAST ONLY	9.1	7.8	6.1	5.8	7.2	7.6	7.3	3.9	5.2	5.5	6.0	6.1	5.7	4.0	7.5	6.2	2.8	3.1
VCR OWNERSHIP	9.4	7.4	6.4	7.6	8.0	7.9	6.7	3.3	5.8	7.1	6.9	6.9	5.8	3.2	6.7	5.5	2.6	3.0
HHLD SIZE																		
1	4.6	6.1	4.6	8.6	7.8	7.1	5.8	3.2	4.4	IFR	6.1	5.8	3.5	2.3^	IFR	IFR	IFR	IFR
2	7.0	7.2	5.3	8.0	7.9	7.1	5.7	3.3	5.0	8.3	7.5	7.0	4.9	3.1	IFR	IFR	IFR	IFR
3+	12.4	7.3	6.7	6.7	7.4	7.9	7.1	3.1	6.0	6.0	6.5	6.8	6.4	2.9	6.3	5.2	2.5	2.9
4+	12.9	6.5	6.3	6.3	6.8	7.4	6.6	2.3^	5.7	5.4	6.0	6.4	6.2	3.0^	6.3	5.3	2.6	2.9
PRESENCE OF NON-ADULTS																		
ANY UNDER 18	12.6	7.8	7.4	7.4	7.8	8.2	7.7	2.5^	6.6	6.7	6.9	7.1	6.7	2.7	6.4	5.3	2.6	2.9
ANY UNDER 12	12.1	7.9	7.5	7.2	7.8	8.3	8.0	2.5^	6.7	7.2	7.0	7.0	6.5	2.8	4.8	4.0	2.6	2.9
ANY UNDER 6	11.4	8.3	7.7	7.9	7.9	8.5	7.4	IFR	6.5	7.2	6.9	6.8	5.8	IFR	4.0	IFR	2.1	2.3
ANY 6-11	12.8	7.8	7.4	6.1	7.8	8.1	8.5	IFR	6.9	6.6	7.2	7.4	7.2	IFR	5.1	4.4	2.6	2.9
ANY 12-17	13.7	6.4	6.4	4.9	6.8	7.2	7.1	IFR	5.9	3.9	6.3	6.5	6.7	IFR	6.4	5.3	2.8	3.1
HOUSEHOLD INCOME																		
$30-39,999	8.5	7.4	6.8	8.2	8.7	8.8	7.6	3.3^	5.9	6.5	6.8	7.1	6.8	3.8^	4.7	IFR	2.8	2.6^
$40-59,999	10.7	8.7	7.6	8.5	9.2	9.1	8.1	3.2	6.5	8.5	7.9	7.8	6.1	2.9	5.4	3.3^	2.7	3.5
$60-74,999	12.5	9.3	8.3	7.9	9.9	10.1	9.3	4.2^	7.4	8.4	8.2	8.4	7.6	3.6^	11.0	IFR	4.5	5.2
$75,000+	10.4	6.5	6.1	8.0	7.4	7.0	5.7	2.9	5.1	5.2	5.9	6.5	5.4	2.5	7.8	5.0	1.9	2.3^
SELECTED UPPER DEMOS																		
$50,000+ WITH NON ADULTS	14.6	7.9	8.0	7.1	8.3	8.7	8.7	IFR	6.3	5.6	6.5	7.0	6.8	IFR	8.1	6.5	2.9	3.5
$50,000+ & HOM POM	12.7	7.7	7.9	8.8	8.9	8.6	7.7	5.5	6.8	7.2	7.6	7.7	6.9	3.8^	8.7	5.6	3.1	3.8
$50,000+ & HOH 1+ YRS. COLLEGE	11.1	7.4	7.2	8.1	8.5	8.2	7.2	3.7	6.3	7.3	7.2	7.6	6.4	2.8	7.8	5.4	3.1	3.7
EDUCATION OF HEAD OF HOUSE																		
NO COLLEGE	6.3	6.8	5.4	6.5	6.8	7.1	6.0	3.3	4.9	5.9	5.8	5.7	5.0	3.4	6.2	5.3	2.4	2.8
4+ YEARS OF COLLEGE	8.6	6.7	6.1	7.7	7.7	7.4	6.2	2.8	5.7	7.6	6.9	6.9	5.5	2.4	7.0	3.9^	2.0	2.1
RACE																		
BLACK	5.1	3.6	3.1	3.1	3.2	3.2	2.9	2.8^	2.6	3.0	2.9	2.6	2.3^	2.4^	1.9^	IFR	1.8^	2.6^

VIEWERS PER 1000 TOTAL U.S. VIEWING HOUSEHOLDS--REFERENCED TO 8.68 MILLION HOUSEHOLDS TUNED TO THIS PROGRAM

	HOUSE-HOLDS	WRK WOM 18+	WOMEN 18+	18-34	18-49	25-54	35-64	55+	MEN 18+	18-34	18-49	25-54	35-64	55+	TEENS TOTAL 12-17	FEMALE 12-17	CHILDREN 2-11	6-11
TOTAL U.S.		394	702	252	546	523	391	113	534	237	469	448	326	81	162	66	116	81
TERRITORY																		
NORTHEAST		95	168	49	137	133	103	22	[illegible]	51	107	101	79	18	35	IFR	23	18
EAST CENTRAL		58	106	43	81	80	57	16	76	31	58	58	42	12^	30	IFR	16	9^
WEST CENTRAL		75	122	47	95	88	67	22	104	43	87	78	57	13^	38	IFR	26	18
SOUTHEAST		68	115	39	87	84	65	20	106	40	82	81	53	18	21	IFR	14	9^
SOUTHWEST		33	62	25	45	45	32	11^	66	26	51	49	36	7^	17	IFR	15	11^
PACIFIC		65	130	50	101	94	68	21	105	42	84	82	59	14	21	7^	22	16
COUNTY SIZE																		
A		155	278	90	218	214	166	42	236	91	182	178	137	31	54	20	39	32
B		123	222	78	173	165	130	32	173	69	137	131	96	25	52	18	33	23
C&D		116	203	84	155	144	95	39	185	77	150	140	93	25	57	28	43	25
CABLE/VCR STATUS																		
CABLE PLUS ADS		306	533	202	422	403	293	80	463	189	370	356	253	55	111	45	79	57
CABLE PLUS WITH PAY		204	350	142	283	275	196	42	298	118	240	232	174	34	66	33	40	30
BROADCAST ONLY		89	169	50	125	120	99	33	131	47	99	92	73	26	51	21	37	24
VCR OWNERSHIP		374	646	240	520	495	365	88	564	225	439	417	302	73	158	63	108	75
HHLD SIZE																		
1		36	77	16	35	37	36	35	51	IFR	40	40	21	9^	IFR	IFR	IFR	IFR
2		128	201	65	130	126	113	56	163	63	102	101	77	50	IFR	IFR	IFR	IFR
3+		230	424	171	381	361	243	23	380	149	326	307	228	22	154	62	110	77
4+		122	249	107	235	218	140	8^	235	88	208	195	145	10^	126	52	94	67
PRESENCE OF NON-ADULTS																		
ANY UNDER 18		195	361	157	344	322	202	6^	276	105	256	241	170	7^	162	66	116	81
ANY UNDER 12		144	274	135	265	247	137	4^	205	93	196	184	111	4^	57	24	116	81
ANY UNDER 6		86	172	114	165	148	57	IFR	122	73	120	108	49	IFR	17	IFR	59	23
ANY 6-11		91	172	58	166	164	111	IFR	136	42	128	127	93	IFR	52	22	93	81
ANY 12-17		80	149	29	139	136	119	IFR	121	20	108	103	101	IFR	162	66	36	31
HOUSEHOLD INCOME																		
$30-39,999		51	94	39	77	72	51	13^	77	32	60	57	42	13^	15	IFR	16	9^
$40-59,999		116	178	68	150	141	105	17	155	72	133	126	81	15	31	9^	26	21
$60-74,999		72	106	32	92	93	72	9^	100	39	80	79	61	9^	38	IFR	23	16
$75,000+		99	153	55	127	123	95	14	137	39	106	116	96	14	46	14	17	13^
SELECTED UPPER DEMOS																		
$50,000+ WITH NON-ADULTS		105	180	56	170	164	122	IFR	142	37	126	130	105	IFR	98	38	53	40
$50,000+ & HOM POM		102	158	54	133	132	101	15	143	47	117	120	95	12^	44	14	26	20
$50,000+ & HOH 1+ YRS. COLLEGE		148	233	81	199	194	147	21	218	77	174	185	138	18	62	21	40	29
EDUCATION OF HEAD OF HOUSE																		
NO COLLEGE		160	318	106	223	213	170	72	253	98	185	166	132	55	80	33	56	38
4+ YEARS OF COLLEGE		105	175	69	148	143	101	18	163	68	133	132	90	15	42	11^	21	13
RACE																		
BLACK		26	44	16	32	28	21	9^	30	13	24	18	13^	5^	8^	IFR	[illegible]	11^

N.B SEE LEAD PAGE OF THIS SECTION FOR EXPLANATIONS OF SYMBOLS
Nielsen Media Research--Printed in U.S.A

Exercise 16

FIGURE 3

Will & Grace
WEEKS 123 5 MINS 120
TUE 9:30PM - 10:00PM CS NBC

NTI NAD REPORT – JANUARY
TABLE 10A – EVENING
AUDIENCE BY MARKET SECTION
INDIVIDUAL NETWORK PROGRAMS (TOTAL DURATION)

RATINGS(%)	HOUSE-HOLDS	WRK WOM 18+	WOMEN 18+	WOMEN 18-34	WOMEN 18-49	WOMEN 25-54	WOMEN 35-64	WOMEN 55+	MEN 18+	MEN 18-34	MEN 18-49	MEN 25-54	MEN 35-64	MEN 55+	TEENS TOTAL 12-17	TEENS FEMALE 12-17	CHILDREN 2-11	CHILDREN 6-11
TOTAL U.S.	7.9	6.8	6.0	7.2	6.8	6.8	6.0	4.6	4.3	4.2	4.6	4.9	4.5	3.5	2.5	2.8	1.1	1.3
TERRITORY																		
NORTHEAST	8.8	7.3	6.8	6.2	7.5	8.0	7.5	5.6	4.3	3.6	3.9	4.7	4.5	4.3	3.1^	IFR	8^	1.1^
EAST CENTRAL	8.5	7.5	6.9	9.1	7.7	8.2	6.7	4.9	4.2	4.2	4.9	4.7	4.2	3.4^	2.5^	IFR	1.3^	1.6^
WEST CENTRAL	9.7	8.7	7.7	10.0	9.0	8.0	7.2	5.8	5.5	4.4	5.9	6.2	6.9	4.7	3.4^	IFR	1.6^	1.9^
SOUTHEAST	6.2	5.6	4.8	5.4	5.5	5.9	5.0	3.4	3.7	4.3	4.2	4.3	3.3	2.9^	1.8^	IFR	1.2^	1.2^
SOUTHWEST	6.1	4.9	4.3	5.3	4.2	4.2	4.1	4.3^	3.2	3.4^	3.3	3.5	3.2	3.0^	2.8^	IFR	.7v	8v
PACIFIC	7.9	6.4	5.5	7.9	6.4	6.3	5.0	3.8	4.6	5.2	5.1	5.6	4.8	2.7^	1.5^	1.0v	1.2^	1.2^
COUNTY SIZE																		
A	8.6	7.2	6.6	7.1	7.3	7.4	7.2	5.2	4.2	3.8	4.5	5.0	4.6	3.2	1.7^	2.2^	1.1	1.2^
B	7.6	7.2	5.8	7.7	6.8	6.9	5.5	3.8	4.5	4.4	4.8	4.9	5.1	3.6	2.4	2.5^	1.0^	1.0^
C&D	7.3	5.7	5.5	6.9	6.0	5.9	4.9	4.7	4.2	4.8	4.5	4.6	3.8	3.8	3.4	3.9^	1.4	1.7^
CABLE/VCR STATUS																		
CABLE PLUS ADS	7.5	6.3	5.8	7.1	6.6	6.7	5.6	4.2	4.0	4.0	4.4	4.7	4.3	3.2	2.5	2.7	1.2	1.2
CABLE PLUS WITH PAY	7.6	5.7	5.7	7.5	6.4	6.4	5.1	4.4	4.0	4.3	4.4	4.5	3.9	3.2	2.3	2.3^	1.3	1.2^
BROADCAST ONLY	9.2	8.8	6.9	7.5	7.3	7.2	7.3	5.9	5.2	4.9	5.1	5.6	5.5	4.6	2.4^	3.0^	1.0^	1.5^
VCR OWNERSHIP	8.4	6.9	6.3	7.8	7.0	7.1	6.0	4.7	4.5	4.5	4.8	5.1	4.7	3.6	2.5	2.9	1.2	1.4
HHLD SIZE																		
1	6.7	10.2	6.4	11.1	11.0	9.9	8.9	4.3	7.2	IFR	9.2	8.9	7.1	4.4	IFR	IFR	IFR	IFR
2	7.9	8.8	6.8	10.4	8.7	7.9	6.2	5.3	4.9	5.5	6.3	6.0	5.5	3.9	IFR	IFR	IFR	IFR
3+	8.6	5.0	5.5	5.9	5.8	6.1	5.4	3.6	3.4	3.1	3.5	3.9	3.7	2.3^	2.2	2.4	1.0	1.1
4+	8.4	4.3	4.9	5.4	5.1	5.4	4.7	3.0^	2.8	2.3	2.8	3.2	3.2	1.8^	2.3	2.5	0.9	1.1
PRESENCE OF NON-ADULTS																		
ANY UNDER 18	8.2	4.8	5.5	6.1	5.7	5.9	5.2	3.2^	3.6	3.5	3.8	3.9	3.7	1.7v	2.5	2.8	1.1	1.3
ANY UNDER 12	8.0	4.7	5.7	6.4	5.8	6.1	5.0	2.9v	3.7	3.7	3.7	3.9	3.7	2.3v	2.0	1.9^	1.1	1.3
ANY UNDER 6	8.0	5.6	5.9	6.6	6.0	6.3	4.6	IFR	4.3	4.3	4.4	4.6	4.5	IFR	1.3^	IFR	0.9	1.0
ANY 6-11	7.6	3.9	5.3	6.1	5.4	5.4	4.8	IFR	2.9	2.2^	2.9	3.1	3.3	IFR	2.1	2.1^	1.1	1.3
ANY 12-17	8.1	4.0	4.6	4.9	4.7	5.0	4.6	IFR	2.6	2.1^	2.8	2.8	2.7	IFR	2.5	2.8	1.3^	1.4^
HOUSEHOLD INCOME																		
$30-39,999	7.5	4.6	5.6	6.8	5.7	5.5	4.6	5.6	3.9	3.9	4.0	4.0	3.8	4.1^	2.9^	IFR	1.5^	2.0^
$40-59,999	9.8	7.6	7.5	8.3	8.5	8.4	7.6	5.3	5.2	5.5	5.6	5.7	5.4	4.1	2.4^	2.6^	1.1^	1.1^
$60-74,999	10.1	8.0	7.3	8.5	7.9	7.8	6.9	5.8^	5.3	5.1	5.5	5.8	5.5	4.4^	4.5^	IFR	1.9^	2.1^
$75,000+	10.6	7.6	6.9	9.5	7.8	7.6	6.4	5.1	4.7	4.3	5.1	5.8	5.2	3.3	2.5^	2.5^	9^	5v
SELECTED UPPER DEMOS																		
$50,000+ WITH NON-ADULTS	10.6	6.4	6.5	7.9	6.8	6.9	5.8	IFR	4.3	4.5	4.6	4.9	4.2	IFR	3.0	3.6	1.3	1.1^
$50,000+ & HOM POM	11.1	8.8	8.0	10.5	8.6	8.6	7.1	5.9^	5.4	5.3	5.8	6.1	5.4	4.3^	2.4^	3.1^	1.1^	7v
$50,000+ & HOH 1+ YRS. COLLEGE	10.4	8.6	7.4	9.7	8.5	8.3	6.8	3.9	5.1	5.4	5.6	6.0	5.2	3.1	2.7	3.9^	1.1^	9^
EDUCATION OF HEAD OF HOUSE																		
NO COLLEGE	6.8	4.7	5.1	5.2	5.3	5.6	5.3	4.9	3.4	2.4	3.2	3.7	4.0	3.6	2.1	1.6^	1.0	1.4
4+ YEARS OF COLLEGE	9.6	9.1	7.5	10.1	8.7	8.6	7.0	4.2	5.3	6.3	6.1	6.3	5.3	3.4	2.9^	4.6^	9^	8^
RACE																		
BLACK	4.7	4.6	3.5	2.9^	3.5	4.2	4.3	2.9^	2.1	2.2^	2.2^	1.8^	1.7^	1.9v	.7v	IFR	8^	1.4^

VIEWERS PER 1000 TOTAL U.S. VIEWING HOUSEHOLDS--REFERENCED TO 7.88 MILLION HOUSEHOLDS TUNED TO THIS PROGRAM

	HOUSE-HOLDS	WRK WOM 18+	WOMEN 18+	WOMEN 18-34	WOMEN 18-49	WOMEN 25-54	WOMEN 35-64	WOMEN 55+	MEN 18+	MEN 18-34	MEN 18-49	MEN 25-54	MEN 35-64	MEN 55+	TEENS TOTAL 12-17	TEENS FEMALE 12-17	CHILDREN 2-11	CHILDREN 6-11
TOTAL U.S.		412	779	282	539	515	399	180	507	165	357	356	284	108	69	39	56	39
TERRITORY																		
NORTHEAST		98	190	52	129	129	108	48	106	29	65	72	61	28	16^	IFR	8^	6^
EAST CENTRAL		58	118	46	79	80	59	26	65	21	49	44	35	14^	10^	IFR	8^	6^
WEST CENTRAL		84	151	59	109	91	73	35	99	26	71	69	67	23	15^	IFR	13^	9^
SOUTHEAST		67	121	40	83	85	64	28	83	31	60	58	39	18^	9^	IFR	11^	6^
SOUTHWEST		33	62	25	39	36	31	18^	43	16^	30	29	23	10^	10^	IFR	4v	3v
PACIFIC		72	137	61	101	94	64	26	109	42	83	84	60	15^	8^	3v	13^	8^
COUNTY SIZE																		
A		183	350	117	244	235	195	78	202	63	148	154	119	37	18^	11^	21	14^
B		133	225	92	165	158	110	43	158	52	112	109	96	32	20	10^	15^	9^
C&D		96	205	73	130	122	95	59	146	51	97	94	69	38	31	17^	21	16^
CABLE/VCR STATUS																		
CABLE PLUS ADS		301	569	210	399	389	291	126	364	118	264	264	207	75	51	28	41	26
CABLE PLUS WITH PAY		190	367	154	267	257	179	71	240	88	181	176	132	43	34	16^	32	19^
BROADCAST ONLY		111	210	72	140	126	109	54	142	46	93	93	76	34	18^	11^	15^	13^
VCR OWNERSHIP		385	704	274	505	486	361	140	467	155	338	339	207	90	66	37	56	38
HHLD SIZE																		
1		66	117	23	55	57	61	51	92	IFR	67	69	47	20	IFR	IFR	IFR	IFR
2		172	280	93	157	154	136	99	178	46	95	96	93	69	IFR	IFR	IFR	IFR
3+		174	382	166	327	304	202	29	237	85	196	191	144	19^	60	32	50	33
4+		90	214	101	193	175	110	11^	127	41	108	108	83	7^	50	27	37	27
PRESENCE OF NON-ADULTS																		
ANY UNDER 18		133	296	143	276	255	150	9^	167	62	153	146	103	5v	69	39	56	39
ANY UNDER 12		95	229	132	218	199	94	6v	126	54	115	112	71	4v	26	12^	56	39
ANY UNDER 6		64	145	104	139	121	39	IFR	89	47	85	79	41	IFR	6^	IFR	28	11^
ANY 6-11		50	136	64	128	120	69	IFR	63	15^	56	59	47	IFR	23	12^	44	39
ANY 12-17		56	117	32	107	103	85	IFR	58	12^	52	49	44	IFR	69	39	19^	15^
HOUSEHOLD INCOME																		
$30-39,999		35	85	36	56	49	34	24	56	21	39	36	26	16^	10^	IFR	10^	8^
$40-59,999		113	194	73	152	144	109	31	138	51	104	101	78	23	15^	8^	12^	8^
$60-74,999		68	102	38	80	79	59	14^	79	26	60	60	49	12^	17^	IFR	11^	7^
$75,000+		128	194	72	148	147	116	28	141	35	101	116	100	20	17^	8^	9^	3v
SELECTED UPPER DEMOS																		
$50,000+ WITH NON-ADULTS		94	161	68	151	143	90	IFR	107	33	98	101	72	IFR	41	24	28	14^
$50,000+ & HOM POM		129	177	71	143	145	102	18^	125	38	98	104	83	15^	14^	8^	10^	4v
$50,000+ & HOH 1+ YRS. COLLEGE		188	265	107	219	216	154	24	192	63	152	159	123	21	24	17^	16^	8^
EDUCATION OF HEAD OF HOUSE																		
NO COLLEGE		123	333	95	191	187	167	119	196	44	114	119	115	64	31	11^	26	22
4+ YEARS OF COLLEGE		159	236	99	185	184	126	30	168	62	128	133	96	24	18^	14^	11^	6^
RACE																		
BLACK		37	55	17^	38	41	34	11^	26	11^	19^	14^	11^	5v	3v	IFR	7^	7^

N.B SEE LEAD PAGE OF THIS SECTION FOR EXPLANATIONS OF SYMBOLS

Introduction to the Nielsen Pocketpiece

Learning Objective

The Pocketpiece is produced weekly by the Nielsen Company for network programs. It is a handy reference that outlines top line information such as household rating, share, VCR recording information, and VPVH data for major planning and buying demos.

Similar to the NAD report, age and gender are arranged across the top of the table in the Pocketpiece. Since the Pocketpiece is focused on program trends and other data, market demos are not included in the left column like NAD. When you encounter the term coverage (CVG%), it indicates the percent of total US Households that have the potential to tune in a particular program (i.e. they are capable of tuning in) not how many actually tune in. For example, look two lines below *West Wing* - its CVG% is 99, meaning 99% of US TV Households are capable of tuning in *West Wing* either via traditional broadcast signal or via cable or satellite.

Find the program *West Wing* again in Figure 1. Directly under the program name on the second line, you'll see the *West Wing's* regular day and time of telecast (WED 9:00 P), its duration (60 minutes), network (NBC) and the number of telecasts (3) and the KEY is B. (More on KEY later). The next line down shows the number of stations (219) that aired the program. The coverage percent of the US (See CVG% column in box at top) is 99, and program type is (GD, or General Drama). The number of telecasts (14) is in the C line (Premier to date average).

Problems

It may be helpful to use a ruler to stay in the proper vertical column or horizontal row.

1. In the box at top left below PROGRAM NAME, find the column labeled CVG% (coverage). CVG% is also referred to as Clearance. Use a ruler to help you stay in the vertical CVG% column. Name which program has a significantly lower clearance than all the others.

2. Go to the top of Figure 1 again, and find the KEY label. (Adjacent to PROGRAM NAME, KEY is printed vertically) Each program has at least one A line, a B and a C line which provide measurements for different periods of time. The A line provides estimates for the current period. Programs longer than 30 minutes also have A lines for each half-hour of the program, so planners and buyers can see how audience flows during the course of the show. The B and C lines provide the same estimates as the A line, but calculated on a quarterly or premiere-to-date (i.e. season-to-date) basis. This allows the analyst to compare current activity to longer term trends.

Find the HOUSEHOLD AUDIENCE column. Just below on the left notice the column labeled AVG AUD. %. Follow that column down to *West Wing* and note the current week's average audience rating is 9.4 (A). How does the current week's AVG AUD% (9.4) compare with the quarter (B), and AVG AUD% for premiere-to-date (C)?

3. *West Wing* is an hour-long program. What happened to the audience in the second half-hour of the show (Hint: In the KEY column, there are two A time periods, one for 9:00, and another for 9:30)

4. Three of the programs in Figure 1 have weaker AVG AUD% ratings for the current week (A) compared with premiere-to-date averages (C). Which programs are they?

	Program Name	**A (Current Week)**	**C (Premier to Date Average)**
1.			
2.			
3.			

5. Find the HOUSEHOLD AUDIENCE column again. Right below in the center is VCR CNTRB % column. It reports the percent of households that recorded the program while the set was turned off or on to another program. The numbers in this VCR column are already added into the numbers reported for AVG AUD%, so they are not an addition to it. About 6.4 percent of the *West Wing* audience came from VCR recording this week. Here's the math formula for calculating the 6.4%. For this example, we'll use the first A row for *West Wing*.

0.6 ÷ 9.4 X 100 = 6.4% VCR Usage

For the current week, calculate the percentage of the audiences for all other programs attributable to recording. They are listed in order below:

	VCR	**÷ AVG AUD% X 100**	**= %VCR Usage**
TWICE IN A LIFETIME			
VERONICA'S CLOSET			
WALKER, TEXAS RANGER			
WEST WING			
WHOSE LINE IS IT ANYWAY?			
WILL & GRACE			
WINNING LINES			
WONDERFUL WORLD DISNEY			

6. Share indicates what percent of viewing homes is tuned to the program. Rating divided by the HUT (Households Using Television) = Share. Share can also be calculated for other demos by using their ratings and the PUT (Persons Using Television) for that demo. Since share is calculated on the HUT/PUT for the program's time period, a program can have a lower rating & higher share than another because it draws more viewers in its time period.

Because ratings, HUTs and shares, are interrelated, we can calculate the HUT if we know the other two. Since the pocketpiece gives the rating and share, the HUT can be calculated. Here's how to calculate the HUT for *West Wing*:

$$\frac{\text{Household Audience Avg Aud\% (rating)}}{\text{SH\% (share)}} \times 100 = \text{HUT}$$

$$\frac{9.4}{14} \times 100 = 67.1 \text{ HUT}$$

(a) Find HH rating and share for *Will & Grace* and *Walker, Texas Ranger*; calculate the HUT for each.

(b) Which program has the highest rating?

(c) Which program has the highest share?

FIGURE 1

PROGRAM AUDIENCE ESTIMATES (Alpha)

PROGRAM NAME / DAY TIME #STNS CVG% DUR NET TYPE	NO. OF T/C	KEY	VIEWERS PER 1000 VIWEING HOUSEHOLDS BY SPECIFIED CATEGORIES: HOUSEHOLD AUDIENCE				TOTAL PERS	WORKING WOMEN		LOH 18-49	WOMEN						MEN						TEENS		CHILDREN	
			AVG AUD. %	VCR CNTRB %	SH %	AVG AUD. 0,000	2+	18+	18-49	W/CH <3	TOTAL	18-34	18-49	25-54	35-64	55+	TOTAL	18-34	18-49	25-54	35-64	55+	TOT. 12-17	FEM. 12-17	TOT. 2-11	TOT. 6-11
EVENING CONT'D																										
TWICE IN A LIFETIME	3	A	0.3	.0	1	33	1596	328^	193v	213v	909^	170v	420^	467^	622^	295^	314^	103v	199v	123v	139v	101v	137v	137v	236^	151v
SUN 10.00P 60 PAX	19	B	0.4	.0	1	44	1455	288^	126^	63v	771	94v	306^	384	544	333^	464	90v	263^	255^	231^	172^	94v	60v	126^	101v
304 72 GD		C	0.4	.0	1	44	1392	392	235	29v	849	129^	384	484	557	341	377	85^	216^	256	226	110^	80^	49v	86^	70^
10.00 - 10.30		A	0.3	.0	1	32	1627	359^	229v	218v	941^	190v	453^	499^	596^	293^	322^	98v	214v	126v	156v	108v	141v	141v	224v	145v
10.30 - 11.00		A	0.3	.0	1	33	1565	297^	157v	209v	878^	150v	389^	436^	647^	297^	306^	108v	184v	120v	123v	94v	133v	133v	248^	157v
VERONICA'S CLOSET		A	7.9	.2	12	795	1400	415	354	70	730	268	535	538	404	122	518	195	371	397	286	78	63	35^	89	53
TUE 9.30P 30 NBC	2	B	7.6	.1	11	763	1385	423	348	78	763	256	534	543	427	154	483	176	354	367	273	75	64	38	76	46
219 99 CS	2	C	7.6	.1	11	763	1385	423	348	78	763	256	534	543	427	154	483	176	354	367	273	75	64	38	76	46
WALKER, TEXAS RANGER		A	9.3	.3	17	941	1529	287	182	36	757	94	299	373	445	359	601	98	280	295	364	270	87	31^	85	54
SAT 10.00P 60 CBS	2	B	8.6	.2	15	869	1542	290	172	35	774	90	284	357	452	394	602	99	284	300	360	264	76	29	91	60
206 99 EW	15	C	8.2	.3	15	831	1510	279	178	39	777	103	299	352	419	400	553	78	255	285	330	246	73	27	107	70
10.00 - 10.30		A	8.9	.3	16	896	1537	301	193	37	766	97	310	383	447	355	595	96	285	302	368	260	89	34^	87	56
10.30 - 11.00		A	9.8	.3	18	985	1522	275	172	35	748	92	289	363	443	363	606	100	274	289	361	279	84	28^	84	52
WEST WING		A	9.4	.6	14	949	1484	419	275	45	813	149	373	466	492	326	596	105	298	353	374	216	32^	16^	43	28^
WED 9.00P 60 NBC	3	B	8.4	.5	13	851	1449	391	254	52	788	142	368	443	474	315	579	102	278	338	361	217	36	13^	46	26
219 99 GD	14	C	9.1	.6	14	920	1419	382	250	46	795	147	364	429	461	338	550	98	262	316	340	210	35	17	39	21
9.00 - 9.30		A	9.1	.6	14	918	1490	419	275	45	812	153	368	457	485	331	599	111	300	350	367	219	33^	18^	46	28^
9.30 - 10.00		A	9.7	.6	15	980	1479	419	275	44	815	144	377	474	499	321	593	100	296	355	380	213	31^	15^	41	27^
WHOSE LINE IS IT ANYWAY?		A	7.0	.2	11	703	1566	360	275	73	747	221	451	444	394	227	534	168	356	375	298	116	130	47	154	112
THU 8.00P 30 ABC	3	B	5.9	.1	10	595	1545	354	280	66	734	211	460	445	388	219	515	157	355	361	284	116	128	57	168	119
214 97 GV	17	C	5.4	.1	9	548	1548	360	280	63	716	182	449	451	400	213	531	154	363	357	299	129	135	62	166	115
WILL & GRACE		A	9.4	.3	14	944	1424	443	359	58	720	253	510	517	406	136	539	193	404	413	314	77	77	44	87	49
TUE 9.00P 30 NBC	3	B	8.0	.2	12	808	1421	451	358	70	763	249	520	533	430	165	506	173	366	381	295	84	79	50	73	43
220 99 CS	13	C	8.5	.3	13	855	1416	440	354	77	752	255	512	531	406	167	510	181	374	375	282	90	78	44	76	45
WINNING LINES		A	4.3	.1	8	433	1567	324	201	31^	761	139	323	388	391	333	567	139	315	309	326	196	94	48^	145	92
SAT 8.00P 30 CBS	2	B	5.5	.1	10	557	1510	278	172	43	775	124	298	339	376	397	561	136	279	273	299	225	70	35^	104	63
206 98 QG	2	C	5.5	.1	10	557	1510	278	172	43	775	124	298	339	376	397	561	136	279	273	299	225	70	35^	104	63
WONDERFUL WORLD OF DISNEY		A	7.1	.1	11	714	1675	348	247	57	833	141	402	443	471	341	464	73	259	282	295	153	92	53	286	209
SUN 7.00P 120 ABC	2	B	8.0	.1	12	809	1781	336	236	66	743	182	417	439	421	246	502	100	313	342	329	133	135	72	400	267
222 99 FF	12	C	7.6	.2	12	766	1743	324	245	69	695	187	424	439	386	207	449	110	296	308	280	113	165	103	432	289

A=CURRENT REPORT B=QUARTER-TO-DATE AVERAGE C=PREMIERE TO DATE AVERAGE

FOR EXPLANATION OF SYMBOLS, SEE PAGE B.

Section III

Case Studies

Village Surf Shoppe

A 1-2 day case study to test your knowledge of three concepts: SWOT, Media Objectives & Media Strategies

Village Surf Shoppe provides an excellent platform for learning the most intellectually challenging part of the business – organizing and writing the plan. Three chapters in Media Flight Plan are especially relevant to this assignment:

- Marketing Driven Media Plans
- The Art of Writing Media Objectives & Strategies
- Award -Winning Media Plan

Your goal is to demonstrate that you can apply the principles in these three chapters. Begin with the SWOT – it will test your organizational skills. Next, translate your SWOT into a set of six media objectives. And finally, the most creative part of the assignment: Translate your objectives into strategies – strategies that prove you can think and write imaginatively. Review these chapters thoroughly, especially the case examples in Chapter 4. Tip: Start early – a first draft on this project will be transparent and obvious to Village Surf's marketing director.

Point Distribution

- SWOT 20%
- Media Objectives . . 30%
- Media Strategies . . . 50%

Village Surf Shoppe – A Retail Case Study

Since 1969, the Village Surf Shoppe and its manufacturing arm Perfection Surfboards, have been leading players in the surfing business near South Carolina's Grand Strand. Located in Garden City (within the Myrtle Beach retail trade area), Village Surf is an authentic surf shop in the classic 1960's tradition; it is a laid-back surfer hang-out as well as a comfortable place for tourists. Its advertising slogan, "Hardcore since 1969" reflects unwavering loyalty to the serious surfer. It stands in contrast to the uniformly corporate retail environments of national chains like Ron Jon's.

The facility is a simple cinder block structure, hand-painted with beach images. The interior retail space is tightly packed with surfboards, beachwear, and related products. Surfing lessons, camps, and rentals are also important sources of income. Village Surf Shoppe is much more than a place of business, however; it's a gathering place for avid surfers, the primary target market. These hardcore wave-riders often hang out at Village, telling stories and checking out the new boards.

Surfing's New "Inland Market"

Surfing is one of the fastest-growing sports and leisure activities with over 5 million surfers worldwide. Currently, the U.S. is experiencing a surfing boom as demonstrated by new surfing communities in places like New York City and the shores of the Great Lakes. The growing target market for Village Surf Shoppe is men and women, 18-24 with active, adventurous lifestyles. They are also heavy consumers of recorded music and spend considerable time on the Web. Incomes are less than $28,000 annually.

Popular culture has aided the growth of this market. TV programs such as North Shore and Summerland have exposed millions to the lure of surfing. Similarly, films like Blue Crush and MTV's reality show, Surf Girls, have attracted female surfers to the sport. Recent documentaries such as Riding Giants and Step into Liquid are two of the highest grossing DVD rentals in the country. Many surfers get information about surfing products and weather conditions on the Internet and regularly network with other surfers via e-mail, blogs, and chat rooms.

These developments have led to the new inland surfing market. This new market is willing to drive 1-3 hours to the ocean on a regular basis. Today, it's no longer necessary to live in a beach town to be a surfer. For example, for Village Surf Shoppe, inland markets are emerging in Columbia, South Carolina, Charleston, South Carolina, and Charlotte, North Carolina.

Marketing: Past, Present, & Future

Beyond personal selling and word-of-mouth, guerilla marketing has been the chief media vehicle for the store. Village Surf stickers and t-shirts have been enormously successful in achieving product awareness. Stickers and decals can be seen on cars, skateboards, schoolbooks, etc. If you wander through Myrtle Beach and surrounding areas, you'll notice teenagers wearing the classic Village Surf t-shirt. The peak selling period is April through September; sales decline considerably during the winter months.

Event marketing has also been important. The company sponsors surf competitions on a regular basis. Traditional advertising has been limited and sporadic. Occasional publicity is generated in local news outlets and national surf magazines.

Village Surf management feels it is time to take the business to a higher level. Local competition from Waller Bear's, Surf City, and Eternal Wave create the need for new markets. For this reason, the inland market appears to have great potential and will, hopefully, increase sales by 20% in the next three years. About $200,000 has been committed to inland advertising and promotion for the upcoming year.

The Assignment

This first case study assignment is designed to explore the connection between the SWOT analysis and the creation of market-driven media objectives and strategies. Your challenge includes three parts. First, to organize relevant information in the SWOT so that it leads to media objectives designed to solve marketing problems. The objectives and strategies flow out of the SWOT and make up the last two parts of your case.

I. Use the information outlined in this case to write a maximum 2-page "mini" SWOT (i.e., situation analysis). For this assignment, organize your paper using the following headings as outlined in the chapter *Marketing Driven Media Plans*:

1. Marketing Objectives
2. Competition
3. Creative History
4. Target Audience
5. Geography
6. Timing
7. Media Mix

II. Write a set of six media objectives based on your SWOT analysis. Write one media objective for each of the following as illustrated in the chapter *The Art of Writing Media Objectives & Strategies*.

1. Target Audience & Media Mix
2. Reach – Frequency*
3. Scheduling & Timing
4. Media Budget
5. Geography
6. Sales Promotion

*Make rough estimates for R/F, and don't worry about nailing the "right" reach/frequency numbers. The important objective in this case is to learn to organize and integrate all six objectives.

III. Write a set of six media strategies – one strategy to accompany each of your six objectives. Strategies are ideas that bring the objectives to life. Also, keep in mind that 50% of your score is based on this part of the assignment. In reviewing the Coca-Cola case (in *The Art of Writing Media Objectives & Strategies*), it's obvious that creative strategic thinking is what makes or breaks the brand – the client values strategy more than anything else. Also, keep in mind that this is the marketing intensive part of the assignment. Intelligent marketing is the linchpin to success in business, whichever path you take. Prove you are up to the task by writing a set of six original strategies that pay off your media objectives.

Suggested Length? Strategy is not about quantity; it's all about quality. Look to Coca-Cola and the winning student case study as good models.

Case study sources: Village Surf Shoppe Management, Myrtle Beach, South Carolina. Village Surf Shoppe web site: www.villagesurf.com. Also, 2004 SRDS The Lifestyle Market Analyst.

Case Study Authors: Professor Daniel Stout, University of South Carolina with Professor Dennis Martin, Brigham Young University.

The New Harley ... Ready to Rumble!

Harley redefined the motorcycle industry as it roared through the past two decades with impressive growth. Now, with aging boomers and a mercurial stock market, what's the best marketing and media strategy to keep the New Harley roaring through 2020?

We live to ride, and we ride to eat

Wearing black leather and riding huge Harleys, a motorcycle gang thunders through northern Georgia as if en route to a rumble. But the only rumble for this gang--the Atlanta Harley Owners Group (HOG)--is the one in their stomachs. It's another Sunday ride in the country for the group, and as usual it ends with a feast. "We live to ride, and we ride to eat," says club assistant director B.K. Ellis, a systems analyst.

Although educated professionals dominate the Hog world, there are still a number of would be hard-core guys with big tattoos and bad tempers, the sort who once typified the Harley customer. Most customers, however, would be playing hooky from $78,000-a-year jobs (the average salary of today's Harley customer), riding $16,000 motorcycles (the typical cost of Harley's biggest bike, a cruiser), and pledging fealty to an open-road cult that doubles as a $4-billion-a-year company.

Owning A Hog is a Lifestyle

Harley today has more to do with fraternity than with machinery. You buy a Harley, you join a ready-made motorcycle gang: the 600 U.S. HOG chapters, operated under the dealers' aegis. Style is as important as speed. On dealers' floors, leather-draped mannequins can outnumber the bikes. Harley has artfully parlayed the romance of the road and the independence of the biker to capture baby-boomers. Its core customers have reprised their 1960s rebelliousness with a product that bespeaks their 1990s success.

By selling a lifestyle while competitors sold mere motorcycles, Harley left others in the dust for leadership in the most lucrative segment of the market, the big cruiser bike. It has a 45% share in the U.S., vs. Honda's 23%. Some critics claim that Harley hasn't built better bikes than its four main Japanese competitors, but it has built a far better brand. It licenses its logo to more than 100 manufacturers, which gives the company ubiquitous exposure. It fosters the HOG clubs, which are rolling convoys of free advertising. So even though it sells a niche product, Harley consistently ranks among the ten best-known American brands, in the company of Coca-Cola and Disney.

Harley's Tank Not Full, But Far From Empty

Harley also ranks among America's top growth stocks since its 1986 IPO. Its 37% average annual gain runs just behind the 42% pace of another '86 debutante: Microsoft. While the earnings of many have gone into the tank, there's still plenty of gas in Harley's. Nevertheless, some of its key growth engines showed signs of sputtering. Its customer base has grayed, as the average age of a Harley rider has risen from 38 to 46 in the past decade. "It's an upper-middle-class toy," says Chad Hudson of the Prudent Bear fund, one of a number of prominent short-sellers convinced that Harley will skid, even as the economy continues to rebound.

Last year retail sales of Harley-Davidson motorcycles decreased 21% worldwide, 28% in the U.S. and 10% in international markets. Industry-wide U.S. retail demand for heavyweight cruiser style motorcycles (651cc+) declined 21% overall. Revenue from Parts and Accessories totaled $144.6 million during the quarter, down 5%. Revenue from General Merchandise like Motorclothes® declined 3% to $66.8 million.

Road Ahead Winding, But Company is Optimistic

Harley-Davidson has ramped up for much higher production in the coming year. Economic forecasts indicate 10-15% higher demand for the category. Company financial forecasters are more optimistic; they expect to ship 60,000 to 70,000 motorcycles in the first quarter of next year, and by year's end anticipate shipping in excess of 260,000 motorcycles to dealers and distributors worldwide. Nevertheless, robust growth and higher stock prices for Harley Davidson will no longer be routine as in the past decade. Not only has the world economy been transformed, but the demographic and lifestyle dimension of Harley's target market is undergoing a tectonic shift.

American sales of light sport bikes, aimed at 25- to 34-year-old men, increased 90% from 1998 to 2001. Suzuki, Honda, Yamaha, and Kawasaki have a combined 92% of that market. The 121,000 bikes sold in the category still pale beside next year's goal of 262,000 Harley cruisers, a segment they own, but a segment that is expected to begin shrinking soon.

But the youth of America have spoken. They prefer sleeker, sportier machines than the Harley hog, and Harley's brass is listening. Demographic data suggests Harley's future business is in Gen-Xers and -Yers, not exactly the forte of a company tuned to baby-boomers' rhythms and values. Naturally the boomers' kids want to ride anything but the old man's model. They're drawn to machines that are the anti-Harley.

The company needs to make inroads with today's twenty-something bikers. The prime age for motorcycle customers is 35 to 44, according to Donald Brown, a consultant to the industry. Brown says this age group's numbers began to decline in 1999 and will continue to do so through 2016. Since Harley can't replace all its boomer customers from a limited pool of baby-busters, it must reach deeper than before into the youth market. The result, says Brown: "It will have to compete more head-on with the Japanese."

Increasing Potential in Minority Markets

As Baby Boomers who transformed Harley's rumbling, lumbering bikes from countercultural totems into American icons entering their senior years -- the leading edge of the generation is turning 60 this year -- they're increasingly in the market for knee and hip replacements, not Harley's notoriously bone-shaking bikes. That's forcing the Milwaukee, Wisconsin-based company to scramble to find new customers among women, blacks and Hispanics -- groups that have not been ignored, but that are seen as more important segments in the next decade.

But as Harley-Davidson tries to adapt to the changing marketplace, analysts say it needs to avoid the pitfalls that other boomer-favored businesses like Levi Strauss & Co. have fallen into as they tried to navigate a similar transformation. "Half their demand is from guys 40 to 50 years old," says Bob Simonson, an analyst for William Blair & Company in Chicago. Joanne Bischmann, vice president of marketing at Harley, admits, "The demographics are changing" though she insists the change isn't as dramatic as some have suggested. "But that doesn't mean there aren't other populations we don't want to tap into."

To reach out to the black community, Harley has begun sponsoring the nationally syndicated show of Tom Joyner, an African American radio host whose program is heard by as many as 8 million U.S. listeners. Harley is also advertising during the nationally televised college basketball tournament that dominates the U.S. sports calendar from mid-March to early April and is sponsoring the Roundup, an African American version of the annual gathering of bikers in Sturgis, South Dakota.

To reach younger Hispanics, the company is advertising in Hombre and Fuego -- two Latino men's magazines -- and participating in low-rider shows. And to reach women, it's putting a four-page insert into Jane, Allure, Glamour and two other Conde Nast magazines, featuring what Bischmann says are "real women riders." It's also hosting garage parties for women -- not unlike the get-togethers that Tupperware, Avon, Mary Kay and other U.S. direct marketers have used to target women successfully for decades.

At a recent event that drew hundreds of African American riders from the greater Chicago area to a club in the city's downtown Loop, the opportunities -- and challenges -- Harley-Davidson faces as it tries to change attitudes and win over new riders were on display. Among the attendees were the 11 members of Ladyz on Krome, an all-female club of Harley-Davidson riders, and another that goes by the nom de zoom "Kuiet Storm."

But the vast majority of the riders at the event, including Max "PT" Brown, a 32-year-old member of the 5th Gear Ridaz, another Chicago club, were owners of screaming street bikes like the Kawasaki Ninja. Brown called Harleys "awesome bikes" but added, "The younger riders don't go for them. As you get older, then that's when you go into the Harley-Davidsons."

Give Harley credit for not burying its head in the sand, as the Japanese did when they were atop the market in the early 1980s. They wrote off a near-bankrupt Harley, failed to respond to its resurgence, and then ceded to it the boomers and cruisers. That won't happen at Harley, vows Bleustein. His message to a national meeting of 650 dealers: "The only thing that can stop us is if we get complacent. Even though we've been successful, we can't stand still."

To that end, Harley has poured money into developing new, youth-oriented models. The $17,000 Harley V-Rod--a low-slung, high-powered number known formally as a sport performance vehicle and colloquially as a crotch rocket--is meant for hard-charging youths. Harley has also tried to go young with the Buell Firebolt ($10,000), its answer to Japanese sport bikes, and the Buell Blast ($4,400), a starter motorcycle. But Buell, a subsidiary Harley bought in 1998, has captured just 2% of the sport-bike market, and Harley will make only 10,000 V-Rods this year. Bleustein insists that those numbers aren't the point: "These aren't one-shot deals. These are whole new platforms from which many models will proliferate." [Note: The Buell line has since been folded into the Harley lineup.]

Making changes is tricky for a company with Harley's cult following: They risk alienating current customers. The V-Rod's water-cooled engine is a big departure from Harley's traditional air-cooled one, and to some uneasy riders a portent of additional unwelcome changes to come. "If they ever do anything with that [roaring] sound, they've lost their customer base," says B.K. Ellis.

Harley's marketing team is working hard to make it easier to hold on to people who catch Harley fever. Many offer Rider's Edge courses for novices. Bleustein began the program two years ago because he felt that lots of people were interested in motorcycling but intimidated by the bikes. About half the Rider's Edge graduates are women. Harley's proportion of woman customers has about doubled in the past decade, to 9%, partly because the company required dealers to transform their grimy bike shops into retail emporiums. Dealers who reaped the benefits of directives like that seem confident that the company can keep reinventing itself. "They've done an awful lot to be forward-thinking," says Chris Houghton of Harley-Davidson in Atlanta.

Yet privately, some dealers worry. The customer waiting list for new motorcycles has shrunk from as much as two years to a matter of months. The big question, asks one dealer, is, "What's going to happen in the next 10 years?" The answer: Harley must get ahead of the demographic curve with new customers while somehow keeping faith with its loyal cruiser base. If it doesn't, the born-to-be-wild company will begin its second century with profit growth that is doomed to be mild.

Your Media Planning Challenge

1) Harley-Davidson will launch two separate and distinct campaigns for next year, both running simultaneously. The first will be a traditional Hog campaign – an umbrella campaign assigned to another agency, not your job. Your responsibility is to prepare the media plan for the second campaign targeting the younger segment – Gen-Xers and -Yers. Using information from the case study and from syndicated data provided online, you need to profile this target audience.
2) Integrate social media into your media plan. If you choose traditional media as the foundation of your plan, that's OK. But, HD has just appointed a new VP of Social Media. She wants you to employ social media and expects a very detailed plan on how it will be integrated into your media plan. Integration is the operative word – don't simply tack it on.
3) Along with the strategic use of any new media, the advertising manager wants to see some examples of your strategy. For example, if you create a viral message, be specific. Likewise, if you create event marketing or point-of-purchase promos, be specific about the event and how it will be integrated into your plan.

Nine Key Decisions for Your Media Plan

Write a media plan applying the principles outlined in the text chapters of MFP. Review the exercises as well. See MFP website (www.mediaflightplan.com) for consumer, competitive spending and other marketing data. Once you login, click on *Ground School*, then open Harley case study section to find links to the data. Data is essential to help support your decisions on targeting, competitive, geographic, and other strategic decisions.

1. ***Target audience & media mix:*** Because of the importance of helping HD transition to a younger and very different target audience, give very detailed information to support your target audience demographics and lifestyle. Study your brand and competitive brands carefully and critically. Write your profile for the target audience using all relevant online sources. *Justify both the target profile and your media mix decisions using quantitative and qualitative data from the case, online data, and other sources you may be able to find.*

2. ***Timing/Scheduling:*** Plan a 12-month campaign; each of the 12 months may or may not include advertising or promotions depending on your timing strategy. HD definitely wants you to include mass media in your plan, as well as social media. You decide which month to launch, and which months to accelerate spending. Your timing/scheduling strategy is vital to your success. Your client expects you to research target lifestyle and to *justify peak spending periods with strong support.*

3. ***Media budget:*** You'll need to recommend a media budget for HD. Analyze the information in the case combined with all available online data to establish a defensible budget. Keep in mind that although HD's marketing team is willing to spend the necessary dollars to be effective, you will need to analyze all available data to justify your budget decision. Your budget should account for traditional media as well as any new media plus sales promotional spending.

4. ***Scope:*** Geographic strategy is especially important for HD. Make a very clear commitment to one of the three scopes in *MFP* software: National, Spot, or Both. Justify your decision by citing relevant data from all available sources. This should include data from the case itself, and the online data, and keep in mind that HD's Marketing Director *is especially interested in your quantitative analysis of relevant data*.

5. ***Factor Spreadsheet:*** If you choose to support local markets, use the method outlined in the MFP Exercise, *Learning to "Weight" Spreadsheets*. Calculate Estimated Value Percents (EV%) for all markets selected, and rank them from strongest to weakest. Data for spot market planning can be found online. Evaluate all markets using a factor spreadsheet, and employ a weighting strategy.

6. ***SWOT or Situation Analysis:*** Competitive spending, consumer profiles, market data, etc., are all available online. The quality of your SWOT, and the effort you invest is the key to unlocking some of the most important issues in this case study. As you prepare your SWOT, follow the points outlined in the chapter *Marketing Driven Media Plans*. HD's marketing director suggests special attention be given to the following in your SWOT:

    - **The four P's (Price, Promotion, Place, Product):** Critical analysis of HD and major competitors

    - **Competitive Spending Analysis with SOV (Share of Voice):** Review the exercise *Competitive Spending Analysis and SOV* if you need help. Share of Voice is of particular interest to HD marketing experts - make sure it ties into your media mix strategy. Include a complete SOV analysis in your SWOT.

    - **Geography strategy:** Should spending be focused or broadened? How can HD maximize its advertising voice in national and/or spot markets?

7. ***Creative strategy:*** Write a creative brief for an integrated campaign that positions HD and write a tag line. Why a creative brief? It's all about intelligent positioning. When integrated thoughtfully, creative becomes a major driving force in your media strategies

8. ***Media Flight Plan software:*** Execute a media buy using Media Flight Plan. Include a flowchart in the body of your work, and other printouts as required by your professor. Make sure all decisions stated on these printouts are supported with logical and intelligent objectives/strategies. *Be sure the buys on your flowchart are consistent with your mediobjectives/strategies. Your marketing/media plan will be judged less on the buys you make and more on the objectives/strategies that drive the buys.*

    - Strategy is everything – write media objectives/strategies for the following:

    - A clear definition of HD's target audience with an intelligent media mix strategy. Media mix should include a list of vehicles, e.g. – radio formats, new media approaches, magazine titles, TV programs, etc.

    - Monthly reach/frequency goals and accompanying strategies.

    - Geography: Should HD be advertised nationally, in spot markets, or a combination of both? Justify your decision with marketing data and facts.

    - Monthly media allocations and budgeting strategy demand logical, factual marketing support.

    - Timing/scheduling decisions are vital to HD's marketing success - justify your timing factually.

    - Nontraditional media & sales promotion: Be original and don't underestimate the value of sales promo.

The authors acknowledge and thank the following sources:
- John Helyar, Fortune Magazine for much of the case background and color: http://www.mutualofamerica.com/articles/Fortune/2002_08_01/fortune.asp
- James B. Kelleher, Reuters for Target Market News (The black consumer market news)
Harley-Davidson Earnings Miss Badly: www.stockbloghub.com/2010/01/23/hog-harley-davidsons-earnings-miss-badly/25805
- Zacks Investment Research
Stock Wizard

NOTICE

As with past editions of Media Flight Plan, new case studies will be posted on our website each Fall Semester.